LABOR, DEMOCRATIZATION AND DEVELOPMENT IN INDIA AND PAKISTAN

In this first comparative study of organized labor in India and Pakistan, the author analyses the impact and role of organized labor in democratization and development. The study provides a unique comparative history of Indian and Pakistani labor politics. It begins in the early twentieth century, when permanent unions first formed in the South Asian Subcontinent. Additionally, it offers an analysis of changes in conditions of work and terms of service in India and Pakistan and of organized labor's response.

The conclusions shed new light on the influence of organized labor in national politics, economic policy, economic welfare and at the workplace. It is demonstrated that the protection of workers has desirable outcomes not only for those workers covered but also for democratic practice and for economic development.

Labor organizations that are based on labor rights affect economic performance and political practices in desirable ways. Rights-based labor organizations strengthen democratic governments, public investment, and conversion of wealth into wellbeing. Organized workers help to ensure that benefits of growth are shared. Worker solidarity is essential for democracy and development.

Christopher Candland is Associate Professor, Department of Political Science and Co-Director of South Asia Studies at Wellesley College, USA. He has served as an advisor on international labor affairs and trade to Democratic Party leadership in the US House of Representatives' Subcommittee on Trade and to a federal advisory committee reporting to the US Secretary of State.

ROUTLEDGE CONTEMPORARY SOUTH ASIA SERIES

PAKISTAN
Social and cultural transformations in a Muslim nation
Mohammad A. Qadeer

LABOR, DEMOCRATIZATION AND DEVELOPMENT IN INDIA AND PAKISTAN
Christopher Candland

CHINA–INDIA RELATIONS
Contemporary Dynamics
Amardeep Athwal

MADRASAS IN SOUTH ASIA
Teaching Terror?
Jamal Malik

LABOR, DEMOCRATIZATION AND DEVELOPMENT IN INDIA AND PAKISTAN

Christopher Candland

Routledge
Taylor & Francis Group
LONDON AND NEW YORK

First published 2007
by Routledge
2 Park Square, Milton Park, Abingdon, Oxon OX14 4RN

Simultaneously published in the USA and Canada
by Routledge
270 Madison Ave, New York, NY 10016

Routledge is an imprint of the Taylor & Francis Group, an informa business

Typeset in Times New Roman by
Taylor & Francis Books
Printed and bound in Great Britain by
MPG Books Ltd, Bodmin

British Library Cataloguing in Publication Data
A catalogue record for this book is available from the British Library

Library of Congress Cataloging in Publication Data
Candland, Christopher.
Labor, democratization and development in India and Pakistan / Christopher Candland.
p. cm. – (Routledge contemporary South Asia series ; 2)
Includes bibliographical references and index.
1. Industrial relations–India. 2. Labor unions–India.
3. Democratization–India. 4. Industrial relations–Pakistan. 5. Labor unions–Pakistan. 6. Democratization–Pakistan. 7. Comparative industrial relations. I. Title.
HD8686.5.C36 2007
331.0954–dc22
2006100804

ISBN 978-0-415-42820-0 (hbk)
ISBN 978-0-203-94675-6 (ebk)

CONTENTS

MAPS, FIGURES, AND TABLES

Maps

Figures

Tables

ACKNOWLEDGMENTS

Hard-won insights of workers and organizers made this study possible. Hundreds of workers, labor organizers, labor scholars, managers, employers, and government officials were generous in speaking with me. Few are named here or in the text or footnotes below. I am grateful to each nonetheless for sharing valuable time, experiences, and thoughts.

I am especially grateful to Nabi Ahmed, Karamat Ali, Colin Gonsalvez, Sujata Gothoskar, Riffat Hussain, B. M. Kutty, N. P. Samy, Arvind Shrouti, Damodar Thankappan, and Girish Vaidya. I am also grateful to Khurshid Ahmed, Zahoor Awan, Khuda Bakhsh, Usman Baloch, Eijaz Beig, R. K. Bhakt, Qadir Broih, Gulzar Ahmad Chudhary, Homi Daji, Raju Damle, Arun Daur, Usman Ghani, Syed Khalil Hussain, Mohammad Ishaque, G. R. Khanolkar, S. P. Lodhi, H. Mahadevan, Babu Mathew, Vasant Nayampally, S. N. Rao, Gul Rehman, and Balgaram Tulpule for explaining to me the history and present challenges workers in India and Pakistan. For sharing research and perspectives I thank Charles Amjad Ali, Subashini Ali, Tariq Banuri, Kaiser Bengali, Praful Bidwai, B. N. Datar, L. K. Deshpande, Roza Deshpande, R. Ganapathy, M. R. Ganapathy Rao, Ajit Ghosh, Syed Hameduddin, A. R. Kemal, Noor Khan, Omar Ashgar Khan, Klaus Klennert, Khalid Mahmood, Ajit Mathur, and Sundipto Mundle.

I am grateful to Philip Oldenburg, for generous and skillful advice from the start of the project. I am thankful to Prabat Patnaik and Aly Ercelawn, my sponsors at Jawaharlal Nehru's Centre for Economic Studies and Planning and the University of Karachi's Applied Economic Research Centre. Karamat Ali, Pranab Bardhan, Usman Baloch, Fatima Burney, Ainslie Embree, Mark Kesselman, Joel Krieger, Tarini Mohan, Craig Murphy, Richard Nelson, George Rosen, Barnett Rubin, Margery Sabin, Saba Sulaiman, and Erisha Suwal read all or part of drafts of the manuscript and gave valuable comments. I also greatly appreciate the generous support from the Fulbright Program in India, the American Institute of Indian Studies, the American Institute of Pakistan Studies, the Center for Institutional Research and Informal Sector, the National Council of Applied Economic Research, the East-West Center, and the Council of Overseas Research Centers and from Sharada Nayak, Pradeep Mahendiratta, Peter Dodd, Mancur Olson, Rakesh Mohan, and Charles Morrison.

Introduction

WEALTH, WELLBEING, AND SOCIAL INSTITUTIONS

> The central problem in the theory of economic development is to understand the process by which a community which was previously saving and investing 4 or 5 per cent of its national income, converts itself into an economy where voluntary saving is running at about 12 to 15 per cent. of national income.[1]
>
> W. Arthur Lewis

The claim that economic growth is the surest way to combat poverty has fallen into disrepute. Some economies have grown very rapidly but have failed to convert that wealth into wellbeing. Other economies have grown less rapidly but provided more opportunity for people to escape poverty. How to achieve growth has long overshadowed how to transform wealth into wellbeing.[2] The question of how economic growth is transformed into general wellbeing – into health, and education and literacy, employment – needs greater attention.

The argument made here is that strong labor organizations and institutions play a central role in distributing the benefits of economic growth and in promoting human development. How and whether governments allow workers to organize has great influence on how well wealth can be converted into wellbeing. Unions and other working class organizations are the keys to building solidarity and breaking cycles of exclusion and underdevelopment. Unions promote decent jobs and fundamental rights at work and elsewhere.[3] In turn, decent jobs and rights at work are the foundations of democracy and broad-based human development around the world. Unions and other working class organizations have been active in promoting and defending democracy, often through prolonged popular struggle and personal sacrifice. Unions and other working class organizations lead to more successful economic transitions as well.

India, Pakistan, and the comparative method

India and Pakistan make an ideal comparative pair for inquiry into the impact of organized labor on democracy and human development. India and

Pakistan share cultures and histories. But the political regimes of India and Pakistan are markedly different. And political regimes fashion the legal institutions for the organizations of labor. India has maintained decades of parliamentary democracy. Pakistan, a decade after Independence, gave way to frequent dismissals of civilian governments and lengthy periods of military rule. This combination of deep similarities – cultural, colonial, administrative, legal, historical, and economic – and of stark differences in political regime type and in the organization of labor make India and Pakistan ideal for comparative analysis. One can more easily identify the influence of different labor organizations on human development achievements.

Studying India and Pakistan alongside one another brings to light important issues in the political economy of development. One can see each political regime keeping and consolidating its hold by amending identical colonial legislation to mold regime-supportive and to weaken regime-rival social institutions. Governments – senior managers of the machinery of the state – do act to stay in government. But political regimes – regular patterns for selection of government (e.g. electoral, military, monarchical) – also tend to seek their own longevity. Successive elected Indian governments built upon British legislation, strengthened social institutions, and facilitated political party competition. In contrast, Pakistani governments, mostly unelected, dismantled much of the legislation that Pakistan, like India, had inherited from British rulers, weakened social and civic institutions, and undermined political parties.

Differing institutional environments had, until the early 1990s, little influence on rates of economic growth. India and Pakistan have had nearly identical growth rates in gross national product (GDP), of about 5 percent per annum on average since their Independence in 1947 (See tables 0.1 and 0.2). Their conversion of that economic growth into public wellbeing, however, has differed very widely.

Literacy and health have risen in India but languished in Pakistan. The average years of schooling in Pakistan is fewer than half of that in India. Occupation accidents and fatalities are twice the rate in Pakistan as that in India. Higher income inequality in Pakistan means that the average Pakistani citizen, while as well off as the average Indian in income terms, lives a shorter life. Differing labor institutions had a powerful influence on each of these dimensions of human development and on the translation of growth into human development.

Table 0.1 India and Pakistan: basic wealth indicators

Pakistan		*India*
5.4 percent	GDP growth per annum (1961–2004)	4.8 percent
555 US$	GDP per capita (2003)	564 US$

Source: United Nations Development Program, human development statistics, on-line at www.undp.org.

Table 0.2 India and Pakistan: basic wellbeing indicators

Pakistan		*India*
2,097 PPP US$	GDP per capita (2003)	2,892 PPP US$
48.7 percent	adult (15 and above) literacy	61.1 percent
35.2 percent	female adult (15 and above) literacy (2003)	47.8 percent
32.6 percent	population living below the national poverty line	28.9 percent
23 percent	births attended by skilled health personnel (1995–2003)	43 percent
103 per 1,000	mortality rate (2003) under-5 live births	87 per 1,000
1.8 percent	annual reduction in under-5 mortality rate (1990–2004)	2.6 percent

Source: United Nations Development Program, human development statistics, on-line at www.undp.org.

Differing labor institutions also have a powerful influence on the implementation of major economic policy changes. Identical structural adjustment programs – a standard package of monetarist economic policies – have encountered markedly more resistance from the public in India than in Pakistan. In India, structural adjustment has been very contentious and thus implemented only very slowly. Rob Jenkins refers to India's economic reforms as a "stealth" operation.[4] The privatization program– a key component of any structural adjustment program – has been in Pakistan far quicker and has involved more corruption than in India because Pakistani labor unions have no voice in formal politics, unlike unions in India (or Pakistan's other South Asian neighbors).[5]

Postcolonial economic policies have influenced contemporary political fortunes. Pakistan's developmental shortcomings – suggested by widespread illiteracy, unemployment, and social discontent – are at the roots of its present political crisis.[6] India's present political fortunes – suggested by its rising status in international political fora and its high levels of foreign investments and foreign reserves – are, similarly, rooted in its developmental achievements. India's prior commitments to development – through high quality higher education, the establishment of institutes of technology, and protection of diverse national industries, to give three examples – allow its new pro-international economic interdependence policies to work. If trade and investment openness were the sole cause of economic growth, Pakistan, the more open and more rapidly liberalized economy in the 1990s, would be the economy with higher growth in the decade following. Instead, Indian growth outpaced Pakistani growth (after the initial recession that the structural adjustment initiates).

It is especially revealing to investigate organized workers' and unions' influence on democracy and development under South Asian conditions. These conditions are not friendly to workers' solidarity. High real unemployment (around 20 percent), high underemployment, decreasing job security, falling real wages, and low and falling unionization rates are the reality for most workers in South Asia. Unions face high unemployment and underemployment as does most of the developing world.[7] Labor law (as explained in chapter five) effectively prohibits all but a small percentage (1–2 percent) of the labor force in either country from bargaining collectively.[8] In many regions and many industries – including the textile industry, the largest employer (examined in chapter four) – most working people have little discretionary income and sell their labor at sub-sustenance levels. In some regions and industries, this trend is getting worse. (See map for the major industrial cities in India and Pakistan.)

Map 0.1 India and Pakistan: major industrial cities in which research was conducted. Christopher Candland and Erisha Suwal, 2007

Workers in South Asia and their unions face tremendous challenges. Despite these conditions – sometimes because of them – workers and unions have exercised a significant and positive impact on the creation and maintenance of institutions of democratic government and of high and increasing human development. Unions play an important role in the transformation of wealth into wellbeing. This book shows how organized labor guides economic change in ways that are broadly economically beneficial.

Political regimes and economic change

For more than a decade, structural adjustment has been a major force in the lives of working people – from farmers to factory workers to bank employees and civil servants. The impact of structural adjustment is great enough that any consideration of Pakistani economic development since 1988 or Indian economic development since 1991 must address the experience with structural adjustment.

Contemporary structural adjustment came to South Asia in the late 1980s and early 1990s, about a decade later than in the rest of those economies that underwent International Monetary Found (IMF) structural adjustment.[9] Sri Lanka is an exception. Sri Lanka has long been largely dependent on export earnings from plantation crops. These declined in value in the 1970s. The government was unable to finance imports and thus adopted an IMF loan in 1977, even before the Mexican debt crisis in 1982 prompted the IMF to set up its Structural Adjustment Facility. (See map in chapter two for countries that have undergone IMF-guided structural adjustment programs.)

In South Asia as a whole, currency controls, relatively low international debt exposure, and relatively high worker remittances kept balance of payment crises at bay until the late 1980s.[10] Many Latin American and African economies had already adopted IMF structural adjustment programs by the late 1980s. The IMF coined the term structural adjustment to refer to national macroeconomic measures designed to restructure the economy to take advantage of opportunities – or to avoid losses – in the international economy. An expanded role for the state might be, under some conditions, the best method for promoting advantages or limiting losses. That state-oriented strategy helped to power rapid economic growth in East and Southeast Asia. For example, the government of South Korea made investments in steel mills, ports, and other industries to promote export-oriented industrialization and effect its own structural adjustment to the world economy.[11] Contemporary structural adjustment programs, however, designed and financed by the IMF, reduce the role of government in most areas of the economy. Specifically, contemporary structural adjustment involves reducing government expenditure, withdrawing the state from ownership and regulation of industry, lowering barriers to foreign products and services, and allowing currency exchange rates to be determined by international currency markets.

The government of Pakistan adopted its IMF structural adjustment program with major financing from the international financial organization in late 1988. The government of India adopted a nearly identical agreement with the IMF in mid-1991. In Pakistan, a military-appointed interim government saddled the incoming elected government of Benazir Bhutto with the country's first major IMF structural adjustment program. Many Pakistanis saw cruel irony in the state's rapid withdrawal from the economy – and from the provision of good jobs and affordable public services – under international pressure just as democracy, after more than a decade of authoritarian government, was given another opportunity to survive. Mrs. Bhutto's government devalued the rupee, lowered import tariffs, reduced government expenditure and budget deficits, liberalized financial operations, privatized state-owned industry, and met the other IMF conditions. When Nawaz Sharif succeeded Mrs. Bhutto, his rival, in 1990, he increased the pace of these economic reforms. In their successive two turns in office, Sharif and Bhutto managed to privatize the entire Pakistani manufacturing and financial sectors.[12]

In India, shortly after the announcement of India's adoption of structural adjustment measures, the finance minister announced the elimination of subsidies for unprofitable state-owned enterprises within two years. Almost two decades later, despite concerted efforts, the central government had not managed to privatize in whole a single central government public sector enterprise. Privatization of central government public sector enterprises in India has been very limited. The Indian government has been able to sell shares of state-owned enterprises, but these efforts have been limited largely to a transfer of debt to other public organizations and to the sale of state-level public enterprises in some states. Indeed, in 2006 Indian Prime Minister Manmohan Singh announced that there would be no further privatization. In contrast, in Pakistan, the government has privatized most state-owned enterprises. All public sector manufacturing factories and government banks have been sold to the private sector. The government continues to privatize telecommunications, water, power, and railways.[13]

What can account for the differing records in implementing nearly identical economic policies in the two countries? Why has privatization, a central condition of India's and Pakistan's similar structural adjustment programs, been implemented only very cautiously and incrementally in India, but rapidly, even recklessly, in Pakistan? Does regime type account for the variance in implementation of economic reforms? Are new democracies somehow able to implement unpopular economic measures – such as cuts in public spending – better than established democracies? Or, are legacies of authoritarianism the key to rapid adjustment? This study finds that institutions matter more to patterns of economic change than do current policies or political regimes types.

The evidence from Indian and Pakistani regime types suggests that social institutions, and the organizations that they foster, not political regimes themselves, explain economic reform outcomes. Pakistan Chief Martial Law Administrator General Zia ul-Haq did not initiate privatization, despite his firm control of government and business displeasure over the nationalization program of his predecessor Zulfikar Ali Bhutto. Zia appointed an interim military government shortly before his death in August 1988. That government initiated the structural adjustment program after Zia was killed. Elections brought a new civilian government, headed by Benazir Bhutto, the daughter of the populist leader (by then hanged). International financial institutions worried that the newly elected Pakistan Peoples Party government under Benazir Bhutto, an economic populist, would not be able to impose the requisite economic austerity. Yet, Bhutto implemented economic adjustment energetically. After Benazir Bhutto's departure, businessman Nawaz Sharif – her political rival and General Zia's former ally – continued the pace and the priorities of the reforms, including the emphasis on rapid privatization. The Privatization Commission sold public enterprises to political friends at prices below the assessed value and with extraordinary credit and buy-back terms. Scandal surrounded many of the sales of banks and public sector manufacturing industries to Pakistani and foreign investors.[14] Murder of the opponents of specific privatization deals accompanied some. General Musharraf, took power in October 1999. As of the end of 2007, he continues to implement the structural adjustment program. In Pakistan, civilian governments – of left and right political parties – energetically pressed reforms. One Pakistani military government did not press for reforms; another did. Thus, there is no clear correlation between type of political regime at the time of reform and the pace or pattern of economic reform.

In India too, no correlation between current regime type and patterns of economic reform is obvious. Indian Prime Minister Indira Gandhi made initial, modest economic adjustments during her 18-month Emergency, a civilian dictatorship she declared in 1975. Two years later, Mrs. Gandhi and her Indian National Congress conceded electoral defeat to the Janata (People's) movement. The Janata Party coalition continued incremental economic liberalization policies until 1979, when Mrs. Gandhi was re-elected. Mrs. Gandhi's government negotiated a major IMF loan in 1981 that fostered some very limited regulatory reforms (e.g., removal of production limits on private companies) but also mobilized political opposition to her policies. In 1985, after Mrs. Gandhi's assassination, Prime Minister Rajiv Gandhi, her son, enthusiastically promoted economic reform. In June 1991, after Rajiv Gandhi's assassination, the coalition Congress-led government of former Prime Minister P. V. Narasimha Rao began reforms that would transform Indian economic ideologies and economic performance. Subsequent governments – Congress, Congress coalition, Bharatiya Janata Party (BJP) coalition, and others – have pushed reforms against stiff social opposition for more than a decade. Despite support for economic reform from all the major non-communist political parties, implementation in every area has been slow and enormously contentious. The Indian Government has managed to liberalize currency transactions, lower tariffs, and lift industrial licensing restrictions. But the central government has not engaged in wholesale privatization of industrial or financial enterprise. Thus, in neither India nor Pakistan does the political regime – military or civilian, authoritarian or democratic, new or consolidated – correlate with vigorous or effective implementation of economic adjustment.

More serious, the correlation of regime type with the pace of implementation of economic adjustment itself explains very little. We still would not know the specific mechanisms that would allow an authoritarian regime to impose economic adjustment or those that would allow a new, struggling electoral democracy to implement unpopular economic measures more readily than an established democracy.

The comparative method in a global economy

> For those who would like to get clear of difficulties it is advantageous to discuss the difficulties well. ... people who inquire without first stating the difficulties are like those who do not know where they have to go.[15]
>
> Aristotle

The ubiquity of structural adjustment in the developing world brings into focus the global forces that drive national and local economic and political change. Do these global forces limit the ability of comparative analysis to understand these changes? Before beginning the comparative analysis, it will be useful to discuss what can and cannot be achieved with the comparative method, pitfalls associated with it when considering national changes that might be global in origin, and strategies for avoiding these pitfalls. Let us take Aristotle's advice to discuss inherent difficulties with the comparative method, to which India and Pakistan are here subjected. What are the difficulties inherent in using comparative historical analysis to answer questions related to transnational economic forces and how can these difficulties be avoided?

The most widely used comparative method in the social sciences is John Stuart Mill's "comparisons by the methods of difference and sameness." Many students of comparative politics argued that Mill's method provides a way to make the study of politics a behavioral science. But Mill himself cautioned against applying the comparative method to the social world. As Mill pointed out, the number of relevant variables involved in social phenomena well exceed the number of cases of these phenomena. No countries or political communities are essentially the same in all respects. Thus, none can serve as representative of a type. The comparative method described by Mill is appropriate in solid physics or plant biology, where a physical mass or biological specimen might be regarded as a model representative for an entire class of objects. The social science researcher, however, must specify and control for such an enormous variety of variables when comparing entities as complicated as whole societies and countries that it leaves comparative historical analysis vulnerable to *post hoc* theorizing. Thus, Mill argued that "It is an imperative rule never to introduce any generalization from history into the social sciences unless sufficient grounds can be pointed out for it in human nature," that is, from a non-historical, non-comparative foundation.[16]

A second methodological problem is especially apparent in *post hoc* theorizing and thus prominent in poorly conducted comparative studies. Findings are often restatements of unstated value assumptions. Values (e.g., a preference for political stability over political participation) make their way into all meaningful concepts in social science. Many American economists in the 1950s and 1960s confused the instrumental value of economic growth (e.g., as a means to welfare) with development itself because value assumptions (e.g., a preference for material goods and individual freedom over non-material goods and social solidarity) were lodged implicitly in their economic development models. The manner in which concepts are formulated, data are selected, trends are interpreted, and evidence is treated can easily reveal one's value assumptions as if they were empirical findings.

How are we to avoid these two pitfalls – of variables that outnumber cases and of values that creep into basic concepts? As for values, I assume that they are inescapable. I agree with Gunnar Myrdal that the social scientist can at best (and should at least) try to lay bare his or her value assumptions.[17] This study involves, even pivots on, two value-laden concepts: democracy and development. I acknowledge that these basic concepts are culturally defined. I consider democracy an ideal – pursued, but never fully attained. I believe in inalienable human rights, not that good governments bestow rights on citizens. I regard individual and collective opportunity, security, and empowerment to be the greatest goods. I presume social solidarity and individual freedoms to require one another. I elaborate on these values – where it seems relevant – in coming pages.

As for the problem of fewer differing cases than differing variables, I do not regard India and Pakistan as members of a set (e.g., established democracies or authoritarian regimes). Rather, I evaluate explanations for patterns of economic change in one country against the experiences of the other country. This way, I can readily disconfirm the conjectures that readily make their way into single-case studies. I attempt to not confuse historical phenomena with rules of social or political life. Broadly, I follow Reinhard Bendix's inclination to "increase the visibility of one structure by contrasting it with another." I attempt "to preserve a sense of historical particularity … while still comparing different countries … to make more transparent the divergence among structures."[18]

With this reflective comparative approach, I hope to avoid the reconstitution of facts according to the needs of theory, to which single case studies can easily fall victim. I evaluate trends in one country alongside trends that should appear similar, or dissimilar in predictable ways, in the other. I do not test a model against the experiences of either or both countries. My approach weeds out incidental explanations and enables one to avoid findings based on spurious evidence. It would be easier, but also considerably less reliable, to make findings based on India's or Pakistan's experiences alone. It would be easy to suggest that unions, say in India, inhibit economic growth and even promote economic inequality. Drawing findings on this same question – the impact of unions on growth and inequality – from India and Pakistan is more difficult, but provides more compelling results.

India and Pakistan allow for a high degree of control for study of the influence both of political regimes on labor organizations and institutions and of labor institutions and organizations on patterns of economic and political change. Each country adopted identical colonial labor legislation at Independence. Each country inherited all legislation, including all labor legislation, in August 1947. Paths diverged only after Independence. The Indian and Pakistani governments modified colonial legislation to restrict and to control the trade union movements to suit differing political regime requirements. Military governments in Pakistan ensured that the trade union movement would be politically weak, factory-based, and fragmented. The transitional martial law regime, preparing the way for the first national elections, promulgated an Industrial Relations Ordinance of 1969. The Ordinance effectively prevented trade unions from representing workers of more than a single enterprise and limited unions from forming bonds with political parties. Without overhauling the labor legislation inherited from the British, the military government was able to de-politicize the trade union movement. By contrast, India's elected governments encouraged the development of politically powerful trade unions to serve as electoral vehicles for the major political parties. In India, elections initially strengthened the national trade union federations that were aligned with the Indian National Congress and with other political parties. Thus, while workers and unions helped to shape economic ideologies and political outcomes, India and Pakistan's different political regimes led to two very different labor regimes.

Neither the Indian nor the Pakistani labor movement has been able to reverse the informalization of terms of employment. Indian labor organizations, however, have managed to contain the deregulation of work and to arrest some adjustment measures, most notably privatization. In contrast, Pakistan's new transitional regimes, burdened with the institutional legacy of authoritarian regimes, while unable to prevent labor protest, have espoused neoliberal economic ideologies and imposed upon labor a system of enterprise unionism, prohibiting the development of a trade union movement that could successfully resist government economic reforms.

The argument ahead

This introduction has posed what should be the central question for political economy: how to transform wealth into wellbeing. This introduction has also presented India and Pakistan as a comparative pair for gauging the impact of organized labor on economic and political development and discussed the comparative method.

Chapter one discusses the impact of workers and union movements on Indian and Pakistani politics and the impact of politics on workers and unions since 1920. The All India Trade Union Congress, the longest standing national union federation in the Subcontinent, was founded that year. The chapter will show that organized workers, their unions, and unorganized labor movements had a powerful impact on political developments in the South Asian Subcontinent. The involvement of the working classes in the Indian Independence movement helped to secure democratic institutions in independent India. A habit of selection of candidates for public office from among union leaders stabilized democracy and laid foundations for relatively better welfare and opportunity than experienced in Pakistan. Workers' movements in Pakistan were not as strong as those in India, but they did make democratic gains possible. In Pakistan as well as India, workers and unions asserted and fought for the political rights of all members of society, including universal franchise and the freedom to associate.

Workers and unionists who migrated to or remained in Pakistan made significant contributions to the Pakistani labor movement but were too few to help shape the ideas or programs of the movement for the creation of Pakistan. What the All India Muslim League argued generally about the rights of workers or the dignity of workers – like other specifics about what kind of a homeland for Muslims Pakistan might be – was carefully left unclear in the details.[19] Nevertheless, the Pakistani labor movement was tremendously powerful at important moments after Independence. Factory workers and their protests in 1968–69 persuaded a decade-old military government to hold elections. Two decades later, workers and unions were central to the Movement for the Restoration of Democracy, which helped to end Zia's military rule and begin a decade of elected governments. Workers and unions could assert themselves in factories or on the streets, only rarely through elections. They did protest forcefully and repeatedly to press for democratic rights and to demand an end to military rule.

Chapter two discusses the contribution of workers and unions to Indian and Pakistani economic development, beginning in 1920 a generation before Indian and Pakistani Independence. Differing ideologies and strategies affected labor institutions and organizations just as workers and unions influenced these state ideologies and strategies. Indian workers and unions helped to secure a commitment, albeit not fulfilled, to a socialist pattern of economic development. In Pakistan, as in other authoritarian regimes without hegemonic political parties, workers and unions could rarely influence national economic goals.

Comparative analysis of Indian and Pakistan economic ideologies, development strategies, and political regimes, discussed in chapters one and two, suggests that the more working classes participate in the struggle for independence, the more social-democratic the economic ideologies and economic development strategies will be and the more democratic the politics will be. The relative strength of workers and their unions is an important contributor to India's enduring democracy. Correspondingly, the relative weakness of workers and their unions is an important contributor to Pakistan's entrenched authoritarianism.

Chapters three and four bring the analysis to bear on recent policies and practices. Chapter three discusses the differing responses of workers and unions to economic adjustment in India and Pakistan since the late 1970s. The chapter provides profiles of the Indian and Pakistani economies and of government efforts to implement structural adjustment programs. It documents the influence of workers and unions on patterns of adjustment, specifically privatization. Even enthusiastic promoters of adjustment admit that organized workers and unions have been the chief obstacle to IMF reforms. Maria Victoria Murillo shows in a comparison of Latin American countries that where unions compete with one another and political parties compete with one another, economic reform is a highly contested process.[20] Comparative analysis of labor's influence over the adjustment process in India and Pakistan, specifically over the privatization process, encourages us to extend and elaborate on Murillo's argument. Strong unions – especially when leadership are selected by workers and when their political advocacy is permitted – can make economic adjustment less pernicious to the least advantaged. Strong unions help to slow the adjustment process, soften economic austerity, and make the privatization process less corrupt. Comparative analysis shows that India's process of adjustment has been less painful, less austere, and less corrupt than Pakistan's. In part, this is because of the political power of Indian unions. Organized labor promotes sounder economic policy and economic administration in a variety of ways.

Chapter four discusses the changing nature of work and the increasingly insecure and informal terms of employment that have accompanied adjustment. The chapter surveys changes in the industrial labor force in India and Pakistan focusing on terms of employment, drawing illustrations mainly from each country's largest industry and employer, textiles. In each country, labor organizations are using new strategies to promote social justice and economic democracy in an environment of increasing job insecurity and informality. Unions have fought informalization at the firm level and at the industrial level. Unions have engaged management to keep factories open, to ensure payment of wages, to keep accounting honest, and to include subcontracted workers in union collective bargaining agreements. Unions are also reforming and democratizing themselves.

Emerging union strategies, while differing from country to country in significant ways, involve greater attention to workers in sectors of the economy once neglected by organized labor, with its traditional base in registered factories, often in the public sector. South Asian unions are reaching out to workers in irregular employment status. Some unions have even bargained successfully to include protections for irregular employers, prohibited from unionizing. As such, unions, in South Asia, as elsewhere, are democratizing, both by enlarging their constituencies and increasing rank-and-file participation in leadership selection and advocacy orientation.

Chapter five discusses union strategies and the viability of durable alliances between organized labor and political parties in an era of increased international economic interdependence in which the hand of organized capital over labor is vastly strengthened. The chapter forecasts, based on the evidence of labor's contribution to democracy and development, labor's strategic advantages and political opportunities in poor economies facing continued fiscal crises. In their totality, the chapters demonstrate that workers' solidarity is an essential condition for political democracy and economic development. Labor organizations help transform wealth into wellbeing.

1

ORGANIZED LABOR AND DEMOCRATIC CONSOLIDATION

> First of all, we must have the Government thoroughly with us, heart and soul.[1]
>
> G. V. Joshi

Political regimes – democratic or authoritarian – shape social organizations and mold the state itself. Political regimes also frame the relationships between those social organizations and the state – the administrative apparatus of government. Accordingly, most labor studies emphasize the impact of political regimes on the organization and representation of labor. Few labor studies show how labor organizations and labor institutions help to produce or reinforce political regimes. This book considers the influence both of organized labor on political regimes and of political regimes on organized labor. This chapter focuses on the former, the impact of organized labor on political regime formation.

Unions and workers themselves helped to shape political regimes as well as economic institutions, and the state itself. Everywhere, political regimes have structured labor institutions and labor organizations to suit their needs. At the same time, but less well acknowledged or understood, workers and unions have themselves influenced political and economic development. Even in the predominantly poor and rural economies of India and Pakistan, where labor's bargaining power is low, workers and their associations helped to determine significant economic and political outcomes.

The history of union opposition to authoritarian governments of all kinds in the South Asian Subcontinent is as long as the history of union organization itself. Workers resisted colonial rule. They shirked the regimentation of factory work when the British established manufacturing shops. Workers gave employer associations in colonizing economies reason to fund study of the problems of absenteeism and backward-bending supply curves for labor (workers wanting fewer hours at higher wages) in the colonial world.[2] In South Asia, workers used the organization formed through factory work – including working class neighborhood associations – to close down industry and crowd colonial jails.

Unions also protest undemocratic decisions by elected governments. The most public displays of trade union support for democracy in India and Pakistan are on the streets in opposition to authoritarianism. Unions are supportive, sometimes vitally, to peace-activism, anti-communalism, and promotion of international human rights. Nearly every major union in India and Pakistan opposed the decision of their governments to test nuclear weapons in May and June 1998. Unions complained specifically about the lack of public input into such a momentous decision.

In independent India, labor helped to ensure a tradition of regular elections to public office and helped to make elections more meaningful. Unions educated workers about politics and mobilized them to support pro-labor parties. Workers then used their unions to ensure that elected representatives enacted policies that would promote social welfare.

In Pakistan, workers and unions could not persuade elected representatives to adopt a constitution or prevent the 1958 military coup. But when Field Marshal Ayub Khan provoked organized labor with official celebrations of the first decade of military rule, workers and others protested and wrested from the military a commitment to hold national elections. Workers' organizations build networks among individuals from differing ethnic, linguistic, national, and religious backgrounds. Workers' organizations are essential to making economic life democratic.

Political regimes

Many think of India as a democratic polity and Pakistan as an authoritarian one. The characterization is correct but not complete. There are strong authoritarian institutions in the Indian polity and strong democratic institutions in the Pakistani polity. At any given moment, millions of Indians are under some form of military or paramilitary rule, a practice in existence since British government. In Pakistan, despite frequent and sometimes decade-long periods of military rule and suspension of civil and political rights, regular elections for municipal government have continued.

India's coalition of dominant proprietary classes

A century of contest and representation through elections shaped social organizations and institutions. Regular elections for public office have been held in India since the late nineteenth century, decades before India's Independence from British rule in 1947. The British Viceroy's Legislative Council and the Provincial Legislatures, established by the 1861 Indian Councils Act, were partially elected. By 1884, some members of municipal committees were elected. The Government of India Act of 1919 brought elections for limited self-government to the provincial level. These pre-Independence elections were conducted on a restricted franchise.

The Indian government has held regular elections for national and state (i.e., provincial) office, on the basis of a universal franchise, since 1950. Mrs. Gandhi declared an Emergency and suspended civil and political rights in June 1975. The Emergency was not lifted until February 1977, when her elder son Sanjay persuaded her to declare elections. But when she was defeated in the election intended to solidify her rule, she conceded to the voters. Thus even India's temporary break with electoral politics indicates the resilience of electoral politics in India.

Given the volume and depth of analysis on Indian political regimes, it is striking that scholarship, Marxist and non-Marxist, maintains a broadly similar view.[3] Publicly contested elections among competitive political parties characterize India's political regime – the pattern of recruitment into positions of state management. But most analysts of India's political regime agree that the state – the administrative apparatus for governance, which among modern states typically focuses on revenue collection, law and order, and policing territorial borders – is the instrument of the alliance of three dominant classes: an urban industrial elite, or large-scale industrialists, a landed class, or rich farmers, and the managerial bureaucratic bourgeoisie, or senior civil servants. Numerous students of Indian politics have characterized the state as serving these three "dominatnt classes."

Harry Blair described the partly autonomous "government bureaucracy, the military and the intelligentsia" as the "third element in the political economy of managing the Indian system." The other two elements, according to Blair, are industrialists and large landholders.[4] Pranab Bardhan's similar theory that three dominant proprietary actors capture the Indian state is better known.[5] According to his class-based approach, state controls in the Indian economy have served principally to protect domestic capital from foreign competition, to secure state subsidies for wealthier farmers, and to secure rents and political patronage for the managerial bourgeoisie. The state is not distinct from society. Rather the state is a social alliance administered by one dominant class, the managerial bureaucratic bourgeoisie, in cooperation with other dominant classes. Bardhan uses this conceptualization of the Indian state to explain the evolution of the fiscal crisis, and its tenacity, in the contemporary Indian economy.

Pakistan's bureaucratic-military oligarchy

The Pakistani state has extended protection to two of these same three economically and politically dominant groups, namely large landholders and industrialists. As in India, in Pakistan, the bureaucracy – the managers of the state apparatus – has been characterized as relatively autonomous from other social classes. In Pakistan, however, the military is the basis for that autonomy. Pakistan has spent most of the nearly six decades since its creation under some form of martial or military rule. Electoral democracy in Pakistan got off to a shaky start. From 1947 until 1956, the Constituent Assembly, elected in undivided India with a highly restricted franchise, served as the national assembly. Pakistan's first independent Constitution was framed in 1956. Between the 1958 military coup and the 1988 death of President Zia ul-Haq, only two short episodes of elected, civilian political regimes emerged. The first episode occurred after Pakistan's first general election in December 1970. The military prevented the Bengali leader Mujibur Rahman from forming a government and attacked his supporters in East Pakistan. At the military's defeat in December 1971, the country broke up. Zulfikar Ali Bhutto assumed control of an elected government in a truncated Pakistan. The second civilian political regime was that of Ghulam Ishaq Khan (1985–88). It was party-less – political parties were banned from the elections – and sponsored by the military. Military governments ruled Pakistan from 1958 until 1971, from 1977 until 1985, three times in the late 1980s and early 1990s, and from 1999 until 2002. Martial law has been in effect for more than 30 years of Pakistan's short history as a state.[6]

The Pakistani state is in the hands of bureaucratic and military elites. Pakistan was the illustrative case used by Hamza Alavi to advance the thesis that colonial powers left overdeveloped states in postcolonial societies.[7] The overdeveloped state, embedded in peripheral capitalist development, promoted industrial development, despite the weakness of the indigenous bourgeoisie and to the detriment of "landowners and peasant producers." Peripheral capitalist development demanded it. To raise revenue and to control the native population, colonial rulers created the state. Thus, the strongest elements of the state in postcolonial societies are those designed for extracting resources and policing people. "Effective power within the state apparatus lay in the hands of a military bureaucratic oligarchy."[8] The autonomy of the state in Alavi's analysis derives from the colonial state's service of foreign classes not from an alliance of domestic classes. Of course, the same could be said of India. Indeed, the British East India Company and British Crown ruled earlier, and thus longer, in most areas of what is now independent India than they did in what is now Pakistan. The Indian state should, according to Alavi, be more overdeveloped, more beholden to foreign than to domestic classes.[9] Comparative analysis, however, allows us to see how much stronger the domestic business classes are in India and how different the basis of the autonomy of the Indian ruling classes is from that of the Pakistani ruling classes.[10]

Labor politics under colonial rule

Understanding colonial labor law and its purposes is vitally important to understanding the obstacles that organized labor in India and Pakistan face today. At Independence, India and Pakistan retained all colonial labor law. Rather than framing entirely new law, as a revolutionary government might do, governments in India and Pakistan merely amended colonial labor law. The details of Indian colonial labor history are well enough documented but uniformly ignore the history of the areas that are now Pakistan and Bangladesh.

Coordinated action by workers preceded the formation of unions in colonial India. Even before the legalization recognizing and regulating trade unionism in 1926, labor action was geographically widespread and used widely varied methods. Labor actions were typically spontaneous, decided upon by workers at a particular residence or work site.[11] When associations did emerge, they typically took the form of strike committees. They mobilized around particular grievances, and disbanded when demands were met or abandoned. Bashir Ahmed Bakhtiar, for an exemplary example, while working for a woolen mill in pre-Partition Punjab, mobilized his fellow workers to protest the stinginess of their employer at the wedding of the employer's daughter. Bashir Ahmed Bakhtiar exerted a major influence in the pre-Partition and in the Pakistani trade union movements. He was the founder and the patron of the All Pakistan Federation of Trade Unions.[12]

Early trade unions in colonial India formed as workers' aid organizations. Philanthropists and social reformers established unions out of concern for inhuman working conditions.[13] Mobilizing Bombay textile mill workers for humane working conditions in the 1880s, N. M. Lokhande organized one of British India's earliest trade unions in 1890.[14] Other early but also short-lived unions included the Amalgamated Society of Railway Servants of India and Burma established in 1897, the Printers' Union established in Calcutta in 1905, and the Kamagar Hitvardhak Sabha (Workers Welfare Union) established in Bombay in 1909.[15] More formal and permanent trade union bodies, notably the Madras Labour Union founded by B. P. Wadia in 1919, formed only after World War I, during a wave of labor militancy.

Much of the labor action at the beginning of the century was stimulated by political events. The Partition of Bengal in 1905 helped to arouse workers' consciousness over the linkages between industrial and political action in Bengal, the region first colonized by Britain.[16] The British government too saw a link between labor and political action. Holding that one strike in Calcutta during that period was dangerous and politically motivated, the government dismissed and arrested its organizers. This helped lead to the formation of the Bengal Press Workers Union, which publicized the interests of workers.[17]

Before World War I, the British government in India regularly repressed labor organizations and met labor agitations with violence. In July 1908, the British tried the Congress leader *Lokamanya* (friend of the people) Bal Gangadhar Tilak for sedition on the basis of his writings in his periodical *Kesari* (Lion). His appearance before the Bombay High Court provoked what is widely considered to be India's first political strike. Workers formed a large contingent of the mass protests that assembled to protest the trial. "During the days of the trial a 20,000 strong procession of workers moved around the city and invited factory workers to down tools."[18] Textile workers closed down mills. Police arrested strikers, who were tried, convicted, and given six-year prison terms for disobeying police orders. The commitment of workers to the 1908 Bombay strike persuaded V. I. Lenin to write "in India ... the proletariat has already developed conscious political mass struggle."[19] But Lenin's assessment was premature.

Labor militancy in British India became politically allied only after the Russian Revolution in 1917 and after Indian nationalists launched the Non-Cooperation Movement in 1920. At the beginning of the century, Indian labor was militant but unorganized. Trade unions and organizers, as we shall see shortly, typically struggled to keep pace with workers' movements. One of the earliest trade unions "engaged simultaneously in both economic and political struggle" was the Girni Kamgar Union (Mill Workers Union) (GKU) of textile workers in Bombay, led by Communist Party of India leader Shripad Amrit Dange and British Socialist Ben Bradley. In protest over a lockout affecting several thousand workers, the GKU staged a strike in April 1928, which lasted for six months. The action gained the support of workers in other industrial towns in India as well as funds from sympathizers in Britain and the Soviet Union.[20]

The manner in which the GKU and Bombay Textile Labour Union (BTLU) attempted to channel workers' demands represents two common forms of labor organization in colonial India. These were the earliest major unions in India's most important industrial city. Their formation led to a number of significant pieces of labor legislation. The BTLU was formed in 1925 "on the enthusiasm of the 1925 general strike in Bombay" by a group of labor welfare leaders, including N. M. Joshi and R. R. Bakhale, and "a handful of workers."[21] The GKU was a more radical organization, led by communists and propelled by the militant mood of workers during the April–September 1928 Bombay general strike. "Whereas the BTLU was primarily an outside initiative, the GKM [i.e., GKU] was formed by labourers themselves."[22] When the BTLU broke with the Joint Strike Committee to negotiate a settlement with the government's Bombay Strike Inquiry Committee, workers returned to work. The GKU meanwhile "continued organisational work and struggle in the factories" and "organised a grievance committee in each mill to deal directly with the management." GKU membership subsequently rose while BTLU membership fell.[23] The GKU and the BTLU aptly characterize the two dominant strains of Indian labor unionism: one led by "outsiders," who are more willing to settle disputes; the other led by workers themselves, who are often less compromising.

Muslims played a strong role in the Indian labor movement in the inter-war years, especially in the areas that would become Pakistan. Some, such as Aminaldin Sindhi, formed associations and joined socialist and Islamic ideals. Sindhi told a group of striking workers in Lahore in July 1920 that "Islam had owed its birth to the poorer classes and it would be reborn as the offspring of the Labour Party."[24] In 1922 a revolutionary group began functioning in Lahore under the leadership of Ghulam Hussain. Hussain published an Urdu-language newspaper *Inqilab* (Revolution) for the group. The office of *Inqilab* "became the center of socialist activity" in Lahore.[25] M. S. Khan, General Secretary of the North Western Railway Workers Union, and Shamsuldin Hasan, Publicity Secretary of the Union, together with Hussain, were the leaders of the group. Between 1923 and 1925, a Marxist circle was also established in Karachi. The trials of suspected socialist "subversives" in Peshawar and Kanpur in 1924–25 and in Meerut in 1929–33 led to the imprisonment of several Muslim labor leaders and severely constrained the work of Muslim socialists.

Colonial labor legislation

As Zafar Shaheed has argued, colonial labor legislation "emerged in response to a complex and in some respects contradictory combination of pressures and needs."[26] The industrial relations system of colonial India gave workers a degree of legal recognition unusual for former colonies. But the government retained ultimate authority to prohibit labor organizations and strikes in key industries. The government also retained the authority to refer cases to industrial tribunals for mandatory arbitration. Thus, the state inserted itself between workers and industry and established itself in the central position in industrial relations.

The labor legislation inherited from the British, which forms the core of labor law in both India and Pakistan, may be seen as fulfilling two related functions. British officials were concerned that labor militancy not be harnessed to communist or other subversive movements. Widespread British ownership of industry, especially in Bengal, meant that workers easily regarded foreign rule and poor working conditions as conjoined. Colonial administrators, responding to the British business community, also worried that if labor exploitation in India were left unchecked, then Indian industries would successfully compete against British industries, particularly against the Lancashire and Manchester cotton mills. Missions to India, sponsored by British textile associations, surveyed and publicized the miserable conditions of textile laborers in and around Bombay. Manchester mill owners were the chief advocates of improving Indian working conditions through India's Factories Act of 1934. The Factories Act of 1934 continues to be one of the three central pieces of legislation defining industrial relations in India and Pakistan today.

The two most significant pieces of colonial labor legislation were the Trade Union Act of 1926 and the Industrial Disputes Act of 1947. Before enactment of the Trade Union Act of 1926, labor organizations had no legal status. Labor organizing was regarded as an "illegal conspiracy."[27] B. P. Wadia, for example, was tried under the illegal conspiracy clause as he attempted to establish the Madras Labour Union in 1919. The Trade Union Act of 1926 permitted workers to associate, a right long denied.

The Industrial Disputes Act of 1947 established permanent administrative machinery for the settlement of labor disputes, laying down deadlines for specific stages of consultation and arbitration. Prior to the Act, the government would appoint tribunals to settle disputes between workers and employers. The Industrial Disputes Act of 1947 also prohibited strikes and lockouts when conciliation is pending and required that industrial disputes in public services be settled by compulsory arbitration. Like the Industrial Employment (Standing Orders), the Industrial Disputes Act of 1947 required employers to recognize and negotiate with trade unions. The Industrial Employment (Standing Orders) Act, passed in 1946, was the outcome of the Sixth Indian Labour Conference, held in 1944. The Act defined procedures for recruitment, termination, disciplinary action, and conditions for work and welfare. As the Standing Order requires employers and trade union representatives to exchange drafts of these procedures and conditions, the act compels workers to collective bargaining.

While the British Indian government refused Indians the right to organize, it encouraged the political representation of labor. Labor representatives served in Provincial Legislative Councils, although their role was merely advisory. Even before legally recognizing trade unions, the Government in India gave labor representation, in Provincial Legislatures and in the Central Legislative Assembly, although the British Viceroy made the nominations. The Government of India's Reforms Act of 1919 authorized the Central and Provincial Governments to nominate labor representatives. One labor representative was nominated to the Central Legislative Assembly, three to the Bombay Assembly, two to the Bengal Assembly, and one each to the assemblies of Assam, Bihar, and Orissa. Madras, the North West Frontier, Punjab, and Sindh were not provided the authority to appoint labor representatives.[28] Thus, the territory that was to make up Pakistan, a generation later, had no labor representation. Incorporation of organized labor by the state and political parties preceded Independence and postcolonial politics in South Asia by a generation. Just as the seeds of a social democratic India were sown by British rule, so too the roots of authoritarianism in areas that were to become Pakistan were strengthened by British rule.

Labor unrest in British India was widespread from the start of World War I until 1920, reaching historic heights in 1919–20. World War I stimulated great demand from Indian industries, particularly textiles and significantly military ordinance.[29] Factories extended working hours, operating around the clock, earning their owners larger profits. This led to strong worker demands for better working conditions. Workers grew particularly militant at the close of World War I. The government accordingly framed a bill in 1920, modeled on the Canadian Industrial Disputes Investigation Act of 1907, with the aim of settling industrial disputes by an Industrial Disputes Board before strikes were declared. The bill was shelved because provincial governments opposed it. In the meantime, the government enacted or amended other acts directed at incorporating and regulating labor. In 1922, the government revived the Factories Act, passed the Workers' Breach of Contract Act, and made changes to the Indian Penal Code to promote workplace discipline. In 1923, the government revised the Mines Act. After the widespread labor unrest, involving the GKU and BTLU, in 1928 and 1929, the government reexamined the Industrial Disputes bill and enacted it as the Trade Disputes Act of 1929.[30] The Factory Act of 1934, which continues to be India and Pakistan's code for labor administration, was framed in the wake of a wave of industrial action by factory workers.

In British India, the Government of India Act of 1935 laid down the rules for the Provincial Assembly election of 1937. In India, the act and its election rules remained in effect until the adoption of the 1950 Constitution. In Pakistan, the Act and the electoral rules laid down by the Act remained in effect until the adoption of Pakistan's first Constitution in 1956. The Act allotted 48 seats to labor, 38 in the Provincial Assemblies and 10 in the Federal Assemblies. Provincial and Federal Assembly members were not elected as individuals, but as representatives of government-recognized trade unions. The Act required for certification as a recognized trade union that the union be in existence for at least two years, be registered for at least one year, have its membership rolls be inspected by the Registrar of Trade Unions, and have a minimum of 250 dues-paying members. The Indian National Congress captured the largest number of labor constituency seats.[31] In the 1937 provincial assembly elections, the Congress won 18 of the 38 seats. And in the 1946 elections it won 23 of the 39 Provincial Assembly seats.[32]

The All India Trade Union Congress and political party unionism

Colonial labor legislation both enabled and constrained labor organizations in pre-Partition India. Indian labor activists created colonial India's first national trade union body, the All India Trade Union Congress (AITUC), in 1920, largely in response to the formation of the International Labour Organization (ILO) in 1919.

The ILO's tripartite structure, with its roles for government representatives, national associations of employers, and national associations of employees, encouraged the formation of national labor bodies in every country, even in colonies. Because the AITUC emerged in response to external opportunities, and not solely as an organized outgrowth of internal needs, even within the relatively well-developed Indian labor movement, some felt that the organization of an all India workers' organization was premature. But the AITUC showed considerable skill in political organizing. Within ten years, it grew to nearly one quarter of a million members.

Although there were divisions, the AITUC was the principle trade union center in undivided India, from its formation in 1920 until the formation of the Indian National Congress' Indian National Trade Union Congress (INTUC) in 1947 on the eve of Independence. There were two, relatively minor, factional splits from the AITUC. The first was in 1929 by less radical trade unionists who formed the National Trade Union Federation (NTUF), and in 1931 by more radical trade unionists who formed the Red Trade Union Congress (RTUC). Both factions, however, foundered and rejoined the AITUC. The Red Trade Union Congress rejoined the AITUC in 1935. The National Trade Union Federation rejoined in 1940.

In 1929 conflicts in the AITUC between rightists (chiefly Congressmen) and leftists (chiefly members of the Communist Party of India) reached such an impasse that the rightists formed a new body, the Trade Union Federation. Contemporary observers, even within the faction that departed, disagree about the causes of the 1929 split of the AITUC. G. Ramanujam, former President of the Congress-aligned INTUC, claims that "Indian communists, following, as usual, instructions from Moscow," launched a campaign to undermine the trade union movement and thereby "forced a section to walk out of the AITUC and to form a new central organization."[33] However, B. N. Datar, Founder and Director of the Ambekar Institute of Labour Studies, an INTUC-affiliated research center, attributes the split to differences between communists and non-communists as to how important political goals were to trade union action.[34] The split is indicative of a divide that continues to run through Indian and Pakistani trade unionism. Non-Marxist unionists tend to believe that labor can obtain justice in the workplace without a change in the economic order. Marxist unionists disagree. They tend to believe that union activities should be aimed at gaining the political power to change the economic order.

The Jharia session of the AITUC meeting in 1928 exposed much of the rising conflict between Congress and communist activists within the trade union movement. The session elected Jawaharlal Nehru as AITUC President for 1929. A few days later in Calcutta he was re-elected General Secretary of the Congress, despite a serious rift in the Congress over accepting the All Parties Report. About Jharia, he made the following observations:

> There were differences in the organization about international affiliation and the extent to which Indian workers should participate in ILO activities; but the more serious differences were on domestic matters. One group led by N. M. Joshi did not want political considerations to interfere with workers struggle and expected industrial action to be taken with due care. The other group led by communist elements was opposed to both these prescriptions . . .

> I was inclined to favour the anti-Joshi line though Joshi and his colleagues were closer to me ... I learnt later in Calcutta that I was elected as the President of the AITUC in preference to an actual worker whom the Communists supported.[35]

At the next session of the AITUC, its tenth, in November 1929 at Nagpur, rightists in the union wanted to prohibit the membership of the communist lead Girni Kamgar Union. This may have caused the breach. By December 1929, the rightists in the AITUC set up their own union, the Trade Unions Federation, under the leadership of V. V. Giri.[36] Significantly, the fact that the rightists preferred to leave the original, united federation foreshadowed what would become the most important attribute of Indian unionism, political party dependent, and thus, factionalized, trade unionism. Four decades later, in November 1969, Prime Minister Indira Gandhi's nomination of V.V. Giri to be President of India, against Sanjiv Reddy, the choice of the right wing of the Congress, would provide the occasion for the split of the Congress party. The control that the Communist Party of India exercised within the AITUC, even before it split into ideologically incompatible factions, constitutes the first movement toward a political party-affiliated labor regime in India. The AITUC's split in 1929 marked the beginning of the institutionalization of political party-dependent trade unionism in India.

Gandhian unionism

Mohandas Gandhi involved himself in many important labor actions in the 1910s and 1920s. Gandhi led popular movements against British colonial rule, as is well known, through his appeals to truth, non-violence, and the purity of intention. He believed that successful trade union action was marked not by labor's ability to force industrialists to accept labor's demand, but rather by labor's ability to persuade industrialists of their responsibility to their workers. Gandhi counseled workers that "there is only one royal road to remove their [industrialists] discontent: entering their lives and binding them with the silken thread of love." "Why should not the mill-owners feel happy paying a little more to the workers?" Gandhi wrote in one pamphlet for workers.[37] Gandhi's involvement in the Ahmedabad textile industry – an involvement based on the principle of non-violent dispute resolution and the practice of restraint of labor militancy – had a powerful and lasting impact on the Indian trade union movement. Concerned about militancy of trade union action, trade unions owing their allegiance to Gandhi remained outside of AITUC.[38]

Without planning it, Gandhi formed one of India's most important labor organizations, the Textile Labour Association.[39] Shortly after his return to India from South Africa in 1915, Anusuyabehn Sarabhai, sister of Ahmedabad textile mill owner Ambalal Sarabhai, sent a request to Gandhi on behalf of textile mill workers in Ahmedabad. Workers had been agitating for higher wages. Anusuya Sarabhai had been inspired by the philosophy of the Fabian Society while visiting England. She sided with the workers. In 1917, plague took the lives of many textile workers in Ahmedabad. Mill owners were forced to promise a plague bonus to keep workers from escaping the plague-ridden city and returning to their villages. The companies withdrew the bonus scheme as the plague subsided in 1918. Instead, owners granted workers a wage increase. The wage increase, however, did not even compensate for increases in the cost of living. At Anusuyabehn Sarabhai's request, Gandhi agreed to intervene, cautioning the workers that their best strategy was to refrain from strikes, violence, and ill thought about the mill owners. Gandhi asked workers to request respectfully a higher bonus. Gandhi requested the textile mill owners to submit the workers' grievance to arbitration, which the owners refused. When workers began to strike independently, Gandhi, with some prodding, backed a city-wide strike. He helped to establish the Textile Labour Association in February 1920. Miss Sarabhai became President of the Association. Gandhi supported the workers in their strike by declaring a fast to death unless workers' demands were met. The mill owners finally agreed to arbitration, which lead to a higher wage increase.

Gandhi preferred arbitration to trade union agitations and strikes. His trade union strategy was not motivated merely by his adherence to non-violence. According to Gandhi, the major task of workers with a grievance is to generate among management a sense of compassion in the workers' situation. The strategy finds its justification in Gandhi's theory of trusteeship. Gandhi argued that workers, who provide labor, and industrialists, who provide capital, are cooperatively engaged in production. Thereby, according to the theory of trusteeship, industrialists have a special duty to provide for the welfare of those who contribute their labor.

G. Ramanujam, a leading spokesperson for Gandhian labor philosophy and long-time President of the INTUC, has characterized Gandhian labor philosophy thus:

> If capital employs labour, labour too employs capital. But the community employs both labour and capital. Therefore labour and capital are mutually employers and employees; are jointly the servants of the community, which is the ultimate employer. All employers and employees are therefore co-servants in the service of the society, or co-partners in the service of society.[40]

Workers' welfare, even their survival, is dependent upon the good conscience of employers. Indeed, Gandhian trade unionism was explicitly modeled on the family. Industrialists were to treat workers as benevolently as they would treat their own children; and workers were to treat industrialists as respectfully as they would treat their own parents. Until today, the Textile Labour Association is still "firmly based on the concept of healthy society of working class which is like a large family."[41] The arrangement might be criticized as paternalistic.

Congress unionism

While the Indian National Congress did not sponsor a trade union until the eve of Independence, Congress had a profound impact on colonial-era trade unionism. In 1919, the Indian National Congress began passing resolutions on the need for better conditions of work and terms of service and the need for the party to organize workers. Following Gandhi's struggle against the Ahmedabad mill owners, the Amritsar Session of the Congress in 1919 resolved to urge provincial Congress committees and Congress-affiliated associations to promote labor unions so as to secure better standards of living for workers and to give labor its "proper place in the body politic of India."[42] At the Amritsar Session, Congress also condemned the repression

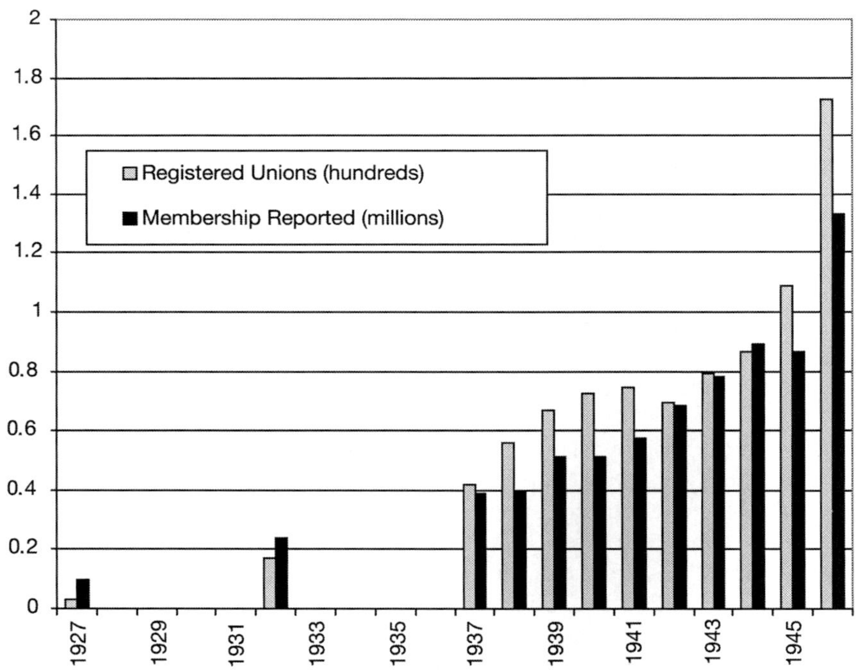

Figure 1.1 Colonial India: union and membership growth, 1927–47
Source: *The Indian Labour Year Book 1947–48*, (Simla: Government Press, 1949), 106.

of workers at the hands of the British Government in India. Later, in 1921, the All India Congress Committee attempted to form a trade union federation with the appointment of C. R. Das, Lala Lajpat Rai, and others. The committee failed to gain the necessary support and decided instead to encourage the formation of a semi-autonomous body. At its Karachi Session in 1931, the Indian National Congress adopted an expansive resolution on labor. The Congress demanded a living wage for industrial workers, fewer working hours, safer working conditions, welfare for old and sick workers, protections for female and child laborers, and freedom of association and collective bargaining rights. In January 1934, with the lifting of the ban on the Congress as an unlawful organization, the Congress Working Committee passed a resolution enjoining Congress workers to be more diligent in organizing industrial labor. Later, in 1937, the Gandhi Sewak Sangh appointed a labor sub-committee to advance Gandhian labor philosophy. The sub-committee formed the Hindustan Mazdoor Sewak Sangh (HMSS) in 1938 "for the purpose of establishing just industrial relations, eradicating exploitation and of applying the principles of truth and non-violence in industrial as preached by Mahatma Gandhi in industrial relations."[43] The HMSS served principally as a training center for Congress workers who would later set out to organize industrial laborers.[44] Unlike the All India Muslim League, which would also become a ruling political party at Independence, Congress established the institution of political party-based trade unionism.

Indian trade unionism

At the Partition of British India, the newly independent states of India and Pakistan adopted the entire legal code of British India, most notably the Government of India Act of 1935, but also all other law including all labor legislation. In 1947, the major labor laws were, in the order of their enactment, the Fatal Accidents Act of 1855, the Emigration Act of 1922, the Workmen's Compensation Act of 1923, the Mines Act of 1923, the Trade Unions Act of 1926, the Factories Act of 1934, the Dock Labourers' Act of 1934, the Payment of Wages Act of 1936, the Employers' Liability Act of 1938, the Employment of Children Act of 1938, the Mines Maternity Benefit Act of 1941, the Industrial Statistics Act of 1942, the Industrial Employment Act of 1946, and the Industrial Disputes Act of 1947. Each is still in effect but has been amended, in most cases only lightly; new laws have been enacted or promulgated. But these are not as significant as the colonial labor laws adopted. Shortly after Independence, in 1948, the Indian Constituent Assembly passed additional labor laws, including the Minimum Wages Act and the Employees State Insurance Corporation Act. These laws remain central components of India's public welfare-oriented employment and social security system.

The 1950 Indian Constitution committed the government to lofty objectives for the protection of the working classes. These objectives are enshrined in the Directive Principles of the State, that section of the Indian Constitution that defines the state's social goals. Three Directive Principles declare that:

> The State shall, within the limits of its economic capacity and development, make effective provision for securing the right to work . . .
>
> The State shall make provisions for securing just and humane conditions of work and for maternity relief.
>
> The State shall endeavor to secure, by suitable legislation or economic organization or in any other way, to all workers, agricultural, industrial or otherwise, a living wage, conditions of work ensuring a decent standard of life and full enjoyment of leisure and social and cultural opportunities.[45]

The 1950 Constitution, which superseded the Government of India Act of 1935, has no provision for labor seats in national and state elections. Trade union leaders, however, continued to contest and, increasingly, to win elections for Parliament and state (i.e., provincial) legislative assemblies.

Aspirant politicians also used workers and unions to persuade political parties to select them as candidates.[46] Trade unions served as vehicles for successful organizers to become political leaders. Fifty-two parliamentary seats, nearly 10 percent of the Lok Sabha, the lower house of the Indian Parliament, are considered to be labor constituencies, where political parties vie for candidates among trade union leaders.[47] One such trade unionist, V. V. Giri, rose to become Minister of Labour and eventually, in 1969, President of India.

Indian trade union centers

Trade union centers are the central figures of Indian trade unionism. Trade union centers are national organizations – composed of federations (i.e., an association of unions), employees of government departments (e.g., railways), and plant unions – that are affiliated to a political party. Some of these parties, such as the Communist Party of India (Marxist-Leninist), are quite small. Three are federations that have broken with the Congress-affiliated Indian National Trade Union Congress (INTUC).

Each of the ten officially recognized trade union centers represent labor in various government–labor consultative forums, such as the Indian Labour Conference, the industry specific Special Tripartite Committees, and the International Labour Organization. Representation in these bodies is in proportion to the claimed (and rarely verified) membership numbers of trade union centers. Each of India's ten major trade union centers, the political party to which it is affiliated, and the year of its establishment is listed in table 1.1. Together these ten centers claim to represent nearly nine million workers.

There is a regular exchange of officials between some trade unions and political parties. This is more common for the trade union centers on the left – where the organization of the working classes is an important component to the party's political program – as with the AITUC affiliated to the Communist Party of India and the Centre for Indian Trade Unions (CITU) affiliated to the Communist Party of India (Marxist).

State patronage by Congress – the dominant political party – benefited the INTUC enormously. In May 1947, three months before the Partition of British India and the creation of the independent states of India and Pakistan the Indian National Congress established INTUC. INTUC claims that it, unlike all other Indian trade union centers, represents the interests of all Indian workers, rather than the narrow interests of a single party-affiliated trade union center. Most other trade unions make the same claim. The Congress's long dominance as the ruling political party of the country has let INTUC maintain this official stance without disguising its direct connection to Congress governments. The weekly newspaper of the Indian National Trade Union Congress, the *Indian Worker*, runs advertisements before elections, proclaiming that only the Congress can protect the working classes. The trade union center's closeness to government is explained, by INTUC's importance as the most powerful representative of the Indian working classes. INTUC's posture as the trade union center representative of the entire working class is also under-girded by its adherence to Gandhian labor philosophy. Yet, INTUC would not have become the country's largest trade union – now surpassed by the Bharatiya Janata Party's Bharatiya Mazdoor Sangh – without government patronage.

After Independence INTUC grew considerably. In the 1970s, however, it was increasingly challenged by the rival trade union centers, particularly the Bharatiya Mazdoor Sangh (BMS), the trade union center affiliated with the Hindu revivalist party, the Bharatiya Janata Party, and the centrist-socialist Hind Mazdoor Sabha (HMS). Indeed, the BMS claims that since the official verification of trade union membership in 1980 it has become the largest trade union center in India.

After the Indian Trade Union Congress formed in 1947, leaders of political parties rival to the Communist Party of India formed rival trade union centers. In August 1947, the AITUC split. M. N. Roy broke from the AITUC to form the Indian Federation of Labour (IFL). In 1948, two other politically affiliated national trade union organizations were formed, the Hind Mazdoor Sabha (HMS) and the United Trade Union Congress (UTUC).

Table 1.1 India: trade union centers and political party affiliations

Trade union center affiliation (by year established)	*Political party*
All India Trade Union Congress (AITUC) est. 1920	Communist Party of India
Trade Union Coordination Committee (TUCC) est. 1939 as Trade Union Cooperation Centre	All India Forward Bloc
Indian National Trade Union Congress (INTUC) est. 1947	Indian National Congress (I)
Hind Mazdoor Sabha (HMS) est. 1948	Janata Dal
United Trade Union Congress (UTUC) est. 1949	Communist Party of India (Marxist Leninist)
Bharatiya Mazdoor Sangh (BMS) est. 1955	Bharatiya Janata Party
United Trade Union Congress (Lenin Sarani) (UTUC(LS)) est. 1959	Communist Party of India (Marxist Leninist)
National Federation of Independent Trade Unions (NFITU) est. 1967	Naren Sen (independent former Congress, West Bengal)
National Labour Coordination Committee (NLCC) est. 1969	Indian National Congress (independent, West Bengal)
Centre of Indian Trade Union (CITU) est. 1970	Communist Party of India (Marxist)
National Labour Organization (NLO) est. 1972	(independent, Gujarat)

Sources: Datar, "Ideology and Trade Unions," in *V. B. Karnik Memorial Lectures*, 1987 and Ghatower, "Answer to Question Number 711," 1992.
Notes: The NLO formed after the INTUC Ahmedabad Textile Labour Association split with the INTUC in debate over the INTUC's commitment to Gandhian objectives and methods.

Trade union power in India

Trade union power in India can be traced, in part, to the strength of its political incorporation. But this incorporation gave greater power to organized labor in the first quarter century of the country's history since Independence. Senior trade union officials in India speak of the decade ending with the declaration of Emergency in 1975 as the heyday of the Indian trade union movement. Unions in many manufacturing industries determined the organization of production on the shop floor. Some labor agreements provided unions with veto authority over the use of labor-saving machinery. Accounts are common from this period of new machinery lying unused, owing to workers' concern that new technology would be used to reduce employment and to concessions from management limiting introduction of such new technology. Union control was most evident in the banking and finance sector. Public sector bank tellers and accountants were able to prevent the introduction of computers for over two decades and to retain labor-intensive account books. Even in the 1990s, Indian bank officers' unions limited the induction of computers at rates of 1–3 percent per annum. In this respect, Indian trade unionism during the height of its power was unusual. For trade unionism allowed workers to determine organization of work and production processes in many areas. This is in contrast to the historic compromise struck throughout most of the advanced capitalist world, which created a reformist trade union movement where workers exchanged demands over work organization and production processes for wage increases.

Such trade union power is now a historical memory in most industries. Trade unions are more concerned with slowing the rise of unemployment and preventing industrial closure than with controlling shop-floor organization. The weakening of Indian trade unionism since the Emergency of 1975–77 is reflected in industrial disputes statistics (See figure 1.2.)

E. A. Ramaswamy, an industrial relations expert, describes organized labor in India as facing a fundamental contradiction:

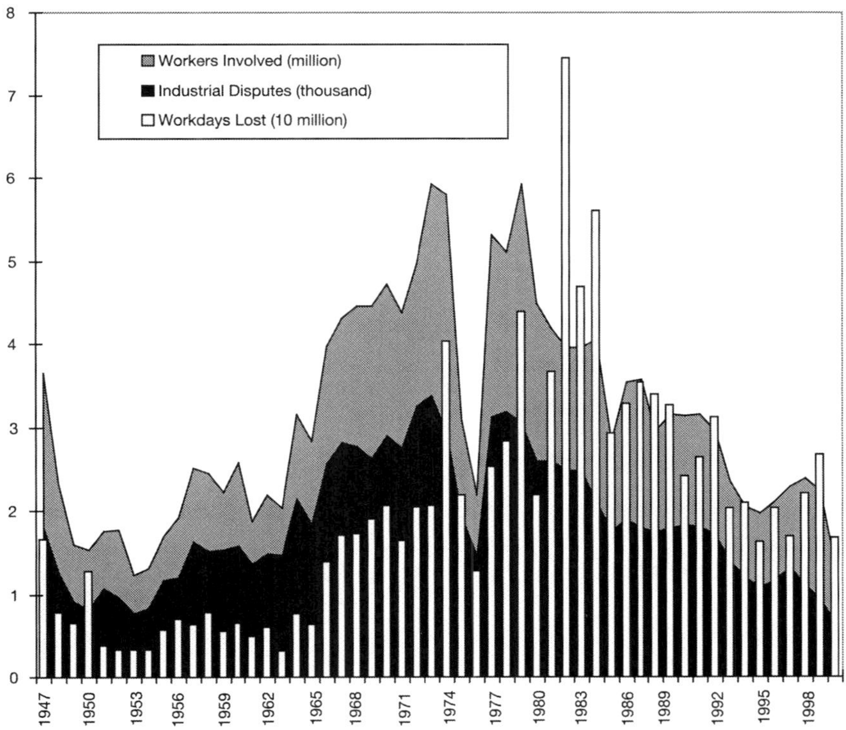

Figure 1.2 India: industrial disputes, workdays lost, and workers involved, 1947–2000
Source: calculated from *The Indian Labour Yearbook*, various issues, 1952–53 through 2002.

> As we contemplate the future of trade unionism [in India], it is important to know that most unions [centers] lack the inherent strength to merit the power they have enjoyed. There are few labour movements anywhere in the world today which are so riddled with problems and so short of credibility, and yet so powerful. For all their apparent might, the fact is that our unions are in the midst of an unprecedented crisis.[48]

The Indian trade union movement is politically powerful and yet inherently weak. What is the basis of this apparent contradiction?

Indian trade unions have attained significant political power, and the consequent ability to oppose government initiatives for public sector restructuring. From the height of the nationalist struggle in 1947, industrial disputes, under existing conditions an indicator of union power fell dramatically and remained low for the first decade of Independence (See figure 1.2.) Industrial disputes rose gradually from the 1950s to their peak in 1973. Industrial disputes fell with the crushing of the May 1974 railway strike, the strike ban under the Emergency in June 1975, and again in July 1981, and with the government's violent intervention in the 1984 dock workers' strike. Of these, the Emergency had the most decisive effect in reducing work stoppages industrial disputes data suggest a deadline of union power.

The number of workdays lost in work stoppages suggests even more strongly the weakening of Indian trade union power. The number of "mandays" or workdays lost may be a more accurate reflection of worker unrest as it incorporates both the duration of industrial disputes as well as the number of workers involved in industrial disputes.

Lloyd Rudolph and Susanne Hoeber Rudolph argue that the 1967–74 period, when the left faction of the Congress was ascendant, was formative for organized labor in India. They point to the rapid rise of workdays lost due to industrial disputes in the 1961–75 period. They claim that:

> freed from the profit and capital accumulation motives of private-sector capitalism, government firms [which rapidly expanded organized employment in the period] could choose to share with their employees rather than appropriate the financial benefits of monopoly, administered prices, and tax-financed subsidies.[49]

The implication is that labor indiscipline is tied to state patronage and rising public sector wages.

By 1967, the year Rudolph and Rudolph date the beginning of the ascendance of the socialist faction in Congress, however, workdays lost were already high. Indeed, the increase in workdays lost might be better traced to 1965–66 than to 1967–74. And between 1967 and 1975, workdays lost did not increase more rapidly than the long-term growth trend since Independence.

Table 1.2 India: claimed and verified membership of trade union centers, 1980

	Number of Union Affiliates			*Number of Union Members*		
	Claimed	*Verified*	*Percent*	*Claimed*	*Verified*	*Percent*
INTUC	3,457	1,604	46	3,509,326	2,236,128	68
BMS	1,725	1,333	77	1,879,728	1,211,345	64
HMS	1,122	426	38	1,848,147	762,882	41
UTUC(LS)	154	134	87	1,238,891	621,359	50
CITU	194	165	85	77,404	31,070	40
AITUC	174	151	87	61,038	27,341	45
NLO	29	21	72	29,896	9,928	33
UTUC	97	31	32	38,193	8,248	22
TUCC	39	11	28	23,675	8,963	38
NFITU	13	7	54	31,568	2,520	08
Total	7,004	3,883	55	8,737,866	4,919,784	56

Source: Calculated from Question No. 711 of Dr. Sudhir Ray in Lok Sabha answered by Deputy Minister in the Ministry of Labour, Paban Singh Ghatower, November 27, 1992, as of December 31, 1980.

The timing of industrial disputes lends more support to a rather different hypothesis. Industrial unrest was not provoked by the public sector patronage but by a loss of purchasing power that followed India's 1965–66 economic adjustments. Wages, including cost of living instruments, had not kept pace with the rising costs of living. Thus, the rise in workdays lost due to industrial disputes might be better correlated to declining purchasing power rather than to state patronage.

The chief weaknesses of the Indian trade union movement and cause of high incidence of industrial disputes is commonly said to be trade union multiplicity. Activists themselves complain that their numbers weaken trade unions. Trade union multiplicity does make solidarity more difficult. It is not uncommon for a dozen unions to operate within a single factory. Rudolph and Rudolph refer to the "loss of vigor that results" from "extensive elaborated ... replication" as involuted pluralism. Adapting Clifford Geertz's concept of agricultural involution, they explain that excessive multiplicity has weakened the Indian trade union movement.[50]

The simultaneous observations of trade union multiplicity and trade union weakness do not in themselves make a convincing argument that these phenomen are causally related. Nor does it illuminate much to characterize Indian unions as weak. Indian unions are not particularly weak in comparative perspective. In what way are Indian unions weak? Their commitment to the non-political interests of their members may be weak but their ability to challenge the state is significant. The real constraint facing the official Indian trade union centers is not their plurality, but their dependent relationship to political party power. National trade union centers are guided by the electoral needs of the political parties to which they are affiliated. This is the source of Indian trade union weakness and the greatest liability of the Indian trade union movement.[51]

In 1971, the Labour Ministry suspended attempts at conducting bi-annual verification of trade union membership. Some major trade union centers opposed an accurate count. In 1980, the government managed to conduct a verification of trade union membership claims in the largest ten trade union centers. The largest official trade union centers were able to verify less than half of their claimed memberships and affiliated unions. On average (weighted by membership), unions could verify only 56 percent of their claimed membership.

An official verification of trade union center membership was conducted in 1980. The verification of trade union membership claims begun in 2000 has not been completed. Official figures collected in 2000 under the BJP government indicate that the BMS has more members than INTUC. Interestingly, the BMS's own 1980 figure on numbers of unions affiliated to it was far more accurate than that of the INTUC.

In India, we do not find such a dramatic decline in industrial disputes in the early 1970s (See figure 1.2), as is evident in Pakistan (See figure 1.3). Rather, we find in India a steady rise in the number of workdays lost and number of workers involved in industrial disputes, until the early 1980s. The decline in industrial disputes in the early 1980s reflects the success of managerial strategies in the labor process, such as subcontracting, that have undermined organized industrial labor. Increasingly informal forms of employment will be discussed in chapter four.

The broad observation about Indian trade unionism is that the political incorporation of the labor movement in India began during the independence struggle through labor's alliances with political parties. Indian labor's role in the independence struggle secured a place for labor in economic development plans and for organized labor in Indian politics. We now turn our attention to organized labor's influence in Pakistan's politics. Unlike the Indian trade union movement, there are very few significant studies of the Pakistani trade union movement.[52]

The Pakistani trade union movement

Organized labor in British India was not mobilized behind the creation of the state of Pakistan. After Independence, Pakistan's political parties and governments attempted to control the labor movement and largely succeeded. Political parties within Pakistan, with the significant exception of the Pakistan Peoples Party under Zulfikar Ali Bhutto, have not evidenced interest in incorporating labor association within the party organization. Even under Bhutto, as chapter two discusses, the government viewed workers and unions with distrust and often sent police and paramilitary forces to meet striking workers.

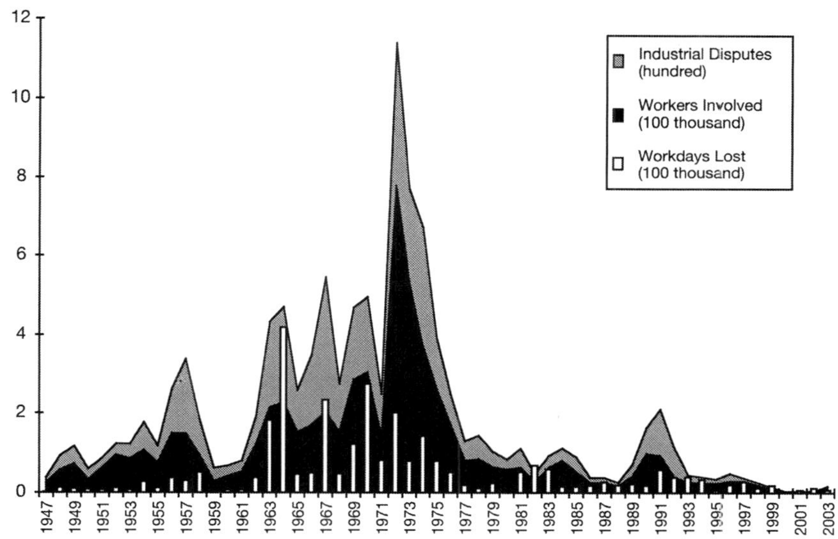

Figure 1.3 Pakistan: industrial disputes, workdays lost, and workers involved, 1947–2003

Source: Government of Pakistan, Ministry of Labour, Manpower and Overseas Pakistanis, *Pakistan Labour Gazette*, July 1996–June 1997, 79–82.
Note: Figures for 1971 and earlier are for West Pakistan only; figures for 1972 and later are for Pakistan after the separation of East Pakistan. The most recent (2–3 years) industrial disputes statistic reported in the *Pakistan Labour Gazette* should be regarded as provisional. They are adjusted upwards in later issues of the *Gazette*, although the earlier figures are not reported as provisional.

Before Pakistan's creation trade unionists were active in areas that were to become Pakistan; Muslim trade unionists were influential throughout British India; and, in areas that were to become Pakistan, despite organizing from a very small industrial base, the Pakistani labor movement developed significant social power soon after Independence. Within two decades, the labor movement was strong enough to successfully challenge authoritarian rule. The military government of Field Marshal Ayub Khan stepped down in March 1969 under pressure from a popular movement in which workers played a central role.

Pakistan's labor laws and trade unions were once identical to India's. The Pakistani government changed its colonial-era labor laws only after organized labor's involvement in a successful movement to end martial law. In response to the threat of an unruly labor movement, the interim military government under General Yahya Khan promulgated an ordinance in 1969 that imposed the system of enterprise unionism on organized labor. Trade unions subsequently proliferated under the successor democratically elected, economically populist government of Zulfikar Ali Bhutto, but labor leaders were imprisoned and workers were met with unprecedented levels of state violence in the factory.

General Zia ul-Haq repressed workers and trade unions for more than a decade. Trade union membership actually dropped 20 percent under the General's rule. Through each of these phases of authoritarian political rule, Pakistani military and civilian political regimes did not seek to incorporate organized labor, bureaucratically or politically. Instead, Pakistani authoritarianism sought to prohibit and limit labor organizing, to exclude organized labor from politics, and to decentralize labor organizationally. Nevertheless, organized labor in Pakistan shows a high degree of social power. This is in surprising contrast to India, where the official trade union centers have benefited from decades of state sanction and encouragement but are widely thought to have declining social power.

Organizing a labor movement, 1947–56

Industrialization had not progressed as far in areas that were to become Pakistan as it had in areas that were to become Independent India. In both West and East Pakistan, according to the most reliable estimates, there were only 75 trade unions at Independence, representing 58,150 workers in a population of more than 32 million people.[53] The small size of the industrial labor force was an initial constraint to trade unionism in Pakistan. Further, Partition badly disrupted Pakistan's industrial development, and the development of Pakistan's trade union movement. Almost one third of Pakistan's labor force at Independence was non-Muslim and migrated to India at Partition.[54] Partition split unions as well. Pakistani unions could not maintain ties with the unions from which they were torn. Within weeks after Independence, even as Partition violence continued, India and Pakistan were at war over Kashmir.

Trade unionism, however, soon had a strong presence in basic industrial infrastructure. In the railways, shipping, hydroelectric power, post and telegraph, cement, and mining, workers organized unions. Growth in the movement after 1947 was strong, partly a reflection of the vigorous leadership mounted by such individuals as Bashir Ahmed Bakhtiar and Mirza Mohammad Ibrahim but also a consequence of Pakistan's rapid industrial growth in the early years after Independence. In only four years, membership in Pakistan trade unions grew by over 650 percent. By 1951, 209 unions had organized a total of 393,137 workers.

In the years immediately following Independence, government initiatives for promoting social transformation in Pakistan were far less vigorous and consistent than in India. The government was much occupied with (failed) efforts to formulate a Constitution, to erect an administrative structure, to establish a military, and promote economic development. That the government frequently announced its intention to adopt a labor policy suggests

Table 1.3 Pakistan: membership of leading trade union federations, 1990

Federation	*Number of affiliated unions*	*Number of members*
Pakistan Trade Union Federation	172	614,800
All Pakistan Federation of Trade Unions (est. as All Pakistan Confederation of Labour, renamed in 1971)	na	520,000
All Pakistan Trade Union Confederation	25	300,000
All Pakistan Federation of Labour	216	262,000
National Labour Federation of Pakistan	230	240,747
All Pakistan Trade Union Federation	185	195,600
Pakistan Banks Employees Federation	11	158,000
Pakistan National Federation of Trade Unions	215	152,300
Sindh Workers Trade Union Council	25	19,060
Pakistan Central Federation of Trade Unions	45	10,345
Pakistan Mazdoor Ittehad Federation	60	9,478
Total		2,482,330

Source: Government of Pakistan, Ministry of Labour, Manpower and Overseas Pakistanis, *Pakistan Labour Gazette*, January–June, 1990, 35, as of 1990.

that it was aware of the social demand for a government program for industrial labor.

While Pakistan had relatively few industrial laborers at Partition, Pakistani unionism did not suffer a lack of committed and experienced labor organizers.[55] Mirza Mohammad Ibrahim, an AITUC member and leader of the Northwest Railway Workers' Union, one of the strongest unions in territory that was to become Pakistan, was one of the leaders of the early Pakistani trade union movement.[56] In 1948, he founded Pakistan's first trade union federation, the Pakistan Trade Union Federation (PTUF). Ibrahim's PTUF affiliated to the Prague-based World Federation of Trade Unions.[57] Other notable figures of the early trade union movement in Pakistan were Bashir Ahmed Bakhtiar, a Punjab-based labor organizer, who led the Lahore-based Pakistan Federation of Labour.[58] M. A. Khatib was a Karachi-based activist. Ali Aftab was a leader of the Seamen's Union in pre-Partition Calcutta and later a leader of the Pakistan Confederation of Labour. M. A. Khan, H. M. Bismal, Khawaja Mohammad Hussain, A. G. Sarhadi, Pir Shamsuddin, and Kaneez Fatma were also active. Ms. Kaneez Fatma remains active today and is the leader of the leftist Karachi-based Pakistan Trade Union Federation.

As a result of rival international affiliations, by 1949 the Pakistan trade union movement was divided into four national federations, two in West Pakistan and two in East Pakistan. In West Pakistan, there were the Karachi-based Pakistan Federation of Labour (PFL) and the Lahore-based PTUF, led by Mirza Mohammad Ibrahim. The PFL represented the unions that had been earlier associated with the "reformist" IFL (International Federation of Labor). The PTUF represented the unions that had been associated with the "radical" AITUC before Partition. In East Pakistan there were the Narayan Ganj-based All Pakistan Trade Union Federation and the Dacca-based East Pakistan Trade Union Federation.[59] In 1950, Abdul Malik formed the All Pakistan Confederation of Labour (APCOL) by the amalgamation of the Labour Federation of West Pakistan and one of the East Pakistan federations.

Pakistani labor leaders remember the period between 1950 and 1955 as one of militancy and protest. "Labour unrest had reached an unprecedented high," according to Zafar Shaheed, a close observer of labor organizing in Karachi.[60] Particularly concerned about the rise of industrial unrest in East Pakistan, the Government of Pakistan adopted a two-pronged strategy, announcing domestically and internationally its intention to meet workers' demands for the right to organize while enacting legislation to control workers and trade unions.

Many senior Pakistani trade union leaders also remember 1952 as the year in which the bureaucracy and industrialists began to collude to repress the industrial working classes. In December 1952, the government promulgated the Pakistan Essential Services (Maintenance) Act. The Essential Services Act, still in effect today, gives the government wide discretion to restrict or ban trade unions and collective bargaining in any industries deemed by the government to be essential to the welfare of the nation. The Act makes absence from or stoppage of work, whether paid or unpaid, in such industries an imprisonable offense. No court has jurisdiction to entertain complaints about the application of the law. In 1952, the government applied the law to the transport, energy, communications, and educational sectors. From 1950 to 1955, the Government of Pakistan also required that at least half of the office bearers in any given union be workers at the workplace of the union. This limited both the number of professional trade unionists permitted to operate in the trade union movement and the time that trade union officers could devote to union work.[61] The ban on the Communist Party of Pakistan in 1954 and the suppression of trade union organization associated with it further impeded the exercise of trade union rights.[62]

The government announced Pakistan's first labor policy on 15 August 1955, a full eight years after the Partition of British India and the creation of Pakistan. Abdul Malik, a union leader from East Pakistan who had been made Minister for Labour, drafted and presented the policy. Earlier, in international fora, the government had agreed to expand its observance of workers' rights. In February and May 1952, the government ratified two of the most important International Labour Organization conventions, the Freedom of Association and Protection of the Right to Organise Convention of 1948 (no. 87) and the Right to Organize and Collective Bargaining Convention of

1949 (no. 98). Malik's professed aim was to raise workers' standard of living and condition of employment and to encourage responsible trade unionism and collective bargaining.[63] The 1955 labor policy aspired to establish responsible industrial relations. Workers would be made more productive by being viewed as partners in industry rather than as ignorant servants of management. However, no substantial legislative measures followed the announcement of the 1955 labor policy. As a result, workers and labor analysts began to assume that all attempts at a national labor policy would be empty official posturing with no real intent to benefit workers. They were correct.

Pakistan's deeply cold war-entrenched alliances heavily influenced trade union development. The government joined the South East Asia Treaty Organization, an anti-Communist US-led military alliance, in 1954. Thereafter, US influence in Pakistani trade unionism increased considerably. The International Confederation of Free Trade Unions (ICFTU) established offices in Karachi and Lahore, extended financial and material assistance to the APCOL, and sent favored Pakistani trade unionists on tours to the United States to study US unionism.[64]

On 7 October 1958, General Ayub Khan declared martial law in Pakistan and abrogated the two-year-old Constitution. A second labor policy, known as the Burki Labour Policy, was announced on 4 February 1959. Following the model of the first labor policy, announced in 1955, the chief aim of the Burki Labour Policy was to discourage labor agitation and encourage peaceful industrial relations. Indeed, at its announcement, it was referred to as the Abridged Edition of the First Labour Policy.[65] The chief consequence of the 1959 labor policy was the promulgation of the Industrial Disputes Ordinance of 1959. The Industrial Disputes Ordinance (IDO) was designed to replace the system of compulsory adjudication through the institution of tripartite Industrial Courts with a system in which the government itself would decide labor disputes. Trade union repression under the first martial law regime, from 1958 to 1968, was relatively mild, compared to that under General Zia ul-Haq in the late 1970s and early 1980s.

The other significant development for labor in the early years of Ayub Khan's rule was that in 1962, the Pakistan Industrial Development Corporation began to sell factories that it had set up in the public sector to private owners. According to trade unionists, this movement of enterprises from public to private sector hands helped spur the development of the trade union movement.[66]

In 1962, the APCOL split into five federations. Fifty-nine dissatisfied trade unions left the federation in 1962 and formed the Pakistan National Federation of Trade Unions (PNFTU) under the leadership of Mohammad Sharif and Khurshid Ahmed.[67] Soon thereafter, the PNFTU applied for affiliation with the ICFTU. The affiliation was granted in 1964. This gave the international trade union secretariat two affiliates in Pakistan. A third was added with the formation of the West Pakistan Federation of Trade Unions

(WPFTU) led by M. A. Khatib and Bashir Bakhtiar. Later in 1971, the WPFTU was renamed the All Pakistan Federation of Trade Unions (APFTU). Workers also formed two leftist federations, the West Pakistan Workers Federation (WPWF) and the small Karachi Workers' Central Committee (KWCC). Despite their leftist leanings, the WPWF and the KWCC did not pursue affiliation with the Soviet-aligned World Federation of Trade Unions.

In 1969, the APCOL split again. Faiz Ahmed Faiz took over leadership of the new APCOL. The renowned Urdu poet was vice-President of the Pakistan Trade Union Federation and had twice represented workers at the ILO in Geneva.[68] An All Pakistan Federation of Labour split off under the leadership of Ali Aftab, of the Calcutta Seamen's Union. Given the turmoil in the Pakistani labor movement, the Western-oriented ICFTU sent a mission to study the problems of the Pakistan trade union movement.[69] As a result of the mission, the international trade union secretariat suspended the affiliation of the APCOL.

With the formal end of martial law in March 1962, a number of Karachi trade unions, previously prohibited from association, formed the Mazdoor Rabta Committee (Workers' Coordination Committee). The Committee "provided a platform for those in the labour movement who were dissatisfied with the way in which many of the established federation leaders had . . . compromised with the government."[70] It included individuals driven underground by the 1954 banning of the Communist Party, radical students, and the leaders of progressive trade union federations, a coalition which would later be instrumental in bringing down Ayub Khan.[71] In March 1963, the Committee helped to mobilize strikes in numerous factories in Karachi, despite the arrest of the federation leaders.[72] The principle grievance of the workers was non-payment of bonuses and wage increases insufficient to meet the rising cost of living. Also significant was workers' displeasure over the restrictive labor laws. Perhaps surprising to employers who had counted on workers from "backward" Northern areas, the procession of workers who called for the strike came from Pathan Colony, the residential area of immigrant Pathans, a major working class community in Karachi. Striking workers were able to secure promises of payment of strike pay. When employers later refused to make good on their promises, a new wave of strikes began.[73] The government intervened by arresting hundreds of workers, shooting demonstrating workers, and "[f]orcing workers to resume production with the use of both police and the army."[74]

The movement against Ayub Khan, 1965–68

With the war with India in 1965, the Pakistan government used the Defence of Pakistan Rules to control trade unions and weaken the trade union movement.[75] At the same time, in the face of widespread public displeasure over the military government's failure in the 1965 war with India, Ayub Khan gave some wage and benefit concessions to workers.[76] Thus the first social security law was introduced in 1965. Ayub Khan also introduced the Companies Profit (Workers' Participation) Act of 1968, designed to give workers a share in their units' profits. Additionally, gratuity allowances were increased.

In 1967, workers at the Karachi Port Trust declared a strike that would signal the beginning of a period of workers' actions that helped to bring down Ayub Khan's government. Karachi Port Trust workers were originally motivated to strike over an unmet wage demand, management's attempts to hinder union formation, and management's employment of workers from outside Karachi. The other major issue was the appointment of M. A. Khatib, then President of the West Pakistan Federation of Trade Unions, over Khurshid Ahmed, President of the PNFTU, to the joint management board of the Port Trust. The Governor of West Pakistan declared that hired thugs had entered the plant, thus justifying continued government repression.[77]

The fall of Ayub and the new Labour Policy, 1969–70

In service of rapid industrial development, the government of Ayub Khan denied workers fundamental rights of association and representation. The denial of these rights together with the working classes' rapid loss of purchasing power caused major industrial unrest in Pakistan.

On January 30, 1969, the WPFTU, the PNFTU, and the WPWF formed a Joint Labour Council. In their founding meeting the Council called upon the government to restore the right to strike and "condemned the lathi-charge[s], tear-gassing, imposition of section 144 of Cr.P.C., and enforcement of curfew."[78] Leaders such as Bashir Ahmed Bakhtiar, M. A. Khatib, Usman Baloch, and Mubarak Haider organized waves of strikes in Karachi, Lahore, and other industrial centers in 1969.[79] On February 22, 1969, union leaders organized a major procession in Lahore attended by workers from the private and the public sector. Workers carried banners with such slogans as "We are not interested in any form of government but food," "Down with capitalism," and "Down with the Jagiridari [feudal] system." Water and Power Development Authority (WAPDA) employees in Islamabad, farmers in Multan, doctors and hospital employees in Lahore, and railway workers in Quetta demonstrated against the government. The major demand of workers at these rallies, was restoration of the right to form associations and the right to form trade unions.[80] Workers' organizations took form, giving organizational expression to a rising tide of social movements opposed to the policies of Ayub Khan. The Democratic Action Committee, on February 14, organized a week-long general strike to begin on March 1.[81] The government attempted to negotiate with representatives of organized labor. These negotiations had little chance of reducing industrial conflict because the labor movement demanded fundamental rights – the right to form associations, the right to bargain, and the right to strike – which would have required the government to dismantle its only legal structure for the control of labor. On February 20, 1969, Labour Minister Malik Allahyar Khan convened a meeting of the West Pakistan Labour Advisory Board, the government's West Pakistan-wide joint body of worker and employer representatives. Labor representatives at the meeting staged a protest over the government's inaction on their earlier demands on the right to collective bargaining, to form associations, and to strike.[82]

In response to the repressive legislation and the arrest and victimization of trade union leaders, trade union organizations called a one-week general strike on March 17, 1969, in which industry and utilities were shut down nation-wide.[83] The movement against Ayub Khan was fought in streets and factories. In March 1969, the police shot demonstrators at the Colony Textile Mills in Multan.[84] The press gave considerable support to the workers' movement. An editorial from the *Morning News* reflected sympathetically on industrial workers:

> Caught in a web of static wages, spiraling prices and shrinking opportunities, these salaried groups have over the years provided the filling for the economic sandwich. They dutifully paid their taxes. With resignation they met the demands of the extortioners in the market. They meekly took their places at the end of the queue. And when belts had to be tightened, it was also theirs that were taken in another notch. ... [T]he workers quite naturally have turned to [mass upsurge] to ring changes in their own position.[85]

In March 1969, President Ayub Khan announced his resignation. He appointed an interim military government to govern the transition to civilian rule. The new martial law government, under General Yahya Khan, quickly sought to appease workers. In response to the challenge posed by the workers' movement, within a month of taking over, the martial law administration of Yahya Khan announced a new labor policy.

Yahya Khan made Air Marshal Nur Khan, Deputy Martial Law Administrator, responsible for restructuring the administration of labor and education. Following three weeks of meetings with trade union leaders, Nur Khan invited labor leaders and industrialists for an open format tripartite labor conference in Karachi. The conference began on May 15, 1969. The product of the tripartite discussions was the Industrial Relations Ordinance of 1969. The Ordinance, announced by the Martial Law Administration in April 1969, subsumed the Trade Union Act and the Industrial Disputes Act. It remains the most important piece of legislation on industrial relations in Pakistan. The policy conformed to the broad objectives.

The Industrial Relations Ordinance of 1969 (IRO) affects the structure of the trade union movement in Pakistan more than any other piece of legislation. Promulgated in November 1969, the Ordinance was the product of six months of deliberation between government and labor, after a broad popular movement, in which labor played an important role, successfully challenged the martial law government of General Ayub Khan. Organized labor forced the military government to negotiate with it, but the military government set the terms. The IRO gave industrial workers the fundamental rights which the labor movement had demanded since 1965: the right to form trade unions, the right to collective bargaining, and the right to strike.[86] Labor was granted a higher minimum wage and assurances for better implementation of labor law (e.g., labor-selected rather than management-selected labor representation on Works Committees). The government, however, retained the authority to ban and to call off strikes. Workers in many "essential services" and public utility services remained prohibited from trade unions. Most importantly, the IRO instituted enterprise unionism in Pakistan. The IRO restricts effective trade unionism (i.e., those with collective bargaining authority) to factory-level unions.

The inspiration for the IRO was Noor Khan's experience in Pakistan International Airlines (PIA). When he assumed control of the military-founded and -run airlines in 1959, standard procedure was to imprison workers who attempted to form a union. Nur Khan decided that PIA would run better if these workers were released from jail, brought back to PIA, and permitted to form a union, provided that the union could be insulated from professional trade unionists.[87]

Workers' agitations continued and trade union leaders continued to complain of victimization by industrialists during the deliberations leading to the institution of the new labor policy. Wages in a number of industries were lowered as the proceedings of Industrial Courts entrusted to adjudicate labor disputes were suspended.[88] While working on the new labor policy, Nur Khan expressed particular concern over Pakistan's low productivity. A team of experts was constituted to develop a profit-sharing scheme by which workers would be induced to increase productivity in exchange for higher wages.

The new Labour Policy, drafted by the Labour and Social Welfare Division of the Government of Pakistan, was officially announced by Air Marshal Nur Khan on July 5, 1969 and promulgated, as the Industrial Relations Ordinance, on November 5, 1969.[89] The major trade union federations of Pakistan welcomed the new policy.[90]

Industrial dispute statistics assist in understanding the impact of the IRO on Pakistani unionism. Workers and workdays lost in disputes climbed steadily until the 1958 military coup, after which they declined (See figure 1.3.) Each began to rise again in the early 1960s, until slowed by the 1965 war.

The IRO instituted the Collective Bargaining Agent (CBA) system. The CBA system determines how trade unions are officially recognized and empowered to negotiate with management on the behalf of labor. The system requires that trade unions gain one third of the workers of a single enterprise as members. If more than one union is so organized, then a secret ballot election is held across the enterprise to select the official CBA. CBA elections are held bi-annually. The government of Pakistan's use of workplace elections to control organized labor may appear paradoxical, in light of democratic India's lack of elected labor representation. The IRO requires that 75 percent of the officers of a registered trade union are able to declare the same employer. Thereby, the CBA system effectively places the responsibility for collective bargaining and worker representation with workers and at the factory level, not with politicians, lawyers, aspiring political party candidates, or other professionals, or at higher levels, as in India.

Bhutto and continued labor unrest, 1969–72

Despite the attempt to institute a more equitable industrial relations regime, strikes, industrial unrest, and the arrest of labor leaders continued in Pakistan. Over 40,000 cotton textile mill workers went on strike in October 1969 demanding a higher minimum wage. A strike was also called by the Security Papers Workers Union. The public sympathy for industrial workers was reflected in an editorial in *The Pakistan Times*:

> Within a fortnight of the promulgation of the new Industrial Relations Ordinance, disputes between labour and employers have erupted in several parts of West Pakistan, notably in Lahore and Karachi. ... little has been done to protect the workers from victimisation during the period between the imposition of martial law and the promulgation of the new labour legislation. It seems that the dismissal of a large number of workers during this period has become one of the major grievances of labour. Another cause of unrest is obviously the employers' hesitation to enforce the minimum wage formula and their attempt to alter the conditions of work – as indicated by the latest strikes in Karachi.[91]

According to an editorial in the *Daily News*:

> The one main factor of the present unrest ... is the non-implementation of the new labour policy of the Government. There is a general complaint of mass retrenchment, creation of unrepresentative unions by the hirelings of the industrialists, and the non-implementation of the minimum wage increase.[92]

The unrest at Valika Textile Mills in Karachi provides an example of the character of the continued industrial unrest. A strike among the nearly 3,000 workers began on October 21, 1969[93] over the dismissal of four employees, including the union President[94] and over the non-payment of wages. Usman Baloch, then President of the Muttahida Mazdoor Federation, led the strike. The Karachi Shipyard Workmen's Union supported the strike and threatened to close the shipyard.[95] As a result, the government repeatedly expelled Kaneez Fatma, the President of the Karachi Shipyard Workmen's Union and General Secretary of the Pakistan Trade Union Federation, from the city in 1968 and in 1969.[96] When the Pakistan Trade Union Federation had divided in 1966, one group fell under the leadership of Kaneez Fatima. The other fell under the leadership of Mirza Mohammad Ibrahim in Lahore.

The strike turned violent. Thirteen of the Valika Mills laborers were arrested and sentenced to various terms of months of rigorous imprisonment by the Summary Martial Court under Martial Law Regulation 21 for failing to disperse when so ordered by a Superintendent of Police while demonstrating in Karachi.[97] The numbers of workers involved in disputes increased dramatically in 1972.

Under Bhutto's authoritarian populism, 1972–77

With its founding in November–December 1967, the Pakistan Peoples Party (PPP) attracted support from labor leaders, such as the Lahore-based leader Ziauddin Butt, a former assistant to Mirza Ibrahim, and the Multan-based leader Mahmud Babar.[98] In 1971 the PPP formed a Peoples Labour Federation, led by Lokhman Mirza and Nazir Masieh.[99] The PPP owed much to the working classes' organizers for its political success. Zulfikar Ali Bhutto acknowledged this support at his inaugural speech to the 19 November 1973 Pakistan Tripartite Labour Committe Conference in Rawalpindi:

> Our electoral success was made possible because the toiling masses, particularly peasants and labourers, co-operated with the Pakistan Peoples Party. We cannot forget their kindness.[100]

But he did forget. Although the Pakistan Peoples Party's Zulfikar Ali Bhutto came to power with the support of mass movements, the relationship between his government and these movements, including organized labor, was not untroubled. As was his strategy with other social movements, such as the student groups, Zulfikar Ali Bhutto chose neither to support any existing trade union federations nor to create a new body. Instead, he believed that workers should support the PPP directly, as party workers rather than as industrial workers.[101] Bhutto's regime simultaneously encouraged the growing assertiveness of labor and violently repressed labor agitations.

Workers and workdays lost in industrial disputes declined dramatically under the Zulfikar Ali Bhutto government. From over two million workdays lost (in 779 industrial disputes) in the first year of Zulfikar Ali Bhutto's government in 1972, workdays lost in industrial disputes in the final year of his rule fell to fewer than half a million involving fewer than 100,000 workers.

Within two months of assuming office, President Bhutto announced his New Deal for Labour.[102] In January 1972, Bhutto had nationalized a number of industries and had arrested prominent industrialists on criminal charges. Announced on February 10, 1972, the new labor policy was proposed as the first step toward a pro-labor industrial regime. Workers were granted participation in management, the right to hire independent auditors to review company accounts and a 100 percent increase in their share of company profits, from 2.5 percent to 5 percent. The New Deal for Labour established Junior Labour Courts for the speedy settlement of labor disputes.

The Industrial Relations Ordinance of 1969 was amended in 1976 so as to discourage the proliferation of trade unions. The IRO of 1969 specifies that in an establishment where two or more registered trade unions are in existence, no additional trade union may be registered unless it can collect signatures from 20 percent of the employees.[103]

Another important feature of the labor regime under Bhutto was his promotion of overseas labor contracts. The PPP government made arrangements with a number of Middle Eastern oil-producing states to export both skilled and unskilled labor. In the 1970s, the remittances from these laborers became the single largest item on Pakistan's current account balance. As one appreciates from the name of the Ministry of Labour, Manpower, and Overseas Pakistanis, labor migration is a significant portion of Pakistan's labor force. The export of labor may also have had the effect of weakening the organizational strength of labor in Pakistan.[104]

Zia's martial law regime, 1977–85

General Zia outlawed strikes and demonstrations under martial law, from July 1977 to August 1985. Trade union activities in public and private hospitals, educational institutions and a number of public sector corporations were banned. Public sector undertakings in which trade union activities were banned include the Pakistan Security Printing Corporation, Pakistan Security Papers Limited, Pakistan Broadcasting Corporation, Pakistan Television Corporation and Pakistan International Airlines. While trade unions were permitted to exist in the nationalized banking system, they were prohibited from collective bargaining. From a union membership of just over one million in 1977, membership declined to 869,000 by 1980.[105]

In the first year of the government of Zia ul-Haq state violence against textile workers at the Colony Textile Mills in Ismailabad near Multan represented the position of the military government toward organized labor. Colony Textile Mills employs over 5,000 individuals, chiefly in cotton spinning and weaving. The workers had demanded a bonus which Moghiz e Sheik, the mill owner, refused. The Worker Union, a pocket union of the management, gave a strike notice which was intended to demonstrate to the workers that the union sided with them. Workers ensured that the strike was organized in January 1978. The Colony Textile Mills called in the police to disband the demonstration. Firing upon the striking workers, police killed 14 workers.

In 1978, Chief Martial Law Administrator General Zia ul-Haq appointed a Labour Commission to recommend to the government a new labor policy. The Commission submitted its report in 1979, but the government was unable to adopt the report because it did not grant unrestained right to hire and fire that General Zia had promised to employers.[106] The 1979 report also noted that a fundamental problem of Pakistani industrial development is that industrialists have never been able to reconcile themselves to working cooperatively with trade unions. General Zia appointed another Labour Commission which submitted its report in 1986. The government was unable to adopt either set of recommendations.

Repression at factories under Zia was high. The connivance of the police and political appointees prevented trade union recognition even in those enterprises where trade unionism was permitted. When the Service Shoe Employees Union, the pocket union of Service Shoe factory, for example, lost the CBA elections to Service Shoe Workman's Union in 1982, the management hired armed men to enter the plant and to intimidate members of the elected CBA, the Service Shoe Workers Union. The Zia government also sought to loosen labor regulations in export-oriented industries and in export processing zones. By notification in the *Pakistan Gazette* of October 10, 1982 (SRO 1003(1) 82 and SRO 1004(1) 82), the government of Pakistan exempted all factory owners operating in export processing zones (EPZs) from adherence to Pakistan labor law.

Labor under Benazir Bhutto and Nawaz Sharif

Benazir Bhutto remained in office, during her first tenure, for merely 20 months. In her address to the country on December 2, 1988, she announced that Pakistan's labor laws would be amended in accordance with its commitments to ILO conventions on guaranteeing freedom of association among workers. On May Day 1989, the government announced the lifting of trade union laws restricting the right of assembly and collective bargaining in public sector enterprises. But Benazir Bhutto's Pakistan People's Party failed to remove the restrictions against organized labor before it was dismissed by the President, allegedly under direction of the military.

The Minister for Labour in the PPP government finalized and planned to announce their new labor policy on August 14, 1990, to coincide with Pakistani National Day. Several days before the announcement, however, on August 6, the government was dismissed by a Presidential order:

> Although little was revealed as to what the package would contain, it was expected that the new policy would be in line with the PPP manifesto aimed to enhance the workers' benefits, strengthen their position in relation to the management and bring the regulations more in conformity with the ILO Conventions and recommendations.[107]

Workers' shares in industry profits were expected to increase from 5 percent to 10 percent.

Since 1980, the government of Pakistan has been unable to formulate a labor policy, despite numerous promises by each of the several governments in power in Islamabad since 1980 that a new labor policy would be formulated and presented. The government of President Zia ul-Haq went so far as to convene two labor boards from prominent industrialists, management lawyers, and trade union federation heads which proposed new legislation. In each case, President Zia opted not to promote the proposed new policy and the policy report was made confidential.[108] The government of Prime Minister Benazir Bhutto did develop a new labor policy, a major campaign promise, but failed to have it announced, much less implemented, before President Gulam Ishaq Khan dismissed her 18-month-old government. Each of the Nawaz Sharif governments made promises for a new labor policy but failed to deliver one.

In an apparent effort to frame a meaningful set of reforms to labor law, the government called for a meeting of the Pakistan Tripartite Standing Labour Committee in December 1992. Its last meeting had been in 1988. The chief agenda items of the 1992 meeting were trade union reform, establishment of a revised minimum wage, and simplification and rationalization of labor legislation. Members agreed to establish a Tripartite Wage Council, a National Tripartite Council on Safety and Health, a National Productivity Council, and a Commission of Experts for simplifying labor law. It was also agreed that contract labor would be brought within the purview of existing labor legislation. The government assured the labor representatives that, contrary to previous official pronouncements, the government would not exempt export processing zones from labor laws. A press statement was issued to this effect, although at the same time the government was informing prospective investors that labor laws were relaxed in export processing zones.[109]

Mrs. Bhutto's unplanned departure from office on 6 August 1990 may explain the failure of her first administration to produce a new labor policy – promised in the Pakistan Peoples Party's election manifesto. Her government lasted for fewer than two years. Mrs. Bhutto's second administration, like her first, was again cut short before it produced a new labor policy. The most notable initiatives in labor affairs under Mrs. Bhutto were lifting of the ban on union among railway employees, which the Minister for Labour and Manpower, Ghulam Akbar Lasi, announced in May 1995,[110] establishment of a Child Rights desk in the new Ministry of Human Rights, and reinstatement of 25,000 federal and authority of provincial level government employees who had been dismissed by Nawaz Sharif in 1990.

Labor under Pervez Musharraf, 1999–2007

The Musharraf government, with two years to frame legislation and enact it by promulgation, significantly amended the Industrial Relations Ordinance. The Amendment created bilateral boards with specializations such as benefits and occupational health. General Musharraf offered charge of the Ministry for Local Government, Rural Development, Labour, Manpower, and Overseas Pakistanis (previously three separate ministries) to Omar Asghar Khan. Omar Asghar Khan was known in his own right as a teacher (at Punjab University), as a recognized scholar on politics and social change in Pakistan, and as a community builder (he founded and led the Sungi Development Foundation). He was also known as the son of Mohammad Asghar Khan. The retired Air Marshal headed the progressive Terikh-e-Istaqlal. Omar resigned from the government in December 2001 to establish the National Democratic Party to contest in the October 2002 election, and was found dead under suspicious circumstances in June 2002. Before Omar Asghar Khan resigned from the Musharraf cabinet, he framed and had the cabinet discuss and approve a new set of policies for large sections of the labor force. The new labor policy is broad and vague and much of it remains unimplemented. Omar Asghar Khan's successor in the Ministry of Labour, Manpower, and Overseas Pakistanis, Abdul Sattar Lalika, died of a heart attack in February 2004. Since 2002, the Musharraf government has used the finance bill to amend labor law and weaken internationally recognized workers' rights.

Trade unionism in India and Pakistan before adjustment

What distinguishes Pakistani trade unionism from Indian trade unionism is not that Pakistani trade unionism is apolitical. Unions in the territory that would become Pakistan were political party-allied before and for a generation after Independence. Nor does a lack of militancy distinguish Pakistani from Indian labor. Further, the Pakistani trade union movement has maintained a steady, critical posture toward the state. Even the giant APFTU – criticized by other federations as too cooperative with government[111] – which relies on the union membership of the Water and Power Development Authority, is nevertheless no less opposed to government economic adjustment programs and privatization plans than other federations. What distinguishes Pakistani trade unionism from Indian trade unionism is that the politics of Pakistani federations are not defined by political party ideologies and rivalries.

Ruth Berins Collier and David Collier argue that the timing of organized labor's incorporation by state or party has a critical effect on subsequent political development.[112] The comparative history of state–labor relations in

India and Pakistan suggests that their hypothesis extends to South Asia. What Collier and Collier identify as party incorporation and state incorporation, I refer to instead as party incorporation and state control to emphasize that party incorporation typically seeks to mobilize workers whereas state control typically seeks to immobilize them.

The evolution of trade unionism in India and Pakistan can not be traced to differences in party-based and non-party-based political systems. Political parties have been an essential part of politics in Pakistan as well as India, though in differing ways. Pakistan itself was created at the insistence of a political party, the All India Muslim League. Political parties have been banned at various times in Pakistan. The Communist Party of Pakistan was banned in July 1954 upon the alleged discovery of an officers' plot to overthrow the government in which the Communist Party of Pakistan was allegedly involved.[113] True, the ban on the Communist Party of Pakistan since 1954 and round-up of its leadership beginning in June 1951 deprived Pakistani trade unionism of the most organized left political party. And General Zia ul-Haq did prohibit participation of political parties in the 1984 elections, even while aiding parties, such as the Jamaat-e-Islami, that had no proven electoral support. Despite these incursions by state agencies, political parties have been very much a part of Pakistan's political development. As Ayesha Jalal argues, attributing "the frequency of military rule in Pakistan ... to weakness in its political party system ... [has] done more to obfuscate than to lay bare the complex dynamics which have served to make military rule the norm rather than the exception in Pakistan."[114] Political parties are weak – in many senses of the word. But that observation is less meaningful than the dynamics that contribute to political party weakness.

It is considerably more difficult to gauge the degree of trade union power in Pakistan; the government does not publish separate figures on the number disputes involving lockouts and those involving strikes. A trend is nevertheless clearly discernible in the figures on industrial disputes. Serial data on trade unions and trade union membership growth in India and Pakistan suggest strongly that the Industrial Relations Ordinance of 1969 had a powerful influence on the structure of trade unionism in Pakistan. It produced more unions, but unions with fewer members.

Before promulgation of the 1969 labor policy, Pakistani employers would often delay their part of the procedure for registering trade unions. It was common for trade union registration to drag on for years. Air Marshal Noor Khan's labor policy made registration within 15 days mandatory.[115] As a result, the number of trade unions almost doubled within a year (See figure 1.4.) As trade union membership grew steadily, the rapid multiplication of trade unions led to a rapid decline in trade union membership density. The Industrial Relations Ordinance of 1969, was amended by Prime Minister Zulfikar Ali Bhutto in 1976 to discourage further proliferation of trade unions.

Like the original IRO 1969, the effects of the 1976 amendment are clearly reflected in membership statistics. Statistics on industrial disputes (See figure 1.5) suggest that the fragmentation of organized labor in Pakistan through enterprise unionism helped to quell labor militancy. Note that the values in figure 1.5 are for West Pakistan only; values for 1972 and later are for Pakistan after the separation of East Pakistan. Industrial disputes statistics also evidence the considerable rise in labor protests over the industrial restructuring, including the privatization measures since 1989.

In India, neither the number of unions nor the membership density changed much in the late 1960s or early 1970s (See figure 1.6), as they did in Pakistan. There is wild statistical variation for total trade union members since 1980 in India, caused by self-reporting and irregular government verification, as was conducted in 1980, of trade union rolls. Union submissions are highly questionable. Statistics on trade union members are also compromised because only those unions that submit returns are included;

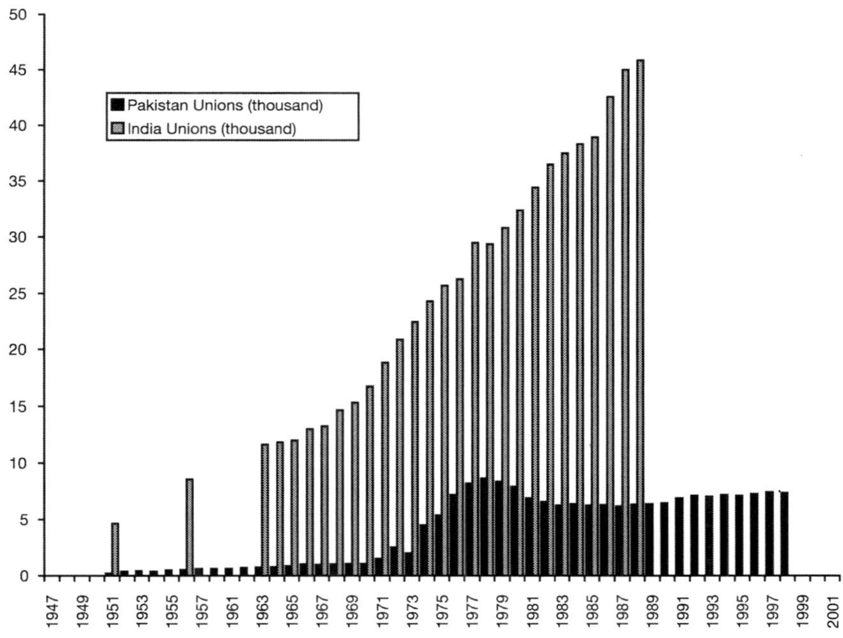

Figure 1.4 India and Pakistan: unions, 1947–1998

Sources: Ministry of Labour, Manpower and Overseas Pakistanis, *Pakistan Labour Gazette*, various issues and *The Indian Labour Yearbook*, various issues, 1952/53 through 1993.

Note: Data before 1972 are for West Pakistan only. The last two years of *Pakistan Labour Gazette* figures are adjusted later and should be considered provisional. Periodic changes to the definition of employment make it fruitless to trace over time union membership as a percentage of employment (union membership density). While data are available for later years, these data are derived in different ways than those for the years given here.

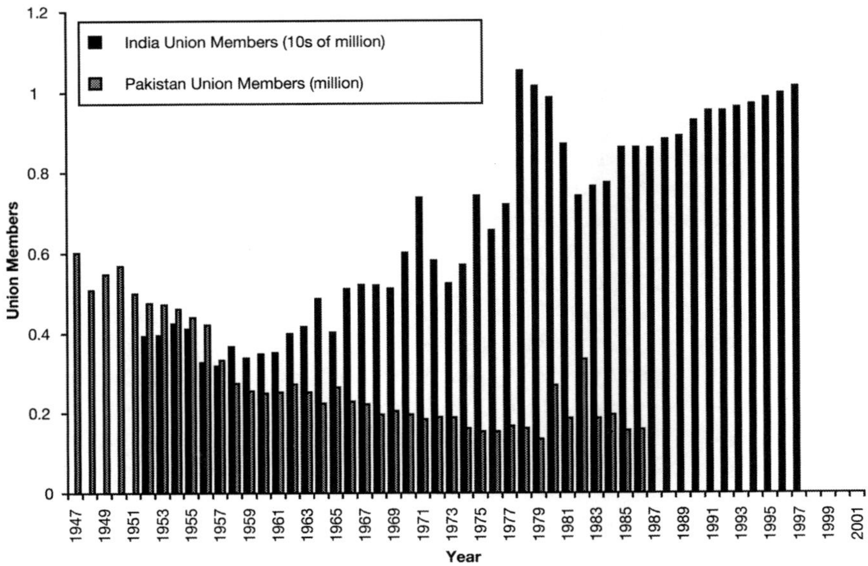

Figure 1.5 India and Pakistan: union members, 1947–1993

Sources: Ministry of Labour, Manpower and Overseas Pakistanis, *Pakistan Labour Gazette*, various issues and *The Indian Labour Yearbook*, various issues, 1952–53 through 1993.

Note: Data before 1972 are for West Pakistan only. The last two years of *Pakistan Labour Gazette* figures are adjusted later and should be considered provisional. Periodic changes to the definition of employment make it fruitless to trace over time union membership as a percentage of employment (union membership density). While data are available for later years, these data are derived in different ways than those for the years given here.

there is no attempt to estimate a trade union membership statistic based on known non-reporting by unions, especially by those unaffiliated to one of the major ten or eleven trade union centers. The proportion of unions submitting returns to existing unions differs greatly from year to year.

In India, the political power of organized labor derives from its participation in the movement against British colonial exploitation and a reputation for being able to protect employment once obtained. That image is now tarnished. In the white-collar sector of organized labor, which includes the two million public sector employees in financing, insurance, and real estate and community and social services, unionism now has a bad reputation. White-collar unionism especially has helped to mark Indian unionism in general with the opprobrium of protecting privilege. Relatively well rewarded professional workers, including doctors and hospital workers, airline pilots, bank personnel and teachers, are often found on strike in India in demand of higher wages or, quite often, in a moral defiance of a slight to a colleague. People also remember that some trade unions supported Mrs. Gandhi's Emergency. While workers and trade union leaders who opposed Mrs. Gandhi's Emergency rule were arrested and

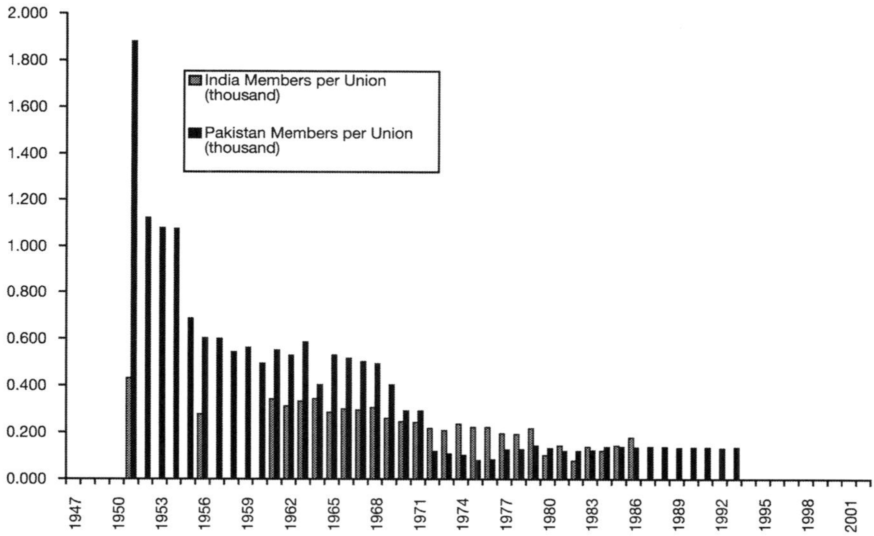

Figure 1.6 India and Pakistan: members per union, 1947–1993
Sources: Ministry of Labour, Manpower and Overseas Pakistanis, *Pakistan Labour Gazette*, various issues and *The Indian Labour Yearbook*, various issues, 1952/53 through 1993.

Note: Data before 1972 are for West Pakistan only. The last two years of *Pakistan Labour Gazette* figures are adjusted later and should be considered provisional. Periodic changes to the definition of employment make it fruitless to trace over time union membership as a percentage of employment (union membership density). While data are available for later years, these data are derived in different ways than those for the years given here.

imprisoned or driven underground, INTUC and AITUC, affiliated to the Congress and the Communist Party of India, respectively, supported Mrs. Gandhi and cooperated with the dictatorial "Emergency" regime.

Fuzzy rules for trade union recognition are a crucial correlate to political party unionism. Unlike Pakistan, in India, there is no legal mechanism for trade union recognition, except in the states of Karnataka, Orissa, and West Bengal.[116] Employers must bargain with all unions that possess a credible threat to disrupt production. Indian political parties are quite effective in mobilizing labor and providing such a threat. The mobilization of workers is the litmus test of a trade unionist's political skill. George Fernandes, for example, India's Defense Minister under the Bharatiya Janata Party, rose to General Secretary of the Janata Dal-affiliated Hind Mazdoor Sabha (Indian Workers Union) because he was able to mobilize railway workers in a national strike against Prime Minister Indira Gandhi in 1974. Fernandes established himself as a trade unionist–politician even though Mrs. Gandhi brutally crushed the strike, paramilitary forces killed workers, and workers' grievances were not addressed. What was important was that he could mobilize workers.

Political party unionism refers to the influence of political party-affiliated unions within the union movement. Political party unionism does not necessarily entail union influence over economic policy or even the welfare of workers. While political party unionism can effectively veto government privatization decisions, it is not able to prevent private sector management from illegally shutting down factories, declaring lockouts, or relocating to areas where workers are not unionized. Keeping a factory in the public sector, which political party-based unionism can achieve, does not guarantee workers employment, good working conditions, adequate pay, or even payment for their work.

Indeed, political party-based unionism can prevent workers from exercising influence over government policy and has often exacted a high cost from workers. The 1982–83 Bombay textile strike is a clear example. The strike is the world's largest as measured in workdays lost. Hundreds of thousands of mill workers took up the strike because they wanted an amendment to the Bombay Industrial Relations Act – a colonial legacy – so that the Indian National Congress-affiliated union, the Rashtriya Mills Mazdoor Sangh (National Mill Workers Union) would no longer be the sole collective bargaining agent for all textile workers. The strike resulted in the loss of an estimated one hundred thousand jobs and sharp decline in labor conditions and in terms of employment throughout the industry. It is officially still in force, although the strike leader, Datta Samant, was murdered, allegedly at the request of the Rashtriya Mills Mazdoor Sangh, which continues to be the sole collective bargaining agent for workers in the Maharashtra and Gujarat textile industry.[117] This legally mandated exclusive representation is still strongly opposed by many workers. Not all Indian workers have embraced political party unionism.

Some social institutions form in reaction to, rather than mirror, the political regimes that attempt to harness or to control them. The government of Pakistan's efforts to de-politicize labor by limiting professional or "outside" leadership, over time, has strengthened organized labor as a social movement in Pakistan. Political regimes lay down deep institutional roots, especially in the formative periods of postcolonial economic change. But these institutions are not replicas of the political regimes that attempt to mold them. Rather – as the absence of workplace elections in India and their presence in much of Pakistan's industry imperfectly suggests – social institutions are often formed in reaction to and thus reverse in form the mechanisms used by governments.

The role of labor in fashioning different development strategies is the focus of the next chapter. The chapters that follow move to contemporary events. Chapter three describes the Indian and Pakistani governments' attempts to implement structural adjustment, especially privatization, and assesses the response of Indian and Pakistani labor to the associated industrial restructuring and to increasingly informal terms of employment.

2

THE STATE AND ECONOMIC DEVELOPMENT

[The enclosed material] is enough to show to you that various suggestions that have been made . . . will have to be analysed and ultimately I consider it is the duty of every true nationalist, to whichever party or community he may belong, to make it his business and examine the situation and bring about a pact between the Mussalmans and the Hindus.[1]

Mohammad Ali Jinnah

I have carefully looked through the various materials to which you have drawn attention in your letter and its enclosures and I find nothing in them which refers or touches the economic demands of the masses or affects the all-important question of poverty and unemployment. . . . The peasantry, industrial workers, artisans and petty shop-keepers form the vast majority of the population and they are not improved in any way by your demands. Their interests should be paramount.[2]

Jawaharlal Nehru

This chapter compares the evolution of Indian and Pakistani development strategies and economic ideologies. India and Pakistan developed modern industrializing economies of roughly similar structure and with broadly similar degrees of state intervention. Each economy is predominantly agricultural but hosts a relatively large (20–25 percent of the total labor force) industrial labor force. Each contains a large public sector, or did before implementation of the International Monetary Fund (IMF) structural adjustment measures. Each economy has a large labor force distributed in similar sizes across industrial sectors. These broadly similar economic structures, however, were developed under markedly different political regimes and economic ideologies. India has maintained a record of regular elections unbroken since Independence and a social democratic economic philosophy. The military and the bureaucracy have ruled Pakistan for most of its existence.

Development strategies

Indian and Pakistani officials expressed widely divergent economic ideologies, but used closely similar economic policies and built public sectors of similar proportions and structures. Pakistani officials, as staunch supporters of the United States' anti-Communist alliance, embraced the "neo-classical" economic policies that the United States then promoted. Pakistanis trained in US universities formulated Pakistani economic planning in close collaboration with American economists. Indian officials, in contrast, promoted "a socialist pattern of development" with the aid of allies in central planning, in Western and Eastern Europe. The economic models were similar, while the expressed ideologies, and the ultimate aims for the public sector, were different.

Despite variation in professed economic ideology, each government was, until the adoption of structural adjustment programs, committed to strong interventionism in the service of rapid industrialization. Although the domestic business classes were far stronger at Independence in India than in Pakistan, in each economy, industrialization and the business classes originated in the public sector.

Only the state had the ability to promote industry. Industrialization was the central element of both the Indian "socialist pattern of development" and of the Pakistani combination of export promotion and import substitution. The Indian strategy aimed for progressive expansion of the public sector, inherited from the British. The Pakistani plan was to build the public sector as a springboard for private sector development. In practice, in each country, the public sector – in manufacturing and mining, engineering, oil, power, petroleum, chemicals, pharmaceuticals, fertilizers, as well as basic research and development – was the foundation for subsequent private sector industrial development. Thus, each government adopted, in the main, statist economic policies, but in accordance with very different articulations of economic development ideologies. Governments in Pakistan in the 1950s and 1960s developed public sector enterprises to create the foundation for the private sector. Indian governments in the same period developed the public sector with the intention of gradually bringing the entire economy into the public sector.

While the economic policies following Independence yielded large public sectors, different economic ideologies helped to produce divergent economic outcomes and markedly different degrees of labor incorporation. The Indian government promoted a statist welfare model and encouraged strong political party-based unionism. Pakistan governments followed US economic models and sought to exclude organized labor, forcing the labor movement to develop social bases of power that were independent of political parties and the political process.

Since the Partition of British India and the creation of Pakistan on August 14, 1947 and of India on August 15, 1947, the two regimes pursued markedly different economic development ideologies. Pakistan, after a decade of indecision, moved toward a strategy aimed at rapid creation of capital through capital-intensive export-oriented manufacturing. The development strategy did not merely tolerate income inequality, but regarded it as essential to economic growth. India and Pakistan exhibit a stark contrast in development ideologies that is rarely seen between neighboring countries, except between countries created by Partition.

Pakistan's Industrial Policy of 1948 described the mandate for state-led industrialization as a "state imperative." The Industrial Policy framed the country's industrialization strategy for over two decades. It declared that in an overwhelmingly agricultural economy, one of the chief mandates of the state was to create industry.[3] Pakistan's industrial strategy was to build a public sector that would serve private sector development, initially in consumer goods. The strategy emphasized export of agricultural products and retained only energy and ammunitions and some transportation and communications for exclusive development by the state.

The rapid creation of a group of Pakistani industrialists, referred to as Pakistan's "22 families,"[4] was one result of the forced industrialization of the 1950s and 1960s. In 1952, the Pakistan Industrial Development Corporation (PIDC) was set up to establish public sector enterprises and industries that, once profitable, would be sold to the private sector. The government operated the unprofitable and unsold factories. Of the 43 large industrial ventures established by the PIDC, 34 were transferred to private ownership, most as public limited companies. Leading industrial families purchased them.[5] The Industrial Development Bank of Pakistan and the Pakistan Industrial Credit and Investment Corporation aided Pakistani industrialists. Pakistani government promoted, with a significant five-year detour in the mid-1970s, a neo-liberal orientation in economic policy.

Within the decade following Independence, India implemented a strategy directed toward the development of heavy industry with socialist features. Whether this was the foundation of socialism or the beginning of state capitalism with socialist pretensions is still much debated. Fabian socialist thought and Soviet industrial achievements inspired many Indian leaders. They adopted an import substitution strategy for economic development, politically buttressed by the rhetorical objective of establishing a "socialist pattern of development."[6]

At Independence, there was very wide official and public support for a strongly interventionist state in India. Government intervention aimed at changing the economic order was the rationale for the Indian state itself. A variety of mechanisms for intervention and programs for economic change were summed up in the concept of planning. Support for economic intervention in India proceeded from the almost unquestionable thesis that as the British state had served British national interests, then an independent Indian state would serve Indian national interests. Centuries of British colonial rule were seen as a corruption of an Indian tradition of government, traced from ancient times (specifically the Ashoka period) when "the welfare of the whole world was to be promoted in every walk of life."[7] In contrast, "the state in India under British rule was functioning purely from the point of view of an alien government, discharging mostly police functions, having no social stake in India."[8]

Similar industrial structures

The level and character of industrialization with which India and Pakistan found themselves at Independence were central, of course, to their leaders' choice of development strategies. Indeed, the differing character of Indian and Pakistani economies heavily influenced that choice. Nevertheless, India's nationalist struggle was to a large extent a struggle over economic autonomy, while Pakistan's was principally a struggle to define the adherents of a religion as a nation. The struggle for Pakistan was a struggle without an economic development plan. Partition left Pakistan militarily vulnerable and in economic disarray. Pakistan arrived at Independence without a coherent development strategy.

India and Pakistan share basic economic features. India and Pakistan are squarely situated in the middle of lower income developing countries, as ranked by the World Bank according to real per capita income. Per capita income is US$460 in India (or US$2,450 in equivalent purchasing power) and US$420 (or US$1,920 in equivalent purchasing power) in Pakistan.[9] Most of the population in each country live in rural areas and most workers are agricultural laborers. In India, 73 percent of the population live in rural areas; in Pakistan, 67 percent live in rural areas.

Income distribution in the two countries is remarkably similar. In India and Pakistan, respectively, 3.9 percent and 3.7 percent of national consumption is done by the poorest 10 percent of the population; 28.5 percent and 28.3 percent of consumption goes to the wealthiest 10 percent, respectively.

The structure of production is also similar, with 52 and 53 percent of Indian and Pakistani gross domestic product (GDP) in services, 21 percent and 22 percent of Indian and Pakistani GDP in agriculture, and 16 and 18 percent of Indian and Pakistani GDP in manufacturing, respectively.

Each country is a petroleum importer and labor exporter. Foreign remittances as a percentage of gross national product (GNP) and overseas workers as a percentage of the total labor force have been substantially higher in Pakistan than India since the mid-1970s. This has helped to weaken trade unionism in Pakistan, as skilled workers have found employment outside of the country.[10]

Table 2.1 India and Pakistan: distribution of gross domestic product by sector, 2002

India	*% of GDP*
Agriculture, value added	21.1
Manufacturing, value added	16.1
Services, value added	51.7
Pakistan	*% of GDP*
Agriculture, value added	22.3
Manufacturing, value added	17.6
Services, value added	52.7

Source: World Bank Development Indicators.

The Indian and Pakistani states also have broadly similar structures of economic intervention. Government consumption is 11 percent of GDP in India and 14 percent of GDP in Pakistan. Each country has a large public sector, a fact which is often obscured by Pakistan's professed economic conservatism. The share of the public sector in total investment is also high in both countries. Prior to the adjustment efforts, in 1987–88, public sector investment was 57.9 percent of total investment in Pakistan.[11] In India, at that same pre-adjustment time, gross domestic capital formation in the public sector was 45.3 percent of total capital formation.[12] Each country commits a far greater portion of expenditure, as a percentage of GDP, to the military than to education or health.[13]

In India and Pakistan, government industrial policy since Independence has encouraged the development of indigenous business classes. Industrial policy in the first two decades of Independence excluded private investors from key areas of industry, but protected Indian industrialization from foreign competition. In the early years, at the same time that the growth of big business in India was being closely regulated, industrial policy sought to provide special opportunities for small and medium sized businesses. The late 1960s marked a transition toward a pronounced antagonism between Indian business and the Indian state. But overall, Indian industrial policy has facilitated the development and consolidation of the private sector in India. While the private sector and government have often opposed and undermined each other, under the guise of socialist ideology, the Indian government has facilitated the growth of the private sector. The creation of an industrial elite in Pakistan was not the product of a long history of indigenous economic development, but rather the product of the post-Independence political elite's strategic efforts to foster an indigenous capitalist class. While it was also central to India's development strategy to strengthen domestic industry and indigenous industrialists, in Pakistan the challenge was far greater.

Industrialization through the public sector

While India's economic ideology favored public sector investment and Pakistan's gave priority to the private sector, each developed massive public sectors. The Indian and Pakistani governments have also maintained the dominant role in industrial financing of private sector development. In Pakistan, before the extensive privatization, government sponsored corporations held assets valued at more than Rs. 700 billion, an amount equal to Pakistan's entire annual GDP.[14] The Pakistani public sector's share of total investment in 1987–88, prior to the adjustment measures, was 57.9 percent. The public sector's share in total non-agricultural economic activity was 13.7 percent in Pakistan in 1987–88.[15] Before the privatization drive, government-owned companies and firms could be found in the automobile, banking, cement, chemicals, engineering, fertilizer, iron and steel, oil exploration and refining, and agricultural processing sectors. The government held monopolies in the telecommunications, power, railways, and air transport services.[16]

In both India and Pakistan, as in most developing economies, a significant proportion of domestic businesses engages in trade, finance, and other activities that require little or no investment in manufacturing. Both the Indian and Pakistani governments have faced a reluctant, short-term-profit seeking, investment-inhibited private sector. Governments have responded with a combination of policies. Some governments in each country have reacted to low investment and high corruption in the private sector by nationalizing industry. They have also backed private sector firms with soft loans and generous credit from public sector institutions with very little oversight. Especially well-rewarded firms are those that threaten to close due to industrial "sickness."[17] The system of industrial credit and tax concessions, however, has encouraged some industrialists to overvalue their investments so as to pocket subsidized loans and to run enterprises as magnets for funds rather than as productive enterprises.

Families, who possess only a minority stake in their enterprises, control and manage India's major business houses in the private sector. According to the Public Interest Research Group, "there are 297 private sector companies in which public financial institutions along with state level industrial development corporations, central and state governments, jointly held 25 percent of more of equity capital."[18] Public financial institutions often possess the commanding share of private sector companies, but government representatives on company boards exert little or no influence over management. Contemporary management in India and Pakistan still owes much to the managing agency system, which operated in the earliest industrial ventures in India, most notably in the textile industry. In the management agency system, a group of individuals manage and operate a business on behalf of the owners. Managers collect a commission based on their performance. Control of company management is not a function of ownership. It is rather a function of the managing agents' ability to raise capital. Indeed, it is widely believed that some government officials who represent public sector financial institutions are bribed by the families that manage these companies. These private sector industrialists allegedly ensure, thereby, that officials from the financial institutions do not interfere in company operations. Public financial institutions and their officials who sit on private sector boards do grant private sector industries credit at concessionary rates. This led one commentator to remark that "the only difference between the private and the public sector is that in the public sector, profits and losses belong to the public; in the private sector, profit is the promoter's while the loss is that of the public."[19]

Nationalism and economic thought in colonial India

Indian economic nationalism

That foreign rule was responsible for India's poverty and that only a strong state – with the ability to deny market access to foreign capital – could assure India of economic progress were popular convinctions in India. These convictions served as powerful impetuses for central planning in India.

Dadabhai Naoroji was the first to assess and document the unequal relationship between British public finance in India and exports from India. Naoroji's model involved an early version of the calculation of terms of trade.[20] According to the de-industrialization thesis, "throughout the eighteenth century and the early part of the nineteenth century, local commercial and manufacturing activity was undermined, first through outright plunder and later by calculated neglect and the use of discriminatory tariff restrictions."[21] The de-industrialization thesis is also now well established.[22] Nationalist leaders and economic historians pointed to the decline of India's textile industry as evidence that colonial economic policy had arrested India's economic development. As a result of the decline in employment, India suffered "re-ruralization," and a rise in rural unemployment.[23]

The de-industrialization thesis was more than an economic argument about the detrimental effects of British tariff and trade policy or "internal drain" through British government public financing on India's industrial advance. It was an argument about the very development of "the mind and spirit of India."[24] As Jawaharlal Nehru put it:

> A society, if it is to be both stable and progressive, must have a certain more or less fixed foundation of principles as well as a dynamic outlook ... Without the dynamic outlook there is stagnation and decay, without some fixed principle there is ... disintegration and

> destruction. In India from the earliest days . . . the dynamic outlook was . . . present . . . When the British came to India, though technologically somewhat backward, she was still among the advanced commercial nations of the world. Technical changes would undoubtedly have come and changed India as they have changed some Western countries. Normal development was arrested by the British power. Industrial growth was checked and as a consequence social growth was also arrested. The normal power-relationships of society could not adjust themselves and find equilibrium, as all power was concentrated in the alien authority, which based itself on force and encouraged groups and classes which had ceased to have any real significance.[25]

This passage from Nehru's *History of India*, written from prison in Ahmadnagar Fort in 1944, expresses the central movement in the orchestration of an economic philosophy that places the state at the center of Indian society's economic equilibrium. As Partha Chatterjee shows in his reconstruction of the derivative maneuvers of Indian nationalism:

> The specific ideological form of the passive revolution in India was an *étatisme*, explicitly recognizing a central, autonomous and directing role of the state and legitimizing it by a specifically nationalist marriage between the ideas of progress and social justice . . . It is an ideology of which the central organizing principle is the autonomy of the state; the legitimizing principle is a conception of social justice.[26]

To Nehru, socialism and the potential of a nationalism based on scientific humanism was also the best weapon against the religious rally of narrow nationalism. Governance over the expanse of an independent India required an immensely powerful and intrusive Indian state.[27] Socialism, for Nehru, was the mechanism by which the state could ensure Indian unity, state autonomy, and economic development.

The Congress first took a stand on the desired direction of India's economic policy in Karachi, at the 1931 session of the All India Congress Committee. While the resolution advocated "nationalisation of key industries and services, and various other measures to lessen the burden on the poor," it was a "mild and prosaic resolution," which "a capitalist state could easily accept."[28] Until the Karachi Congress, according to Nehru, who spoke at the Congress for the resolution on Fundamental Rights and Economic Policy, "Congress had thought along purely nationalist lines, and had avoided facing economic issues, except in so far as it encouraged cottage industries and *swadeshi* generally." The Congress resolution on Fundamental Rights and Economic Policy angered the British government, which saw the move as the work of M. N. Roy, a well-known Indian communist and member of the Soviet Comintern.[29] Depending on the source, later Roy either "drifted from the orthodox Comintern" or was expelled. Roy wrote a program for trade union unity that helped to unite the ranks of the All India Trade Union Congress and the Indian Federation of Labour. Roy himself, in keeping with his analysis of Nehru and the Congress, considered the resolution a "typical product of a *bourgeois* reformist mentality." Nehru wrote the resolution, with substantial assistance from Mohandas Gandhi. The precedent for formulating such a resolution, according to Nehru, was the United Provinces (UP) Provincial Congress Committee which had been "agitating ... to get the AICC [All India Congress Committee] to accept a socialist resolution" for some time. In the 1929 session, the UP Provincial Congress Committee had persuaded the AICC to accept "to some extent" a socialist economic policy resolution.[30]

The Bombay Plan and the needs of industry

Some critiques of India's central economic planning have treated Indian planning as if government control over the economy were the design of a newly independent nationalist political elite bent on autarky. It is often neglected that central economic management was instituted by the British Colonial Office as an instrument of colonial management in British India.[31] The British Labour government's White Paper, issued in 1945, originally defined in detail a system by which the state would exercise direct control over "strategic" areas through public enterprises and indirect control over the rest of the economy through industrial licensing.

India's nationalist leadership placed high priority on protecting the newly independent country's economy so as to guarantee national independence. But central planning was not a government initiative imposed upon an unwilling business community. State control of the country's financial institutions, management of commerce and ownership of basic industry were accepted features of capitalist development, supported by strong constituents in the business community. Economic planning was not merely the defensive reaction of a newly independent state to colonial exploitation. Economic planning had its origins in colonial administration, and was supported by Indian business leaders. The Indian business community, prior to Independence, demanded that these instruments of central planning be strengthened rather than minimized. That Indian industrialists were generally strong advocates of state planning is typically ignored by much scholarship on economic reform in India, which often promotes the view that the state is by nature predatory and business is free-market minded and progressive.

Indian industrialists, somewhat concerned about the socialist rhetoric of a few nationalist leaders, were nevertheless strongly in favor of a planned economy. According to analysis by Raghabendra Chattopadhyay, "the Indian business community . . . play[ed] a crucial role in developing the concept of planning, particularly during the two decades before Independence."[32] Indeed, as early as 1934, G. D. Birla, India's leading industrialist, in a speech before the annual session of the Federation of Indian Chambers of Commerce and Industry (FICCI), made a plea for central planning.[33] While a group of Bombay liberals and British loyalists did criticize Nehru's support for a socialist solution to Indian poverty, a solution for which he argued passionately at the Lucknow session of the Indian National Congress in 1936, most industrialists opted to work with Nehru to temper the more radical of his economic proposals.[34] What concerned Indian industrialists was not a centrally managed economy but the threat of expropriation through government nationalization.

The most important pre-Independence document on India's economic development was the *Brief Memorandum Outlining a Plan of Economic Development for India*, popularly known as the Bombay Plan. India's leading industrialists and economists wrote the plan, presented in separate parts in January 1944 and January 1945. The authors included Purshotamdas Thakurdas, J. R. D. Tata, G. D. Birla, Ardeshir Dalal, Shri Ram, Kasturbhai Lalbhai, A. D. Shroff, and John Matthai.[35] The industrialists argued that "a central directing authority" in economic affairs was integral to India's political unity. The plan also claimed that:

> During the greater part of the planning period . . . in order to prevent the inequitable distribution of the burden between different classes . . . practically every aspect of economic life will have to be so rigorously controlled by government that individual liberty and freedom of enterprise will suffer a temporary eclipse.[36]

The principal objective of the Bombay Plan was "a doubling of . . . per capita income within a period of fifteen years," which with an estimated additional annual population of five million people would require "a trebling of the present national income."[37] The Bombay Plan devoted considerable attention to calculations on what constituted "the minimum requirements of human life," estimating this in numbers of calories, yards, square feet, clinics and schools, and houses per capita. In addition, a committee of the Indian Federation of Labour, the predecessor of the Indian National Trade Union Congress, drafted a People's Plan. Both the industrialists' plan and the labor plan recommended a commanding role for the state.

The labor plan, like the Bombay or business plan, emphasized comprehensive economic planning to engineer industrialization, employment, and growth. The movement in favor of centralized planning was not without its critics. There were Marxist critiques of central planning. K. B. Krishna issued a short, sharp critique of the "cult of planning."[38] The Gandhian

Plan, the alternative to both the labor plan and the industrialists' plan, which did not advocate a commanding role for the state, received less attention.

Economic nationalism in the movement for Pakistan

Indian economic planners and nationalist leaders were powerfully influenced by the economic theory and ideology of early twentieth-century Europe, and the Soviet Union. Pakistani nationalist leaders had no ideological moorings or firm convictions on the Pakistani economy, other than that it should grow and that it would need to industrialize. The demand for Pakistan was a reaction to the British government's strategy of gradually devolving a measure of political authority to indigenous elites in British India according to the religious community they were assumed to represent. The All India Muslim League made the demand for Pakistan in March 1940,[39] a mere seven and one half years before the British would agree to Partition India into two independent states. The Muslim League was formed by conservative Muslim landlords in December of 1906 in reaction to promises by the new Liberal Viceroy, Lord Minto, that Muslim loyalty would be rewarded by an "administrative reorganization" that would safeguard the "political rights and interests as a community" of the "Mohomedan community."[40] Muslim parties of British India did not support the movement for Pakistan. Indeed, the Jamaat-ul-Uleme-e-Hind, Jamaat-e-Islami, and Ihrar opposed the creation of Pakistan.

The provision of separate electorates for the Muslim community was made in the 1909 Indian Council's bill, which provided for six reserved seats for Muslims on a central council of 28 non-official members. Minto appointed an additional two Muslim members to raise the number to eight, a ratio greater than Muslims in the total population of British India in 1909.[41] Over the next three decades, the movement for separate Muslim representation would lie dormant. Mohammad Ali Jinnah himself, the father of the country, would play the role of "Ambassador of Hindu-Muslim Unity" until the middle of the 1930s. But the principle of providing separate electorates for Hindus and Muslims was upheld in the constitutional reforms of 1919 and the Government of India Act of 1935.

From its origins to its precipitous conclusion with the founding of Pakistan, economic nationalism was not a significant component within the All Indian Muslim League's movement for Pakistan. If economic independence did inspire Muslims to support a separate Muslim state, this was largely lost on the All Indian Muslim League representatives of the Indian Muslim population. The All India Muslim League's economic program never went further than the Lucknow session's resolution of 1937, to institute a program of economic reforms, including the fixing of a minimum wage and maximum daily working hours, to improve health and hygiene, to clear slums and abolish usury and debt.[42] Some have argued that the origin of the movement for Pakistan was "the realization of being an underprivileged socioeconomic community."[43] According to Hasan Gardezi, the movement for Pakistan, like the struggle for an independent India, had economic underpinnings. "The founder of the Muslim League, as well as many workers in the movement," he argues "portrayed the struggle for independence from colonial rule as freedom from exploitation by the big-city financial and capitalist interests."[44] Gardezi makes the point to lend weight to his general assertion that Pakistan has constituted a "betrayal of the people" whom it was intended to protect. Muslim peasants, particularly in Bengal and elsewhere in Eastern India, may have embraced the movement for Pakistan as a struggle against economic exploitation by Hindu landlords. However, no such commitments are found in the arguments for Pakistan advanced by the Quaid-i-Azam (Great Leader), Mohammad Ali Jinnah, or in the resolutions of the All India Muslim League.

The deliberations and the resolutions of the All India Muslim League between 1906 and 1924 do reveal some material of interest to the consideration of the origins of Pakistan's early industrial development strategy. Speaking as President of the First Session of the League in Karachi in 1907, Muslim industrialist Sir Adamjee Peerbhoy concurred with the assumption that progress requires industry. "The history of the British people has shown that industrialization leads the way and on that foundation they build great superstructure of the arts."[45] But, this was largely by way of an excuse for his "laboring" in industry rather than in politics and a means to underscore the value of education and to remind listeners of his generous contribution to the Aligarh Muslim University. At the 1910 session, Maulana Syed Ahmad, the Imam of the Juma Masjid of Delhi, said that:

> commerce and trade that have made European countries prosperous and powerful ... if we aspire to our legitimate place in the British Empire, we must concentrate our mind on our economic development. ... For our people the question of economic development overshadows all others.[46]

Other sentiments in favor of economic development of the Muslim community through industrialization are sprinkled through the speeches, resolutions and documents of the All India Muslim League. But no coherent economic development program was articulated.

This characterization of the social and economic thinking of the All India Muslim League has been challenged by Ian Talbot in a consideration of previously unexamined material of the All India Muslim League Planning Committee, formed in September 1944.[47] The Muslim League Planning Committee's program for poverty alleviation and economic reform, recommended in the draft of a first volume of an economic plan, clearly questions the textbook account of the Muslim League as completely lacking an economic plan and social welfare concern. That the Planning Committee did not produce a final draft and that the promised second volume, which was to focus on Muslim majority areas, was not issued, however, suggest that although the Committee may have given voice to progressive social policy, the League's commitment to social welfare and radical economic reform was rather weak.

India's "socialist pattern of development" 1947–91

The economic nationalism that animated the Indian nationalist movement structured the approach to development chosen by the Indian state.[48] The "developmental" Indian state, spearheaded by the establishment of a large public sector in basic and capital goods, succeeded in stimulating high levels of growth in manufacturing until the mid-1960s. Both external crises, including a border conflict with China in 1962 and a war with Pakistan in 1965, and internal crises, including a serious drought and devastating famine in 1965 and 1966, forced India to readjust its development strategy and to curtail planned public sector investment in the mid-1960s. After consolidating her hold on the Congress, Prime Minister Indira Gandhi's populist economic policies in the early 1970s, which involved a spate of nationalizations of financial institutions and failing private sector enterprises, further distorted the developmentalist orientation of the Indian state. In 1975, Mrs. Gandhi declared a state of Emergency, which she ended 18 months later, but this nevertheless raises questions about the compatibility of Indian democracy and command capitalism.

The ideological foundations of Nehruvian socialism

Jawaharlal Nehru was a leader of the Independence movement and Prime Minister of India from its Independence in 1947 until his death in 1964. He was the chief architect of India's political economy. His vision of the economy of an independent India was self-professedly socialist. Although Nehru described himself as non-doctrinal, even poorly schooled in socialist theory, he regarded himself as a socialist worker.[49] Nehru expressed sympathy and agreement with the socialist thought of British Fabians, a society founded by Sidney Webb and Beatrice Webb in 1918. Fabians then held an "organic" view of social change. Fabians argued for social ownership through a program of gradual nationalization beginning with utilities, thus earning them the name "gas and water socialists." Socialism would be realized through economic democracy. Fabians argued for the turning over of rents from land and capital to experts in science and statistics who would provide for the public good.[50]

In keeping with Nehru's conviction that progress was dependent upon the state's decisive role in economic management, the state's role in securing the social good was enshrined in the 1950 Indian Constitution. Nowhere is the commitment to workers' welfare as explicitly articulated as in the Directive Principles of State of the Indian Constitution. According to Directive Principle of the State Thirty-Nine:

> The State shall, in particular, direct policy toward securing: (a) that the citizens, men and women equally, have the right to an adequate means of livelihood; (b) that the ownership and control of the material resources of the community are so distributed as best to subserve the common good; (c) that the operation of the economic system does not result in the concentration of wealth and means of production to the common detriment.

The well functioning economy in the developing world, where investment in infrastructure and basic industry was low, required strong state intervention. Concentration of wealth was thus seen not only as a social evil but as economically undesirable.

Sukhamoy Chakravarty provides a rich account of the tenets of Indian economic planning. Chakravarty presented six foundational tenets, economic assumptions, which inclined Indian economists and planners to adopt "a socialist framework of economic policy in the mid-fifties."[51] First, a serious deficiency of capital was perceived as the chief structural constraint to development. Second, a low propensity to save limited capital accumulation. Third, even if savings could be raised their conversion into productive investment was unlikely. Fourth, agriculture faced diminishing returns and low employment potential, whereas industry had no such constraints on returns or employment generation. Fifth, market forces would produce excessive consumption by the wealthy. Sixth, although income inequality was perceived as negative, "a precipitate transformation of the ownership of productive assets was held to be detrimental to the maximization of production."[52]

These tenets were largely in keeping with British economic thought of the 1930s and 1940s. The last tenet, that growth should precede equity, requires elaboration, especially in comparison to Pakistan's early development strategy where growth was seen to require inequity. As Chakravarty points out, "while Nehru and others did talk about letting the national cake grow larger before an adequate standard of living could be provided for all, they were not growth maximizers in any sense of the term."[53] Since the institution of central planning, Indian economic managers have been concerned with preventing the growth of income inequality. A number of the industrial regulations established in the 1950s and 1960s aimed to prohibit the concentration of capital.

Planning for development, 1950–65

In 1937, the National Planning Committee was founded under the auspices of the Indian National Congress. The principle objective of the Planning Committee, chaired by Jawaharlal Nehru, was to help eliminate poverty in India by promoting industrialization. It was thought that the only way to reduce poverty was to shift the sectoral distribution of labor away from agriculture and into industrial production. Economists M. Visvesvaraya and K. T. Shah, as well as numerous industrialists, served on the Committee, indicating the broad support with which Indian industrialists greeted state planning. In 1947, the Indian National Congress established an Economic Program Committee, headed by Nehru, which in 1948 recommended the establishment of a permanent Planning Commission. It first met and issued the First Five-Year Plan in 1950. The Planning Commission was created by executive order, drawing on the justification of the Directive Principles of State, the guiding principles of the Indian Constitution.[54] The Planning Commission has been responsible for formulating both annual and five-year plans for the development of the Indian economy for nearly five decades. Each plan is considered, modified, and approved by the National Development Council, a body composed of the Prime Minister, in his or her role as Chairperson of the Planning Commission, and the chief ministers of all Indian states and union territories.

The First Five-Year Plan (1950–54), issued shortly before India's first general election, was as much a statement of the Congress's broad economic development goals as it was a concrete economic program. The plan was declared a success because of particularly good monsoons in 1954 and 1955, and because its overall target growth rate was achieved. Toward the end of the First Five-Year Plan, India's development strategy was more clearly articulated. In December 1954, the Parliament adopted a resolution declaring a "socialist pattern of society" as the goal of economic policy. In 1955, the Avadi session of the Congress endorsed the program of a large public sector. The Industrial Policy Resolution of 1956 excluded private enterprises from specified basic and strategic industries, giving emphatic support for a strong and exclusive public sector.

> The adoption of the socialistic pattern of society as well as the need for planned and rapid development require that all industries of basic and strategic importance or in the nature of public utility services should be in the public sector.[55]

The Indian state reserved for the public sector future enterprises in electricity, irrigation, coal, steel, fertilizer, pharmaceutical and chemical plants, mineral and metal exploitation, and heavy engineering. According to one Western economist who served as a technical advisor in India in the 1950s, "[t]he most important fact of government of this past decade [the 1950s] is the great widening of the area of government responsibility in the field of economics."[56]

Comprehensive planning began in earnest with the Second Five-Year Plan, presented in 1956. The Second Five-Year Plan placed increase in per capita income at the center of the planning process. Other principal goals of the plan were to ensure that economic growth would be self-sustaining, to shift dependence away from foreign aid and extractive and traditional industries, to increase employment, and to diminish income inequality between individuals, groups, and regions. Central to these objectives was the state-guided build-up of heavy industry. According to official thinking at the time:

> the rate of industrialization and the growth of [the] national economy would depend on the increasing production of coal, electricity, iron and steel, heavy machinery, heavy chemicals, and the heavy industries generally which would increase the capacity for capital formation.[57]

Nevertheless, modernization was understood in a richer though solely economic manner. India's economic development placed high priority on the tenets of a welfare state, one of which was the promotion of labor rights and standards. Government planning at the highest levels has defined the welfare of working people as a central purpose of the Indian state. A strong trade union movement was central to the project of uplifting the poor and working classes. "The attitude towards trade unions," according to the government's First Five-Year Plan (1950–55), "should not just be a matter of tolerance but they should be helped to function as part and parcel of [the] industrial system."[58] The second plan was theoretically explicit. It recognized the "utter necessity of a strong trade union movement for safeguarding the workers' interest and achieving the targets of the plan," declared that the "creation of industrial democracy is a pre-requisite for our cherished goal of establishing a socialist society," and stressed that industrial democracy would not be possible without a "strong and healthy" trade union movement.[59] Subsequent plans similarly endorsed and encouraged strong trade unionism, giving greater emphasis in later plan documents to the potential for unions to promote efficiency and productivity.

The challenge to Nehruvian planning, 1965–66

The Swatantra party, founded in 1959 on a platform of opposition to the Congress's commitment to state control of the economy, performed well in the 1962 elections, replacing the Communist Party of India as the largest opposition party. The Communist Party of India had criticized the Congress for not proceeding toward socialism quickly enough.[60] An even greater challenge to Nehru's economic development strategy came in the form of the 1962 Sino-Indian war. The Indian debacle resulted in the resignation of Nehru's "most ardent socialist colleagues from the cabinet," including the Defence Minister, Krishna Menon. Further, the war was devastating to the philosophy of Third World solidarity and prompted a dramatic recognition of government expenditure; within the year, military expenditure was doubled.[61] Nehru forced the resignation of conservative ministers within the party and was able to secure a reaffirmation of the socialist commitment of the Congress in a resolution on "Democracy and Socialism" at its annual session in January 1964. But while Prime Minister Nehru was able to maintain the Congress's rhetorical commitment to socialism, by his death in May 1964 the Indian socialist development model was faced with a serious economic crisis combined with political opposition, both against and from within the Congress.[62]

The failure of both the 1965 and 1966 monsoons caused massive food shortages in India, resulting in a drop in agricultural production of 20 percent and requiring India to purchase food supplies from the United States. Food shortages and increased military expenditure after the 1962 Sino-Indian war fueled inflation. In fiscal year 1964–65, inflation rose by 10 percent, followed by 7.6 percent in 1965–66, and 14 percent in 1966–67, the highest level in India since the introduction of economic planning.[63] With the war with Pakistan over Kashmir in September 1965, the United States suspended foreign aid to both countries. In June 1966, Mrs. Gandhi announced that the rupee would be devalued. The measure was designed to secure renewed foreign assistance.

The economic crises of the early 1960s considerably weakened the Planning Commission's role in economic policy making. A three-year "holiday" from the Five-Year Plans was declared in 1965. Even with their resumption in 1970, the Planning Commission never regained its commanding role in directing Indian economic development. The Planning Commission and its development goals would become increasingly irrelevant to Indian economic development. Instead, the fundamental economic decisions and guidance would come from the Prime Minister's Office and the Finance Ministry. The Planning Commission has traditionally been at odds with the Ministry of Finance, a relatively conservative gathering within the Indian government. The Minister of Finance from 1950 to 1956, C. D. Deshmukh, later became a leader in the Swatantra party, which had challenged Nehru's economic strategy.[64] Another conservative, Morarji Desai, served as Finance Minister, in the belief that without his supervision Prime Minister Indira Gandhi "would sell the country to the communists."[65] The relocation of economic decision making to the Finance Ministry would later become important both to attempts to strengthen the socialist features of the economy and, later, to liberalize the economy in the 1980s.

On Nehru's death in 1964, Lal Bahadur Shastri was made Prime Minister of India. Shastri was a Gandhian who enjoyed the respect of the business community. The economic policies of his 19-month tenure, ended by his death in January 1966, were considered by leftists to be a "deviation" from Nehruvian socialism. For the famine caused Shastri to divert government expenditure from industrial development toward agriculture and required greater reliance on market-driven controls. For example, the recognized inefficiency of fertilizer production, which had been the exclusive domain of the public sector, was opened to private investors, both domestic and foreign. But these "deviations," which Shastri defended as a necessary part of democratic governance, were marginal.[66] What is most remarkable about India's handling of the severe economic crisis of the mid-1960s was the decision, despite considerable political pressure on the Congress from within and without, not to abandon or to substantially re-negotiate Nehruvian socialism.

Indian socialism and economic populism, 1967–73

With the death of Prime Minister Shastri, the Congress Parliamentary Party chose Nehru's daughter, Indira Gandhi, who had served in Shastri's cabinet, to succeed him as Prime Minister. A general election was held in February 1967. The Congress, which had previously dominated parliament, was reduced to so slim a majority that "the defection of only 25 members could [have brought] about the downfall of the government."[67] Further, the Congress faced not only its traditional opposition from the Communist parties, but also the opposition of two strong rightist parties, the pro-business Swatantra party and the Hindu-chauvinist Jan Sangh. More fundamentally, the Congress faced a deep division within the party between leftists, committed to deepening Nehruvian socialism, organized under the Congress Forum for Socialist Action, and rightists, a collection of older Congress cabinet ministers and chief ministers known as the Syndicate.

In the June 1967 Working Committee of the Congress, Mrs. Gandhi was able to persuade the party to adopt a Ten-Point Programme aimed at deepening Indian socialism. The program committed the government to state control of banking for the social good, the nationalization of general insurance,[68] expansion of state trading of import and export goods, public food grain distribution, consumer cooperatives and fair price shops, regulations to curb the growth of monopolies and the concentration of capital in the private sector, guaranteed provision of goods to fulfill minimum living requirements, reduction in poverty, rural works programs, land reform, credit to landless agricultural laborers, supply of clean drinking water, and withdrawal of the privy purses granted to former princes. But despite the appearance of unity in June 1967, the division within the Congress over Indian economic development deepened.

In an opening move to oust Mrs. Gandhi, the Syndicate was successful in nominating Sanjiva Reddy for the Presidency of the Republic of India at the All India Congress Committee in Bangalore in July 1969. The Syndicate had calculated that Mrs. Gandhi could be removed from office with Sanjiva Reddy's assistance. Mrs. Gandhi, after a three and a half year period in the Prime Minister's office in which she managed to maintain a distance from an obvious alliance with the left faction of Congress, directly challenged the Syndicate by dismissing the conservative Morarji Desai as Finance Minister and assuming control of the ministry herself. She also promulgated an ordinance to nationalize the 14 largest banks in India, which was greeted by wide public support. The Syndicate began negotiations with the two national rightist parties, the Swatantra Party and the Jan Sangh, and secured the necessary support in parliament for the election of their Presidential candidate. Mrs. Gandhi, in turn, gained the support of the Communist Party of India and regional parties so as to secure the election of her chosen candidate, V. V. Giri, as President of India. "[I]n the maneuvers to censure and discipline her ... the party split into two in November 1969."[69] The rightist faction that opposed Mrs. Gandhi, which consisted of 60 of the 283 members of the Congress, formed the Indian National Congress (O).[70] Given the constraints of an electoral democracy, Mrs. Gandhi made a decision about the direction of the Congress. Referring to the conservative elements in the party, she explained years after the Congress split that:

> if their way would have been followed, Congress would have been completely finished. As you saw, in the next election, that part of the Congress was practically finished. Had we been with them, we would also have [been] finished.[71]

In an electoral political system, entailing periodic public evaluation of government policy at the polls, Mrs. Gandhi calculated that Indian public opinion was moving to the left. Her evaluation was enthusiastically reconfirmed by the 1971 general election, in which her Congress Party (R) secured more than two-thirds of the seats in the Lok Sabha.[72] The electorate continued to support the Communist Party of India, while strengthening the Communist Party of India (Marxist), but cut down the Jan Sangh and especially the Swatantra party and the Indian National Congress (O). By delinking state elections from the national election, Mrs. Gandhi assured that the national election would serve as a popular referendum on her, in which her slogan of *garibi hatao* (remove poverty) was designed to appeal to the masses. What is most significant about the division of the Congress over the two factions' differing economic philosophies is that it was played out in an electoral political system.

The move to bring 85 percent of bank assets into the public sector through her bank nationalization program had been a long-standing demand of the left. The report of the All India Congress Committee's (AICC) Economic Programme Committee in January 1948 had recommended that banking and insurance be nationalized, and had been adopted later in the year by the AICC. The central bank, the Reserve Bank of India, was nationalized in 1949. And in response to demands through the 1950s for nationalization of all commercial banks, the Imperial Bank of India and eight banks belonging to formerly princely states were nationalized in 1956. "Two resolutions were moved in Parliament during 1963 for bank nationalization."[73] Thus, Indira Gandhi's 1969 bank nationalization ordinance had precedence in government policy. It was followed by a series of economic policy maneuvers which would command Mrs. Gandhi popular support for her commitment to socialism. Other such policies include the Monopolies and Restrictive Trade Practices Act of 1969 and the Industrial Licensing Policy of 1970, which expanded the domain of industries excluded from private sector investment. The real "triumph of ideology" over economic rationality came with the nationalization of the entire coal industry, the Indian Iron and Steel Company, as well as two refineries needed for the newly acquired steel plant, the Indian Copper Corporation, and over one hundred textile mills.

Stagnation before Emergency 1974–75

India was faced with a new and serious economic crisis in the early 1970s. The average annual growth in India's GNP between 1970 and 1975 was less than 1.3 percent.[74] With a population rising at nearly 2.5 percent per annum, per capita income was declining. The United States suspended both economic aid and the supply of food grains at concessionary rates in response to the Indian intervention in the civil war in East Pakistan in 1971. The cost of caring for nearly ten million refugees (and nearly one hundred thousand Pakistani prisoners of war) also considerably taxed the Indian economy. The October 1973 hike in oil prices by the Organization of Petroleum Exporting Countries (OPEC) further added to inflationary pressures and government expenditure.

In addition to these renewed economic challenges to Indira Gandhi's socialist economic program, the Prime Minister was also faced with serious political challenges. A student agitation had toppled the Congress government in Gujarat. And the subsequent elections brought to power one of Indira Gandhi's chief rivals, Morarji Desai. Under the leadership of Jayaprakash Nayaran, popular political movements threatened the entire Congress. Further, in May 1974, the socialist trade union leader George Fernandes led a railway strike which paralyzed the country. In this context of economic crisis and political unrest, Mrs. Gandhi's economic policy moved rightward, while holding to the underlying economic position that economic growth necessitated capital accumulation in the state sector. The railway strike was crushed by force. Thirty thousand workers were arrested. In July 1974, the government impounded state workers' wage and cost of living increases, or dearness allowances.[75]

A decisive shift rightward occurred in the early hours of June 26, 1975 when Mrs. Gandhi declared a national state of Emergency. Two days earlier, the Supreme Court of India found the Prime Minister guilty of minor election violations by which the courts had no choice under the Constitution other than to annul her election and bar her from public office for six years.[76] Official rationale referred to mounting foreign and capitalist threats to India's independent socialist development. But the government's economic initiatives were decidedly pro-business. The government lowered the maximum tax rate for industry and permitted investment allowances against corporate taxes. The government also removed the dividend ceiling, which had accompanied the earlier measure impounding workers' wages, cost of living increases, and dearness allowances. Further, industrial licensing was relaxed and unauthorized capacity installation was legalized. But the relaxation of controls on industry was not as great as the tightening of the controls on organized labor. Strikes in what were defined as essential industries, such as civil services, power and water supply, police and railways, were banned. At the same time, Mrs. Gandhi appealed to the leaders of the Indian National Trade Union Congress and the All India Trade Union Congress to prevent strikes for a period of one year.[77] Leaders of the rival Centre for Indian Trade Unions and the Hind Mazdoor Sabha had already been "crushed into submission."[78] The government arrested or drove underground Marxist and socialist labor leaders, except those affiliated to the AITUC. The number of officially recognized labor disputes dropped dramatically.

In Latin America, more than ten years before the Emergency in India, democracy had also suffered authoritarian intrusions. Guillermo O'Donnell's well known thesis on the rise of bureaucratic-authoritarianism argued that the military coups in Brazil in 1964 and in Argentina in 1966 were the structural consequences of import substituting industrialization. O'Donnell's thesis that import substitution industrialization provokes authoritarianism is an economistic extension of Huntington's thesis that modernization creates levels of political participation that can not be politically incorporated without government created institutions of mass control. "If high modernization results in mass praetorianism," argues O'Donnell in his tenth proposition, then "the assessment by technocratic role-incumbents of their combined capacities is likely to generate a coup coalition."[79]

There were two major differences between Mrs. Gandhi's Emergency and the rise of bureaucratic authoritarianism as theorized by O'Donnell. These suggest that the Indian Emergency was not a bureaucratic authoritarian intervention provoked by the exhaustion of an import-substituting pattern of industrialization. In the first place, India's import substitution was not concentrated in easily achieved but quickly exhausted domestic substitution of consumer good imports as O'Donnell argued it had been in Brazil and Argentina.[80] Indian import substitution was concentrated in the capital goods sector. More importantly, the Emergency did not generate a coup coalition. The Indian military remained neutral during the Indian Emergency and resisted attempts by Mrs. Gandhi's son Sanjay Gandhi "to insinuate himself into national security decisions."[81] Perhaps the distance that India was able to maintain from the United States and the US military help to explain India's resilience to authoritarianism. The Emergency, however, did confirm a fundamental shift in the state's treatment of organized labor, in evidence since the police break-up of the 1974 railway strike. The gradual adjustment of the Indian economy and the dissolution of a relationship between organized labor and the state began under the Emergency. We consider the transformation of state–labor relations in greater detail in chapter five, where the rationalization of labor and organized labor's responses are examined.

Pakistan: neoliberal growth models 1947–88

The Partition of British India in 1947 left Pakistan with very little modern organized industry. Official sources describe Pakistan at Independence as an "economic wasteland."[82] Per capita income in Pakistan at Partition was 32 percent lower than in India.[83] The principal manufactured products in Pakistan at Partition were cotton yarn in West Pakistan and jute and tea in East Pakistan. The cotton crop from Pakistani Punjab continued to feed the mills in Ahmedabad and Bombay, while the jute crop from East Pakistan fed the mills in Calcutta. But Pakistan's decision not to join the United Kingdom and India in a currency devaluation led to India's suspension of this trade in 1949.

At Independence, most of the industry, commerce, and finance in the regions that became Pakistan tended to be in the hands of Hindus, Parsis, and Europeans, most of whom migrated at Partition. There were only two major industrial families in Pakistan after Partition, the Ispahani and Adamjee, both in tea production.[84] The pressing concern of the Pakistani state in 1947, therefore, was to assist in the development of industry and business. As Angus Maddison summarized:

> [t]he new industrial class in Pakistan was formed largely of a small group of refugee families who had previously been traders in India, and who were able to discern the new industrial profit opportunities. The landlord class which was predominate politically in the first decade of Independence had almost no role in industrial development.[85]

Stimulating original industrialization, 1947–58

After Partition, Pakistan met the challenge of developing basic industry without a well-defined industrial policy or coherent economic philosophy. Although there was an emphasis on import-substituting industrialization, as called for in the Industrial Policy Document of 1947, it did not appear as a matter of economic strategy, but as a necessity for government revenue. Tariffs were not high enough to stimulate widespread import-substituting industrialization.[86] Pakistan's early import restrictions were motivated less by import-substitution convictions than by the compulsions of a serious foreign reserve crisis.[87]

When the United Kingdom devalued the pound in September 1949, India followed suit. Allegations that Pakistan had refused to devalue its currency to assert its independence from India, its largest trading partner, were countered by the Pakistani government. The Finance Ministry argued that the decision not to devalue was made "entirely by economic considerations," that "conditions favorable to industrialization should be created and maintained."[88] "The prominence given to industrialization was symbolized by the controversial decision of not devaluating the rupee in 1949."[89] Maintaining an overvalued currency allowed Pakistan to receive higher selling prices for its exports, chiefly composed of such raw materials as jute and cotton, while reducing the cost of imported machinery and capital goods. But as a result of Pakistan's decision not to devalue its currency, India suspended trade with Pakistan.

The Government of Pakistan developed a strong public sector in the attempt to develop an indigenous capitalist class. It was not a public sector based on an ideological commitment to state ownership, as in India. Rather, the Pakistani public sector was intended to be the foundation for the development of private industry. In 1950, the Pakistan Industrial Development Corporation (PIDC) was set up to establish public sector industries that, once viable, could be sold to the private sector.[90] Of the 43 large industrial ventures established by the PIDC, 34 were transferred to the private sector, most as public limited companies. Some were sold to leading industrial families.[91] Pakistani industrialists were also aided by liberal credit from the Industrial Development Bank of Pakistan and the Pakistan Industrial Credit and Investment Corporation. Despite considerable political instability, Pakistan made major progress in economic development prior to 1958. The country was almost self-sufficient in food grains, pulses and flour, except during the crop failure of 1952–53. Only in 1956 did food imports begin to rise dramatically. In 1947, Pakistan was an importer of textile goods, but by 1952 was a substantial exporter of textiles. The percentage of growth of GNP originating in manufacturing in 1953–54 reached 29.6 percent, a level higher than at any time during Ayub Khan's development decade, despite a machinery import bill five times lower than in 1959–60.[92]

The development decade of Ayub Khan, 1958–69

A general election was scheduled in Pakistan for February 1959. The most senior managers of the state bureaucracy, however, were generally not prepared to face voters. The bureaucracy had formed a political party with an eye to ensuring that the Muslim League would be defeated, but their Republican Party lacked the popular support necessary to win an election. More importantly, the emergence of the National Awami Party in East Pakistan created "the danger of the non-Punjabi electorate in West Pakistan voting for parties committed to dismantling the one unit system" which under-girded the control of the state apparatus by a predominantly (West-Pakistan) Punjabi civil bureaucracy and army. The potential for popular unrest in both rural and urban areas caused President Iskander Mirza to request that the Commander-in-Chief of the Armed Services, Field Marshal Mohammad Ayub Khan, assume political power. In a gentlemanly affair, Ayub Khan agreed. The Field Marshal asked the president to resign, which he did on 27 October 1958.[93] Ayub Khan declared martial law, banned political parties, and pronounced himself Chief Martial Law Administrator.

The 1958 coup was more an orderly transfer of power from a civilian to a military leadership than a struggle between an elected government and the armed services. The bureaucracy maintained its grip on government. This perspective is widely shared by scholars of Pakistani politics. This observation is central to the consideration of the affinity of political regime type to economic policy. It signifies that the 1958 declaration of martial law did not transform the political regime.

Ayub Khan would remain in office for ten years. One of the most significant features of his self-proclaimed development decade was his reliance on Western economic techniques to solve to Pakistan's problems. According to one senior Pakistani economist "to him the economic profession has reasons for remaining profoundly grateful because of the honor [Field Marshal Ayub Khan] has conferred on it, and the responsiveness he has shown toward professional advice."[94] In keeping with this professional approach to economic development, Ayub Khan not only made use of Pakistani economists who had been trained in the United States but also invited US economists to assist him in engineering rapid economic growth. Numerous American advisors worked in Pakistan during Ayub Khan's development decade.[95] According to one such advisor, the National Planning Commission was "insidiously take[n]-over" by American advisors.[96] In the wake of World War II, the United States was attempting to demonstrate that its political and economic systems could serve as the model for developing countries. Technical assistance to Pakistan in the 1960s provided the US government, US educational institutions, and major private foundations an opportunity to prove the benefits of US economic management. Ayub

Khan also invited Western financial assistance. In 1954–55, foreign loans constituted 1.1 percent of GNP. Under Ayub Khan, dependence on foreign loans increased sharply to 8.7 percent of GNP by 1964–65.[97]

On March 1, 1962, after three and one half years in office, Field Marshal Ayub Khan proclaimed a new constitution for Pakistan. The 1962 Constitution dissolved Pakistan's parliamentary system and instituted a Presidential system, with Ayub Khan at its head. In its limited curbs on the powers of the President by the legislature, according to Huntington, "the system approximated more the model of a *Rechtsstaat* than of a liberal democracy."[98] The 1962 Constitution provided for indirect elections through Ayub Khan's system of Basic Democracies. Political parties were banned.[99] Samuel Huntington at this time was preparing his argument that public participation in politics, unstructured by order-preserving institutions, is a danger to political development. Field Marshal Ayub Khan's system of basic democracies, found great promise "for the tempered expansion of power."[100]

Field Marshal Ayub Khan's political leadership combined political command and control with an effort to stimulate growth by facilitating the concentration of capital. Under his economic development strategy, capital accumulation was the main goal of Pakistan's economic policies. "The private capitalist was expected to perform an important function through savings and reinvestment of profits. Thus the government was prompted to encourage the private sector through a variety of incentives with little or no curb on profits."[101] Pakistan's economic strategy, characterized as a "functional inequality" approach,[102] did not view the concentration of capital as a social danger, as did India's early development strategy, but rather saw capital concentration as necessary to rapid growth. It was argued by the Western economists who advised the Pakistan government in the late 1950s and 1960s that economic growth required an inequitable, but temporary, concentration of wealth.[103] Economic models of the period laid great stress on domestic investment as the source of economic growth.

Habibur Rahman, Chief of the Economic Research Section and then the General Economic Section of the Pakistan Planning Commission from 1959 to 1962, wrote a brief but telling tract on Pakistan's economy, assessing which leading economic development model was best suited to Pakistan.[104] Telling is his approach, in which the answer to Pakistan's problem of underdevelopment is to be found in the selection and fitting of one of eight possible Western economic models to Pakistani conditions. The Keynesian, or government spending driven, model is rejected. For while it includes "a prescription for dealing with the curse of *unemployment*" it assumes a level of idle industrial capacity which is not found in underdeveloped countries. The classical, neo-classical (i.e., neo-liberal), and Harrod-Domar models are similarly rejected for being unsuitable to underdeveloped countries. The only model suitable to Pakistan, he argues, is Lewis's model, which, like the classical model, assumes that it is only the capitalists who save:

> The landlords do not save ... The middle-classes and the wage-earners also do not save. ... Saving for the purpose of investment is done *only* by one class in the community, and that is the *capitalist* class. And they can progressively save more only "if the share of profits in the national income is increasing." This is why the capitalists' profit is the *king-pin*, the *primum mobile* of economic growth in the Lewis model. Public policy for economic development must, therefore, be oriented towards creating the circumstances which lead the *share of profits* in the national income to *increase*. ... All private and public policies must be geared to this continuous expansion of the capitalist sector.[105]

The Lewis model challenges the Nurksian assumption that savings are low in underdeveloped countries because people are poor. According to Lewis, people are poor because savings are low.[106]

Lewis's model postulates two sectors, a capitalist sector and a subsistence sector. "The former is the *progressive* sector; the latter is *stagnant*." Because workers are drawn from the subsistence sector, their wages are subsistence wages, "equal to the average product per man in the subsistence agriculture, plus a margin" large enough to draw them away from their villages.[107] At such wages, "[t]hey will always produce more than what they are paid; the *residue* builds up the capitalist profits as in the classical model."[108] In the Lewis model the state:

> abandons the classical requirement of *laissez-faire* and ... play[s] a vigorous role in economic development investing directly in business, regulating industries, trade commerce and using all its powers ... bringing about rapid economic growth.[109]

As chief research economist Rahman acknowledges, these ideas were not his own invention, but reflected the thinking within the government. In the late 1950s and early 1960s, Pakistani economists and officials viewed Pakistan's economic options in the dichotomous terms of growth through capital concentration or equity and the vague notion of a welfare state. In 1963, Mahbub ul Haq, Chief of the Planning Commission and Pakistan's most influential economic planner, underscoring Pakistan's "need for a growth economy" summarized Pakistan's development challenge as follows:

> It would be tragic if policies appropriate to a Keynesian era were to be tried in countries still living in a Smithian or Ricardian world ... the best (and, perhaps, the only) form of social security is ... through the creation of sufficient capital by some. There exists, therefore, a functional justification for inequality of income ... The

> road to eventual equalities may inevitably lie through initial inequalities.[110]

Gustav Papanek declared Pakistan's efforts to use private incentives to achieve social goals a success.[111] Papanek, an economist and advisor to Pakistan's Planning Commission, espoused the "social utility of greed," without which, he argued, no economy could develop.[112] He and contemporary economic planners claimed that "the real [development] problem [was] the creation of surplus value." Thus, regional and functional disparities were welcomed. Papanek pointed to the fact that Pakistan had tripled its foreign investment between 1960 and 1965 and showed strong industrial growth through the Second Five-Year Plan.

American advisors as well as Pakistani economists trained in US institutions were able to direct Pakistan's economic policy toward an export-oriented industrialization strategy. Under General Ayub Khan, Pakistan revised its import substitution-oriented development strategy and promoted exports. The chief institutional vehicle for this shift of productive capacity was the Export Bonus Scheme of 1960. The Export Bonus Scheme employed a system of multiple exchange rate vouchers granted to firms according to the share of exports in their overall production.[113] The aim of stimulating exports of manufactured goods constituted an incentive for capital intensive techniques and a bias against agricultural exports.

Grants and loans from sympathetic governments, chiefly the United States, were a central requirement of Pakistan's early development strategy. In 1954–55, foreign loans constituted only 1.1 percent of GNP. Under Ayub Khan, dependence on foreign loans increased sharply to 8.7 percent of GNP by 1964–65. With the political unrest after Ayub's removal, foreign borrowing as a percentage of GNP declined to 3 percent in 1969–70.[114] The 17-day war with India in 1965 over Kashmir lead to a drastic fall in foreign investment.

As a result of a strategy of generating surplus capital, capital in Pakistan became highly concentrated in the hands of a small group of industrial families. Government statistics are unreliable. But the then Chief Economist of the National Planning Commission in 1968 estimated that "the top twenty industrial families control about 66 percent of the total industrial assets, about 70 percent of the insurance funds and about 80 percent of the total assets of the banking system."[115] Contrary to the predictions of the doctrine of functional inequality, growth in large-scale manufacturing in Pakistan was actually higher under the parliamentary regimes preceding General Ayub Khan's coup than during his development decades. From 1950 to 1957, growth averaged 18.6 percent as against 12.8 percent from 1958 to 1968.

While Ayub Khan's decade of development may have fostered economic growth, it also contained the seeds of its own destruction.[116] Ayub Khan's strategy of "functional inequality" demonstrated that even under a military dictatorship, income inequality and rapid growth can not be sustained indefinitely. In March 1969, a broad popular movement against Ayub Khan, in which students, industrial labor and other sections of the urban middle classes participated, forced him to step down. In evaluating Huntington's thesis that institutionalization should precede participation, it is instructive that Ayub Khan's system of Basic Democrats, which Huntington embraced as an ideal for institution-building in the developing world,[117] rather than achieving any success in institution-building was overthrown in 1969 in a massive national upheaval that the military, the strongest institution in Pakistan, could neither ignore nor suppress. After six months of street protests and failed attempts to crush the movement through arrests, prohibitions against demonstrations under the Defence of Pakistan Rules and military actions which left hundreds dead, President Ayub Khan handed over power to his Commander-in-Chief, General Yahya Khan, on March 25, 1969.[118] The following chapter details the role of industrial labor in the unrest that brought down Ayub Khan and discusses how Yahya Khan's regime instituted more effective mechanisms for controlling organized industrial labor. The interim military government's chief tool in this regard was the Industrial Relations Ordinance of 1969 which legally ensured the political marginalization and organizational fragmentation of labor in Pakistan.

General Ayub Khan's development strategy was based on myths and oversights. Economists of developing areas believed that the native farmer was unresponsive to price incentives; that the capital required for national economic development could only be generated by extracting surpluses from agricultural laborers; and that coercion could guarantee successful implementation of government policy. Further, the military regime underestimated the social and political consequences both of fostering industrial concentration and of creating a small, well-paid labor force above a large underemployed labor force.[119]

As Pakistan's economic policy makers worked under an authoritarian political regime, they did not propose policies with a view to elections. Such economic calculations later had significant political consequences, as evidenced by the mass protests against Ayub Khan. Economic policy in Pakistan from 1947 to 1969, however, was largely insulated from popular pressures. Only toward the end of that period did rural and urban popular movements gain strength. When economic populism was harnessed by Zulfikar Ali Bhutto's campaign against Ayub Khan and his victory in Pakistan's first general election, Pakistan's economic philosophy and policy mechanics were transformed. Just as Indian economic policy under Nehru was largely managed by the Planning Commission but became centralized in the Ministry of Finance under Indira Gandhi, so too Pakistani economic policy became centralized in the Finance Ministry and eventually the Prime Minister's Office, with Pakistan's first transition to electoral democratic rule.

Zulfikar Ali Bhutto's populist detour, 1970–77

Pakistan's first national election in 1970 and the subsequent ascendance of Zulfikar Ali Bhutto in 1972 re-oriented of Pakistan's economic philosophy. Bhutto campaigned on a platform of Islamic socialism, promising to return to the working classes the wealth which was properly theirs. The often repressive and reckless manner of his economic populism through a program of nationalization ultimately helped to strengthen the hand of his political opponents. Pakistan's second experiment with a large public sector was undermined by his authoritarianism and his party's indulgence in vote-rigging during the 1977 election.

Zulfikar Ali Bhutto began his career in politics in October 1958 when Pakistan's first President Iskander Mirza appointed Bhutto, an attorney, to be the central government's Minister of Commerce. President Mirza was ousted within the month by General Ayub Khan, but Ayub Khan retained Zulfikar Ali Bhutto. In January 1960, Bhutto was moved to the Ministry of Information and in January 1963 was made Pakistan's Foreign Minister.[120] The 1965 war with India over Kashmir gave Bhutto national recognition. Field Marshal Asghar Khan, who served as Commander-in-Chief of the Pakistan Airforce in the early 1960s and founded both the Justice Party and the Tehrik-e-Istaqlal (Red Banner Movement), claimed that Bhutto encouraged Ayub Khan to go to war with India in 1965 so that Bhutto could advance his own political career.[121] Official reports from the front in Kashmir led Pakistanis to believe that the war was being won. "[W]hen it transpired that they had, after all, not won, public opinion attributed this result to betrayal at the highest level in government."[122] Bhutto's hostility toward India during the cease-fire negotiations in the United Nations Security Council and his well performed displeasure with the peace accord negotiated by President Ayub Khan at the Soviet-sponsored negotiations in Tashkent gained Bhutto a considerable degree of public support.[123]

Asked to leave Ayub Khan's administration in June 1967, Bhutto was greeted as a national hero.[124] In anticipation of Ayub's fall, Bhutto announced the formation of the Pakistan Peoples Party in September 1967 and held a founding convention in November and December 1967. The program of the party was drawn up with the assistance of J. A. Rahim, Mubashar Hasan, and K. H. Meer in Lahore.[125] The program, called the *Foundation Documents*, consisted of a series of papers which analyzed the nature of economic development instituted by previous regimes and made the case for the nationalization of heavy industry so as to ensure greater social welfare than had been previously achieved.[126] The industries to be nationalized, according to document four, were "banking and insurance, iron and steel, metallurgy, heavy engineering, machine tools, chemicals and petrochemicals, shipbuilding, armaments, automobiles, gas and oil, mining, generation and distribution of electric power, shipping, railways and air and road transport."[127]

Responding to long-term demands by Pakistan's trade union federations, the *Foundation Document* also called for a national minimum wage, a guarantee of the right to organize and to strike, and the formation of nationwide unions in major industries. These had been legally pre-empted by Yahya Khan's Industrial Relations Ordinance of 1969.

The Pakistan Peoples Party *Election Manifesto* was issued shortly after Yahya Khan announced in November 1969 that elections to the National and Provincial Assemblies would be held in October 1970.[128] The *Election Manifesto* went far further than the *Foundation Documents* in its analysis of the Pakistani political economy as a feudal system and its argument that only the nationalization of "all major sources of the production of wealth" could restore the surplus value of labor that rightfully belonged to workers and peasants.[129]

The 1970 election was Pakistan's first national election, coming some 23 years after Independence.[130] The election was held in December 1969, having been postponed from October 1969 due to severe flooding in East Pakistan. In addition to the Pakistan Peoples Party (PPP), the Awami League, three factions of the Muslim League and four Islamic parties, together with numerous independents contested. The PPP captured nearly two-thirds of the seats in West Pakistan, while the Awami League, led by Mujibur Rahman, took 160 of the 162 seats allocated to East Pakistan.

Neither Bhutto nor Yahya Khan was prepared to accept the Awami League's demand for provincial autonomy in East Pakistan, despite the fact that the 1970 election gave the Awami League 160 seats in a National Assembly of 300. Yahya Khan had made it a condition for convening the National Assembly that the new government be agreed upon first. Thus, it was not until December 1971, after the breakup of Pakistan and the creation of Bangladesh, that Zulfikar Ali Bhutto was sworn in, in a truncated Pakistan, as President and Chief Martial Law Administrator. Public dissatisfaction over the loss of East Pakistan demanded that Bhutto create "a new regime, substantially different from its predecessors in both structure and orientation. ... it would comfort the disadvantaged, while they had made the rich richer."[131]

In his first address to the nation as President of Pakistan, Bhutto promised to usher in a period of social and economic justice. He enjoined industrialists not to dismiss workers and, in words echoing his *Election Manifesto*, referred to workers as "our masters" and the "producers of wealth."[132] Within two weeks of assuming office, Bhutto made good on his election pledge to nationalize most basic industries, assuming the management of 33 private businesses through the proclamation of the Economic Reform Ordinance of 1972. "[T]he brunt of the nationalizations and economic reforms fell on the large family conglomerates controlled by the twenty-two families who had become the target of economic reprisals and public attacks."[133] As many of these businesses were of low productivity, suffered financial losses, or were badly managed and were only a modest proportion of the economy, the Economic Reform Ordinance was based more on "high drama than hope of substantial material gain for the common man."[134]

Two weeks after the nationalization under the Economic Reform Ordinance, Bhutto abolished the managing agent system, whereby an industrialist "family could dominate and control a large number of publicly owned companies by acting as a conglomerate holding company,"[135] often with the benefit of public financing. Other nationalization proclamations followed, despite repeated assurances to the business community that each measure was to be the last. In March 1972, Bhutto nationalized the life insurance companies and private schools and colleges. In June 1973, the government assumed control over the rice export trade and the procurement of raw cotton. Later, Bhutto nationalized the vegetable ghee industry, which had raised prices dramatically in the wake of the devastating monsoon of 1973. Finally, in January 1974, domestic banks, which had already been placed under stricter control by the state, were nationalized. Then, in June 1976, after he had relieved from office the economic advisors who might have been able to steer the state's newly acquired assets toward better management, Bhutto nationalized thousands of small wheat flour, rice-husking and cotton gin mills. It was this challenge to the small entrepreneur who had supported him in 1970, as opposed to the major industrial families, which caused irreparable political damage to his government.

Bhutto's assault on big business in the form of his seemingly relentless nationalization programs succeeded in achieving an organizational solidarity among Pakistani businesses which they had previously been unable to forge themselves. The Karachi Chamber of Commerce and Industry made "repeated representations for reversing the policy of nationalisation." But it was the regionally based, industry-specific business associations which were most active against Bhutto, particularly the Pakistan Pharmaceutical Manufactures Association and the All-Pakistan Textile Mills Association. Galvanized against Bhutto and the Pakistan Peoples Party by the time the 1977 elections were declared, "[b]ig business ... supplied financial support to the PNA,"[136] the PPP's chief rival. The PPP may have been the response to the disastrous consequences of authoritarian economic development, but the party was unable to sustain authoritarian populism.

After five years in office as Prime Minister, Bhutto declared new national elections, as prescribed by the 1973 Constitution, expecting to consolidate PPP rule. The elections were rigged, giving the nine-party alliance against Bhutto, the Pakistan National Alliance (PNA), the grounds for organizing a national movement against the election results. Traders, shopkeepers, and urban middle class professionals formed the backbone of the PNA agitation against the PPP. The PNA's call for military intervention was granted on July 5, 1977, when Army Chief of Staff Zia ul-Haq placed Prime Minister

Bhutto under detention and declared himself Chief Martial Law Administrator. Bhutto was hanged later.

Despite Zia's declaration that the military would step out of politics within 90 days, after overseeing a fair election, the General remained in office for 11 years, until his death in a plane crash in August 1988. The longevity of the Zia government owed much to the Soviet invasion of Afghanistan in December 1979, which elevated Pakistan to the status of front-line state to Soviet aggression. Thus, the Government of the United States, other Western, and Middle Eastern governments provided the Zia government with billions of dollars in economic and military aid. The Zia government was also able to defuse potential social unrest over unemployment by successfully increasing the export of mostly unskilled laborers to oil-producing Gulf states.[137] By 1984, remittances from Pakistani workers in the Gulf amounted to 8 percent of Pakistan's gross national product.[138]

Economic ideology and organized labor

The evolution of differing development strategies and the selection of economic models in India and Pakistan were largely shaped by the different nationalist movements and political regimes in the two countries. India's electoral democratic regimes supported populist economic programs. Pakistan's authoritarian regimes dispensed with economic populism and followed the guidance of technocratically inclined economic advisors. Democratically elected regimes in the developing world have tended to support social welfare ideology, often embracing a strong public sector and import substitution industrialization. In South Asia, modern economic populism has resulted in government nationalization campaigns and the extension of state welfare programs (e.g., Sri Lanka from 1970 to 1977 under Prime Minister Mrs. Sirimavo Bandaranaike, India from 1971 to 1975 under Prime Minister Indira Gandhi, and Pakistan under Prime Minister Zulfiqur Ali Bhutto from 1972–77).[139] Authoritarian regimes in the developing world have been more inclined to support market ideology and to pursue export-oriented industrialization. Modern authoritarian regimes have aggressively promoted export industrialization (e.g., Pakistan under Ayub Khan from 1958–68, South Korea under President Pak Chung Hee from 1961–80, and China under Deng Xiao Ping since 1979).

Economic ideologies are not simply adopted by political regimes according to their predilections upon assumption of office. In formerly colonized societies, economic policies are infused with the ideologies of the Independence movement and influenced by the incentives of existing and past regimes. Thus, more significant than the regime type operative during the implementation of a structural adjustment program and policies adopted, or not adopted, are social institutions and organizations.

India's nationalist struggle and Nehruvian socialism placed national economic sovereignty at the center of the ideological project of constituting an Indian nation. The "fissiparious tendencies" that were predicted to divide India,[140] one of the world's most culturally, linguistically, and religiously diverse countries, were to be contained largely by the Indian government's ideological commitment to national economic sovereignty. Similarly, India's political independence in the postcolonial world was to be secured by economic independence. According to the leadership of the national movement, this required massive state's intervention in heavy industrialization.[141]

In contrast, the movement for Pakistan, at least as articulated by the All India Muslim League, gave virtually no attention to its economic foundation. Only after the economic catastrophe caused by the Partition of British India did the Muslim League leaders define a program for Pakistan's economic development. This strategy nevertheless fell short of a national economic philosophy. The absence of a national economic program was among the major causes in the eventual break-up of Pakistan in 1971, for it allowed economic advantage to flow to the politically empowered in West Pakistan.[142] Consequently, the economic content of the Indian nationalist struggle and its virtual absence from the movement for Pakistan have left a powerful legacy for subsequent efforts in the two countries to restructure and liberalize the economy.

The character of the nationalist movements, and their underlying social bases, led to the Partition of British India and the creation of the independent states of India and Pakistan. It also powerfully influenced choice of postcolonial development strategies and economic ideologies. The regimes that emerged after Independence organized labor differently, according to their political requirements. The development of trade unionism under an electoral regime, especially given its professedly socialist ideology, facilitated the development of political party-based unionism in India. An authoritarian political system, which was confronted by labor and mass movements, led Pakistani leaders to design enterprise unionism in Pakistan. Indian and Pakistani political regimes, and the economic ideologies that they adopted, molded organized industrial labor as a social institution.

Organized labor and the state before 1975

State-guided industrial development was an imperative of the post-Independence period in the former colonial world. In South Asia, as elsewhere in poor countries, the legitimacy of the state vitally depends upon its ability to generate economic growth and employment and to advance social justice and welfare. The Indian and Pakistani regimes tackled this double-edged legitimacy challenge quite differently. India's economic model, based on comprehensive economic planning and state ownership and management of heavy industry, was rooted in British national social welfare economic thought of the 1930s and 1940s. Pakistan's economic model, based on state facilitation of industrial growth through the concentration of capital, was rooted in American neo-liberal economic thought of the 1950s.

The models shared some important assumptions but also differ in consequential ways. Both models assumed a linear path to economic development and regarded a shortage of capital as the chief cause of underdevelopment. Whereas the Pakistan state explicitly privileged economic growth, the Indian state placed greater emphasis on social welfare. Moreover, Indian planning under Nehru, despite its faith in technocratic solutions, carried a moral imperative.

India and Pakistan, despite the differing economic development models, managed to build rather similar economies with large public sectors. Their economic development models shared important assumptions. Both models assumed a linear path to economic development and regarded a shortage of capital as the chief cause of underdevelopment. But while the Pakistani state explicitly privileged economic growth, the Indian state placed greater emphasis on social welfare.

The fiscal crises facing the poor states of the world are not necessarily the consequences of unsound economic policies. Rather, structural adjustment programs are brought on by a tendency within the international financial system. That tendency produces balance of payment crises in most poor economies. Extrication of the state from its central role in the economy and in industrial relations is a common response to fiscal crisis.

The depth of the fiscal crisis of the Indian and Pakistani states are especially acute, reflecting the degree of difficulty in achieving both legitimization and accumulation objectives within a lower income economy.[143] In direct competition with their legitimization tasks, the central justification for the current economic adjustment in India and Pakistan is that the state must withdraw from economic engineering. This is a complete reversal of the former justification for a strong state in developing societies, namely that social groups in the developing world are weak and therefore incapable of independently forming strong social institutions.

The character of the fiscal crises faced by India and Pakistan differ markedly because the character of state-ness differs markedly. As the Indian state withdraws from its social welfare responsibilities, what can substitute for the autonomous state committed to promoting the social welfare of the masses? The question is of consequence for the very integrity of India. As Nehru argued, "without some fixed principle there is likely to be disintegration and destruction."[144] While the avowed goal of Indian development, a "socialist pattern" of growth, remains unfulfilled, common public expectations and institutional mechanisms have been developed. Thus, the economic liberalization being touted by senior government officials does not merely involve a re-allocation of the distribution of wealth and power in Indian society; it necessarily entails the reform of the Indian state.

The Pakistani state, in contrast, has not fostered *étatisme* as its legitimating ideology. The threshold for legitimate performance is far lower for the state in Pakistan. The public sector, before the privatization measures accompanying structural adjustment, was as large as India's. But the rationale was to build industry and then transfer it to help establish a Pakistani bourgeoisie. Economic liberalization in Pakistan, therefore, is not as much a program to reform the Pakistani state. This may have made it easier in the short run for Pakistani governments to effect structural adjustment.

The relative economic conditions prevailing in India and Pakistan in the aftermath of their Partition explain many of the differences in their early economic development strategies. Indian planners could envision a strategy of import substitution industrialization that would promote the self-reliant development of Indian industry because they had the economic resources to do so. In contrast, Pakistani planners had the more essential and difficult task of establishing a central administrative apparatus and a defense force capable of securing two territories separated by over a thousand miles across an unfriendly neighbor and creating the basic industry that could finance these apparatuses. Had India found itself with such a weak economic infrastructure, it might have pursued a more heterodox combination of export promotion and import substitution, as Pakistan did. Similarly, had Pakistan found itself with significant industrial infrastructure it might have pursued a more inward, state-guided industrial development strategy. The political options available to the leadership of the Indian nationalist movement, of the movement for Pakistan, and of the two postcolonial governments were presented by the economic structure upon which each regime was based.

Economic conditions, however, were not the only factors. The economic agendas that nationalist movements articulated were crucial to the subsequent negotiation and consolidation of newly independent states' economic development programs. A socialist economic ideology combined with economic populism under electoral democracy provides, as in India, compulsions for the formation of economically important social organizations, such as political parties and trade unions. That India opted for state-controlled central planning while Pakistan opted for rapid economic growth through "functional inequality" is well enough known. The reasons for the difference in development strategies, the focus of this chapter, have not been thoroughly studied, especially from a comparative historical perspective.[145]

3

ORGANIZED LABOR AND ECONOMIC REFORM

> Pakistan's industrialist Prime Minister [Nawaz Sharif] followed his natural instincts and began liberalising his economy almost a year ahead of us despite stiff opposition from his coalition. ... The Pakistanis, who have always been in awe of India's industrial prowess and envious of our democracy, can today be proud of having stolen a march on us. For once, we have something to learn from them. ... Unlike India, where reform is taking the slow, ponderous pace of an elephant, Pakistanis are zipping toward liberalisation. ... Clearly, Pakistan is plugging itself into the global economy faster than India.[1]
>
> Aroon Purie

Like most countries, India and Pakistan moved away from extensive state ownership and regulation of the economy at the end of the twentieth century. Before the 1990s, India and Pakistan's economic development philosophies contrasted markedly. But each exhibited high levels of state intervention in the economy. In the late 1980s and early 1990s, governments of India and Pakistan were attempting to exit the economy. But patterns of actual economic reform have differed considerably.

Explaining these divergent patterns is the focus of the first half of this chapter. Attempts to implement nearly identical International Monetary Fund (IMF) structural adjustment measures (detailed below) exhibit the influence of solidarity-building social institutions and organizations, more abundant in India than in Pakistan. Labor unions and other significant social organizations have played an essential role in responding to government measures and patterning changes in economic outcomes. This is evident in the privatization processes, discussed in the second part of the chapter.

The major elements of structural adjustment in South Asia were trade liberalization, privatization, and promotion of foreign direct investment (FDI).[2] The memoranda of understanding signed by the IMF and each government were almost identical. Indian and Pakistani currencies were to be devalued and ultimately made freely convertible. The IMF agreements committed the Indian and Pakistani governments to reduce budget deficits by reducing public subsidies, to deregulate industry and commerce, to relax foreign ownership and monopoly restrictions, to open areas to private business, to lower tariffs, and to privatize state enterprises. Generally, the state's authority in the direct management of the economy was to be reduced. Foreign investment was to be encouraged and the financial sector was to be deregulated, denationalized, and opened to foreign banks. Most of these policies have been effected and have begun to transform the role of the state in the economies of India and Pakistan.

The 1988 IMF structural adjustment loan to Pakistan, the first in a series, was negotiated quickly and signed, after General Zia ul-Haq's death, by an interim government. Zia had appointed that interim government after he dismissed Prime Minister Mohammad Khan Junejo's government. India began its structural adjustment program a couple of years later, in July 1991.[3] A fragile Indian National Congress (I) coalition government negotiated the IMF agreement to correct a severe balance of payment crisis. The Government of Pakistan was able to move rapidly in adjustment, notably in its privatization program, with little public resistance. In India, adjustment has been gradual, "half-hearted,"[4] and privatization has been thwarted at the central (federal, in US parlance) and provincial (state) levels. Why have the similar structural adjustment programs been implemented so differently, especially the privatization programs?

Structural adjustment

Contemporary structural adjustment began with the Mexican international private loan default of August 13, 1982 and the consequent establishment of an IMF Structural Adjustment Facility. The immediate concern of the IMF and other Mexican creditors was to maintain the capacity of Mexico, and other debtor developing countries, to make payments to financial institutions and private banks. In this sense – as it relates to balance of payments – the term structural adjustment is a misnomer. Adjustments are made in government expenditure. There is not a structural change in the conditions that lead to balance of payments crises in developing economies.

IMF structural adjustment is based upon monetarist principles. The IMF makes reduction of government expenditure – and thereby reduction of aggregate demand – a condition for release of funds. Tight monetary policies (e.g., higher deposit requirements for commercial banks), and reduced fiscal deficits, dampen inflationary pressure.[5] At the same time, subsidies are cut, leading to higher prices of commodities and services for improved long-term allocative efficiency. By design, structural adjustment dampens demand (in "the short-term," I hasten to add) through significant cuts in government consumption. Structural adjustment thereby depresses employment (again, in "the short-term").

Speculation about the efficiency and distribution tradeoffs of various models of mixed economies should not prevent one from looking at the record. Nearly everywhere that it was deployed, structural adjustment encouraged, if not forced, governments to cut public services, including education and health. These were not small cuts. In many countries, they injure an entire generation.[6] Structural adjustment in India and Pakistan pushed millions into poverty, not unlike the structural adjustment programs of a decade earlier in Latin America and the Caribbean. Structural adjustment programs have failed to promote sustained growth or the intangible foundations for development – such as investment in education and health.

The arguments for structural adjustment may be sound, but the assumptions behind them are not. Indeed, the assumptions underlying structural adjustment theory do not conform at all well to human life. An imaginary unregulated market is posited. The actors in this imagined market are assumed to be individuals (or corporate bodies legally recognized as individuals), with perfect information and equal capacity. An imperfectly informed government that issues distortion-causing regulations for "political" purposes is posited in opposition. This false dichotomy between the fictionalized state and the fictionalized market leads to the conclusion that state regulations can only be perverse in delivering net economic benefits.

Regulation can have a positive impact on efficiency and growth, putting aside positive impact on civil rights for the moment, as health and safety standards do. The existence of regulation does not itself demonstrate that its impact is negative.

Indeed, all markets require states to regulate them. In advanced capitalist societies, such regulation may be less obvious than in postcolonial societies. Vast networks of regulations are necessary to sustain markets, including regulatory bodies for stock and security exchanges, bodies for adjudication of disputes, processes for securing entitlement to intellectual property or patents, as well as regulations related to the numerous necessary direct monetary and macroeconomic interventions, such as interest rate determination. Governments also subsidize selected corporations and industries by bailing out troubled companies or, less publicly, by providing tax write-offs and other financial benefits. Such government intervention in the marketplace – essential to the operation of the so-called free market – comprises the majority of government spending in the advanced industrial world.

In the developing world, government intervention is typically more obvious. Governments often dictate maximum prices on important consumer goods, directly control financial organizations, and restrict designated industries to the public sector. Developing countries do tend to rely more on managerial controls than on macroeconomic controls. By itself, however, this is not proof that states in developing countries are more interventionist. It may be an indication that governments in the developing world are less capable of exercising control over the economy through regulatory and

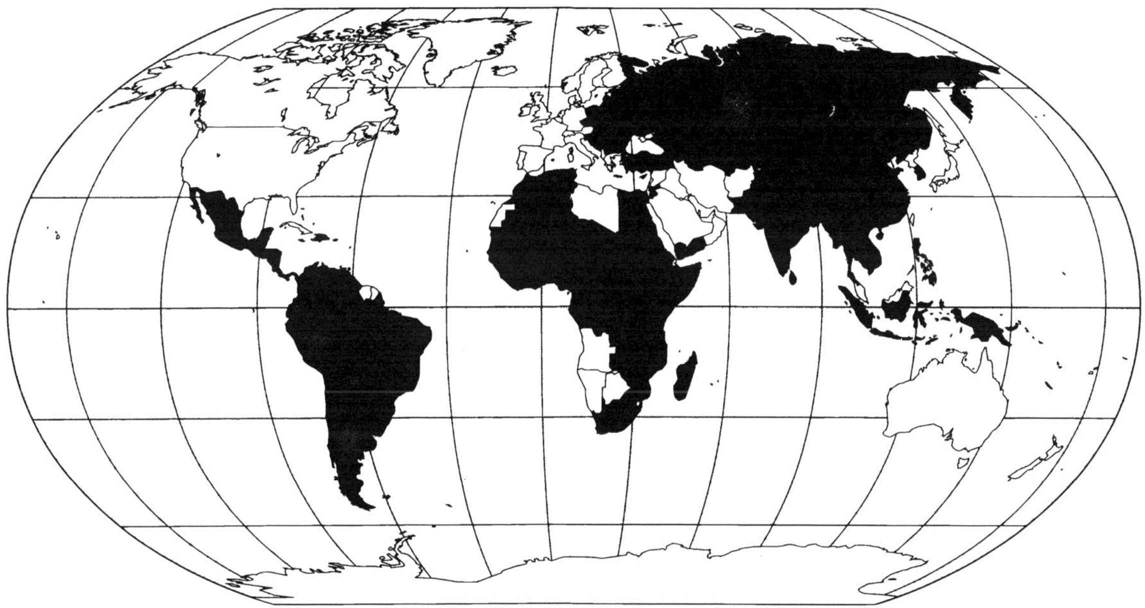

Map 3.1 World: countries having undertaken IMF structural adjustment 1982–2007

Source: adapted by Fatima Burney from Walden Bello, Shea Cunningham, and Bill Rau, *Dark Victory: The United States, Structural Adjustment, and Global Poverty*, London: Pluto Press, 1994. With permission from the authors.

macroeconomic intervention. The significant macroeconomic policy component of structural adjustment of the 1980s and early 1990s shows that governments in the developing world are shifting to more control through macroeconomic and financial policies and less through public management of the economy. At the same time, state protections and supports are being withdrawn from areas of the economy, with harsh effects on significant portion of the population.

Fiscal realities in poor economies

Increasing international economic interdependence is evidenced by the creation of the North American Free Trade Agreement (NAFTA), the World Trade Organization (WTO), and the proliferation of bi-lateral trade agreements. This interdepence renders governments, in both the developed and the developing world, less capable of forcing capital to make pacts with workers. Businesses often opt for investment in areas where no restrictions are placed on employers (nor guarantees placed on worker productivity, worker commitment, or worker discipline), rather than investment in areas where a compromise between the state and workers requires a significant degree of regulation to maintain a productive, rule-structured, and market-obedient work force. Just as Japanese and US corporations shifted their production facilities to Thailand, South Korea, Malaysia, and Indonesia decades ago, Indian and Pakistani industrialists have shifted their production from towns and cities, where workers have experience in organized action, to rural areas and small towns, where workers are not organized.

Governments throughout the world have abandoned once seemingly ubiquitous state-guided economic development strategies. Even in early neo-liberal development models and in their application, the state played a crucial role.[7] Economic ideologies were wide ranging but levels of market intervention in the economy were extensive in all economies, excepting those that have begun to fail as viable modern states. What caused the state's abdication from economic management?

The catalyst for the state's retreat from national economic planning, since the debt crisis was officially declared, has been balance of payment crises. Mexico's inability to meet its foreign debt payments in August 1982 officially inaugurated the debt crisis. IMF structural adjustment programs were designed to allow foreign creditors to recover their loans.[8] But the impetus for structural adjustment runs deeper than such fiscal imperatives. Over the past three decades, the very nature of industry, employment, and production has changed, especially in lower income countries, where economic policy makers once assumed that all economic activity could one day be regulated and formalized.

Structural adjustment does not merely address balance of payment crises. Structural adjustment programs have reduced government spending and opened protected national economies to international competition. Structural adjustment has legalized changes in labor production processes and has institutionalized deregulation and informality that threatens the very institutions of sustained development. Structural adjustment changes the state and its role in society. The chief challenges to societies in industrializing countries may be overwhelmingly fiscal. Nurturing democratic institutions built on cooperation and mutual protection, rather than abdication, is the best response to the inevitable fiscal crises of industrializing economies.

India's cautious adjustment (since 1975)

As with any incremental process, the origins of India's economic adjustment might be disputed. The beginnings of economic reform in India can be traced variably to 1974, when wholesale trade in wheat was denationalized, to 1980, when Mrs. Gandhi loosened industrial licensing requirements, to 1981, when the Indian government negotiated a nearly US$6 billion IMF loan, or to 1984, when Rajiv Gandhi, an advocate of technology and liberalization, was made Prime Minister.

I trace the origin of Indian economic reform to 1975 because the experiment with authoritarian rule known as the Emergency produced the most direct government overtures to the business community and new relationship between organized labor and the state. While the state used unprecedented violence against organized labor and its leaders, some of India's national labor unions also exhibited an unprecedented willingness to collaborate with an authoritarian state in spite of the interests of labor.

Early adjustment under the Emergency

In June 1975, Prime Minister Indira Gandhi declared a state of Emergency.[9] An executive ordinance amending the Maintenance of Internal Security Act permitted Mrs. Gandhi to imprison her political opponents without charge, to censure the press, and to outlaw strikes. Mrs. Gandhi announced that the Emergency was required to protect against external imperialist threats and internal capitalist ones. She announced a 20-point program with such populist features as lowering retail prices, seizing the luxury goods of tax evaders, and enforcing the ceiling on land holdings.[10] The Emergency, however, marked not a deepening of economic populism but a decided pro-business turn.[11] Relaxation of production capacity controls and restrictions on monopolies constituted the first efforts at economic adjustment. In 1975, the government permitted most industries to expand capacity by 125 percent, and to produce in related areas (a practice called broad-banding). In 1975, Mrs. Gandhi also had lifted the ceiling on what constituted a monopoly under the Monopolies and Restrictive Trade Practices Act.[12]

Left front liberalization

Mrs. Gandhi heeded the advice of some in her inner circle to conduct the scheduled 1977 general elections and to stand on a platform of government strength in defense of national independence and socialist principles. In the event, she was soundly defeated. The Janata (People's) Party, a hastily assembled coalition of political parties and protest movements, took office with a political platform in favor of extending Nehruvian socialism through a more strongly interventionist state and a more dominant public sector. The Janata coalition held Gandhian development sentiments and took a negative view of big business. The socialist labor leader of the Janata Party, George Fernandes, who told representatives of big business at the Federated Indian Chambers of Commerce and Industry (FICCI) that they behaved during the Emergency like rats rather than like men, became India's Minister of Industry. The industries of the largest 20 business houses, including the Tata Iron and Steel Corporation, were threatened with nationalization.

Despite the socialist rhetoric, a significant faction of the Janata Party regarded the public sector with the same suspicions as they did big business. Charan Singh, who served in the newly created office of Deputy Prime Minister and later as Home Minister and Finance Minister in the Janata Party government, led a Janata Party section representing middle-caste agriculturists. The Janata Party directed substantial state expenditure to agricultural and small-scale industry development. One major faction of the Janata Party, the Jan Sangh, represented "shopkeepers and traders and the new middle class of small industrialists and white collar workers."[13] "The main thrust" of the Janata Party's economic policy was the position that to of secure livelihoods for the rural masses "whatever can be produced by small and cottage industries must only be so produced."[14]

The fortunes of the Janata Dal at the center coincided with the rise of significant industries at the state level. The consensus apparently forming in the late 1970s among business people, journalists, and government officials that India could perform better in the international economy was encouraged by the major expansion in the middle sized business community in the 1970s. Medium sized businesses, with the political support of regional political parties and state governments, such as the Telugu Desam Party of N. T. Rama Rao in Andhra Pradesh and the Communist Party of India (Marxist) of Jyoti Basu in West Bengal, grew rapidly and challenged the major business houses which were more closely allied to the Congress.[15]

Indira Gandhi's gradual adjustment, 1979–1981

In July 1980, the Congress adopted a new Industrial Policy Resolution designed to bring coherence to de-licensing, broad-banding, capacity expansion, and the other *ad hoc* adjustment measures already announced.

The Industrial Policy Resolution of 1980 marked a clean break with the 1956 Industrial Policy. It dropped the previously obligatory reference to building a strong public sector that would occupy the "commanding heights" of the Indian economy in favor of reference to a public sector that would serve as the "pillars of infrastructure."

Despite the Indian government's cautious pursuit of a more open economic policy, there was economic discord between India and the United States. In August 1980, the US accused the Government of India of unfair trade practices on account of the use of export subsidies.[16] In January 1981, the World Bank announced the cancellation of a US$250 million loan to India to be used to establish two fertilizer plants. The loan was arranged on a concessional interest rate of 7.9 percent, payable over 20 years.[17]

Under some pressure from the US government and from the World Bank, India began negotiations with the IMF on an Extended Fund Facility loan in January 1981. Later in 1981, the government took several anti-inflation measures, including raising the bank lending rates and raising the minimum reserve on deposit required of banks.[18] Also as an anti-inflation measure, in July 1981, during a year of record wheat harvests, the government announced that it would purchase 1.5 million metric tons of US wheat.

Early IMF adjustment, 1981–1983

The negotiation of a US$5.8 billion loan with the IMF was a significant turn in economic development strategy. Then Finance Minister, Ramaswami Venkataraman, announced on August 11, 1981 India's application for the loan. It was eventually approved on November 9, 1981. To be distributed in three installments, the IMF loan was the largest that the international financial agency had ever cleared. The loan consumed one-sixth of the IMF's hard currency reserves. The US government abstained from the IMF vote on the loan, and the Reagan Administration lobbied other governments to block the approval, on the grounds that the loan was development aid rather than financing for structural adjustment. Officially, the loan was granted to relieve India's balance of payments problem, greatly exacerbated by the rising cost of imported oil.

At the same time, the conditionalities of the loan were strongly opposed in the Indian Parliament. Finance Minister Ramaswami Venkataraman was at pains to assure Members of Parliament that the conditions agreed to were in India's own interests. While the Indian government did not agree to a currency devaluation, as is customary, the government did agree to substantial changes in its financial policies. In April, the government eased its import policy in accordance with the conditions of the IMF program. Beginning with the coming fiscal year, fully export-oriented industries were permitted to import all requirements.

In anticipation of the resistance it would face over its economic adjustment policies, the government banned strikes in key industries on July 27,

1981 for six months. The law was promulgated as an ordinance, signed by the President under a Constitutional Provision permitting the President to enact ordinances when parliament is not in session, thus avoiding the outcry that would have occurred in a parliamentary debate on the measure. The industries in which strikes were banned included railways, electrical services, telephones, post, ports, airlines, banking, petrochemicals, hospitals, and defense-related industries.

In the wake of the November 1981 IMF loan, public criticism of the IMF and the World Bank continued. During a visit of the World Bank President, A. W. Clausen, in early February 1982, Indian economic planners voiced their criticism of the high commercial component of a US$1.9 billion World Bank pledge. In January 1982, eight national trade unions called a general strike against the "anti-labour policies of the government." The chief demand of the strikers was that the government lift the 1981 law giving the government the authority to ban strikes. The strikers also wanted the repeal of the National Security Act of 1980. Over 6,000 activists, chiefly in Andhra Pradesh and Tamil Nadu, were arrested on the eve of the strike. By the day of the strike, 25,000 activists and striking workers were in jail.

The government reorganized in favor of politicians inclined toward adjustment. On January 15, 1982, Prime Minister Indira Gandhi reshuffled her cabinet. Pranab Mukherjee, "a close associate of the Prime Minister with little experience in economic administration,"[19] was given charge of the Finance Ministry, while Ramaswami Venkataraman was moved to the Defence Ministry. Political observers saw this as Indira Gandhi's attempt to bring "economic management closer to her inner circle of advisors."[20]

Rajiv Gandhi's supply-side "liberalization," 1984–1990

Ten weeks before the completion of her third term as Prime Minister, Indira Gandhi was assassinated. She had ordered the Indian army to enter the holiest place of the Sikh faith, the Golden Temple, to capture or kill an armed party of Sikh separatists. Her younger son, Rajiv Gandhi, groomed for succession since his brother Sanjay's death in 1980, was quickly chosen to be Prime Minister by Parliament. While Rajiv Gandhi's efforts at economic adjustment were not the first or the most extensive, he is regarded by some as the chief proponent of economic reform among India's prime ministers because he explicitly articulated the position that India's Nehruvian development strategy had outlived its usefulness.

The Congress (I) government lost the November 1989 general election. A coalition government, headed by the Janata Dal leader and former Congress Finance Minister, V. P. Singh, held office until the Hindu chauvinist Bharatiya Janata Party withdrew its support in October 1990, causing the Janata Dal to lose a vote of confidence in parliament in November 1990. The Janata Dal's National Front coalition government was succeeded by a new coalition government, headed by Chandra Shekhar, the leader of a faction of the Janata Dal, the Janata Dal (Socialist), until it lost the support of the Congress (I) in May 1991.

The 1991 IMF agreement and the 1991 new economic policy

The Government of India publicly explained its decision to enter into a structural adjustment agreement with the IMF in July 1991 as the unavoidable response to a serious fiscal crisis.[21] Taking office in June 1991, the Congress (I) government found itself in an unsustainable fiscal situation, a situation which Congress governments had helped to create in the 1980s. The fiscal deficit of the central government for fiscal year 1990–91 was estimated at 8 percent of gross domestic product (GDP), having climbed from roughly 4 percent in the mid-1970s. Interest payments on internal debt alone constituted nearly 20 percent of total central government expenditure. Inflation had reached double digit levels, a historically high and politically dangerous level for India. The consumer price index for fiscal year 1990–91 increased by 13.6 percent, with the sharpest rises in foods, fuels, and other essential commodities. The balance of payments situation was also very serious. Foreign exchange reserves had dwindled, while governments changed three times in New Delhi, to Rs. 2,500 crore,[22] an amount sufficient for only two weeks of imports. In October 1991, the government of India signed an agreement with the IMF for a standby loan of 1.656 billion SDR (Standard Drawing Right) (approximately US$2.1 billion).

The fiscal crisis can be traced to a combination of domestic and international, economic and political factors. Although the government of India had been cautious with foreign and domestic borrowing since Independence, it began running large fiscal deficits, in excess of 6 percent of GDP, in the late 1970s. The deficits, which increased under the Congress (I) government of Prime Minister Rajiv Gandhi, were based upon sharply rising expenditure on interest payments on domestic and international borrowing, defense purchases, government salaries, and domestic subsidies on food, fertilizers, and exports. Large current account deficits, in the range of 25 percent of exports between 1980 and 1984 and 40 percent thereafter, were met through a large loan from the IMF, dispersed between 1982 and 1984, and large commercial borrowings.[23] To manage its fiscal deficits, the government reduced the growth of real spending on capital investment and increased its short-term external commercial borrowing. The Iraqi invasion of Kuwait in 1990 and subsequent conflict in the Persian Gulf made this precarious situation worse. The return of Indian workers from Kuwait and the loss of their remittances added to the foreign exchange crisis.[24] The price of petroleum and petroleum products, India's single most costly import item, increased sharply.[25]

In September and October 1990, Standard and Poors and Moody's lowered their rating of short-term debt to Indian financial institutions.[26] Moody's October 1990 report listed six factors responsible for the decline in their credit rating: (1) the increase in public debt; (2) the increase in external commercial borrowing and subsequent higher interest payments; (3) the increase in the external debt to export ratio; (4) the impact on export earnings and foreign remittances of the Iraqi invasion of Kuwait; (5) the increase in budget deficits and the subsequent increase in interest payments and inflation; and (6) the recession in Overseas Economic Cooperation and Development countries and subsequent decrease in export potential.[27] The July 1991 agreement with the IMF brought nearly US$4.8 billion in credit. While this solved the immediate foreign exchange crisis, the concerns enumerated by Moody's – especially increasing budget deficits, interest payments, and inflation – remained.

In July 1991 the Government of India's Finance Minister, Manmohan Singh, announced in the Lok Sabha, the lower house of Parliament, the removal of most industrial licensing requirements and the lifting of location and capacity restrictions on industry. The new industrial policy reduced the number of industrial sectors reserved for public sector investment from seventeen to eight. The new industrial policy also abolished requirements for government approval of domestic investment in all but 18 sensitive areas, specified on a "negative list," and granted automatic approval of foreign technology agreements and foreign investment of up to 51 percent of equity in 34 sectors, specified on a "positive list." The government declared two major currency devaluations in early July 1991, amounting to a devaluation of the rupee by approximately 20 percent. A further devaluation was made in March 1993.

The government announced in June 1991, and often thereafter, that it would stop supporting unprofitable public sector enterprises. Almost twenty years later, however, the central Government has initiated very limited direct privatization and failed at wholesale privatization. The government has sold shares in public sector enterprises, but most of these shares have gone to government financial institutions, effectively transferring public debt from public sector enterprises to public sector financial institutions. Of the 248 public sector enterprises managed by the central government, only 31 have been subject to disinvestment, and these at an average of only 8 percent of equity.

Pakistan's rapid adjustment (since 1988)

> According to Prime Minister Nawaz Sharif, the free market economy introduced in this country would serve as a model to other Muslim countries. ... His Federal Industries Minister ... said that this was a

challenge to the world as even UK's Margaret Thatcher could not go for such a massive privatization programme.[28]

Nawaz Sharif, Prime Minister of Pakistan, 1992

General Zia's aborted economic liberalization

In his 11 years of rule, General Zia ul-Haq did not significantly restructure the public sector economy that he inherited from Zulfikar Ali Bhutto and General Ayub Khan. From July 1977 until August 1988, Zia managed only to complete the privatization of those public sector enterprises – wheat flour, rice husking, and cotton ginning mills – that Bhutto had slated to denationalize.[29] Zia failed to meet Pakistani industrialists' demand that all nationalized industries be returned to the private sector. Writing in the last month of General Zia's 11-year rule, journalist Shahid Zahid comments that "[d]espite years of ballyhooing about privatization, hardly any change has come about in reducing the size of the public sector."[30] General Zia's economic behavior contradicted the thesis that authoritarian interventions are driven by the logic of dependent capitalist development and betrayed the economic objectives he himself declared in 1977.

Despite the professed interests of the military government, the intervention of the military in Pakistani politics did not mark a transition away from statist economic development. General Zia kept the bulk of Pakistan's newly nationalized industries in the public sector. With the 1985–86 budget, it was announced that shares of public sector enterprises valued at Rs. 2 billion would be sold to the private sector. Fourteen public sector enterprises were later identified for divestiture, but by 1989 only six companies had been divested of public shares. Pakistan International Airlines could only be divested by 10 percent and this was only possible when the government guaranteed returns on the investment. Ironically, only after General Zia's death and the election of Benazir Bhutto's Pakistan Peoples Party (PPP) did Pakistan move rapidly to dismantle the statist structure that Zulfikar Bhutto had helped to solidify.

As soon as the government of Pakistan took a US$835 million IMF loan in 1988, a large loan by any standards, the pace of economic adjustment picked up. Years earlier, in 1980, Pakistan had arranged a, relatively small, US$2 million loan from the IMF.[31] The loan was made from the IMF's Extended Fund Facility, a predecessor to the IMF's Structural Adjustment Facility, established in 1986.[32] The disbursement of the 1980 loan was made contingent upon the lowering of government subsidies on such essential commodities as wheat, cooking fuel, and fertilizers, increasing the administered price of electricity and other public utilities, lowering import tariffs, and halting further investment in public sector undertakings. The loan was extended several times, but eventually lapsed due to lack of implementation of the conditions attached to it. Until a serious foreign exchange crisis forced the government to go to the IMF again in 1988, no substantial progress was made in implementing these conditions.

The caretaker government and the 1988 IMF agreement

The 1988 IMF agreement, which would spur Pakistan's rapid economic policy reform, came at the close of a significant year for Pakistan. On May 29, 1988, President General Zia ul-Haq dismissed the federal government and the national assembly, on charges of corruption and inadequate attention to Islam, under the authority of the Eighth Amendment. On the following day, under Zia's direction, the Governors of Pakistan's four provinces dismissed the provincial governments and provincial assemblies on similar grounds. Zia appointed an interim Pakistan Muslim League-dominated caretaker government and promised to abide by his own 1985 Constitution in holding elections within 90 days, but on a non-party basis. A little more than two weeks after the dismissal of the national and provincial governments, on June 15, 1988, President Zia promulgated a Presidential decree repealing all existing civil law and introducing the *Shariah* as the foundation for Pakistan's legal system. Rather than instituting a system of guided democracy as the promised non-party elections suggested, President Zia deepened authoritarianism under the ideological cover of an Islamic theocracy. Within one month, however, General Zia ul-Haq, his senior military officers, and the US Ambassador died with the detonation of a device aboard a plane on which they were flying.

Before General Zia's death, the Finance Minister, Dr. Mahbub ul-Haq, presented the 1988–89 budget. Twenty years earlier, Mahbub ul-Haq served as Chief Economist for Field Marshal Ayub Khan's Planning Commission. Ul-Haq, the "caretaker surgeon" as he described himself, presented the budget on June 26, 1988.[33] He addressed people directly on television and radio rather than through the conventional address to the National Assembly. The budget provided for major increases in defense expenditure, income and sales tax, and excise duties and as well as the introduction of a value added tax. Fourteen public sector enterprises were to be privatized immediately and others, including the nationalized banks, were to divest shares. In mid-August 1988, foreign exchange reserves dwindled to US$150 million, an amount sufficient for less than one week's worth of imports, the lowest level in ten years. Declining export growth and increasing debt servicing contributed most to the crisis.[34]

The caretaker government thus began negotiations with the IMF on a structural adjustment loan under the IMF's Extended Fund Facility. Mahbub ul-Haq discussed the prospects of securing an IMF loan with the IMF Managing Director in September 1988. Earlier that year, Pakistan had taken a US$18 million standby loan from the IMF to meet balance of payment difficulties.[35] On December 28, 1988, the IMF announced that it had approved a structural adjustment facility loan of 620.05 million SDR, equivalent to US$836 million. An initial tranche of US$147 million was disbursed in December 1988. Three hundred and sixty eight million dollars were to be drawn over a 15-month period on a typical IMF standby arrangement. Funds were to be drawn as adjustment targets were met. The remaining US$467 million was made available as a three-year structural adjustment loan, contingent upon the Pakistan government's achievement of specific economic targets. These were standard IMF conditions, including elimination of subsidies, reform of pricing and tax policies, liberalization of imports, widening the role for the private sector, and contraction of fiscal deficits. With each new fiscal year, the government and the IMF was to sign a new letter of intent, based on satisfactory progress in the previous year.

Economic pragmatism under Benazir Bhutto

On November 16, 1988, Pakistan had its first political party-based elections since 1977. With 38.7 percent of the vote, the PPP emerged with almost twice as many seats as its rival, the Islami Jamoori Ittehad (Islamic Democratic Alliance) (IJI). The incoming PPP government regarded the December 1988 IMF loan's conditions as "a bitter pill, the last legacy of Zia." The new Finance Minister, Ehsanul-Haq Piracha, described the conditions "as the harshest ever contracted by Pakistan" and declared that the PPP should not be held responsible "as it was already signed before [Bhutto] became Prime Minister."[36] The financial crisis it inherited, her government argued, gave it no choice but to honor the IMF agreement. On December 7, 1988, the Finance Minister announced that "the government has agreed to abide by the IMF."

The international financial community seemed inclined to give some leeway to Pakistan's first democratically elected government in over a decade. Pledges by members of the World Bank-sponsored Aid to Pakistan Consortium, meeting in Paris in April 1989, committed US$3.095 billion for 1989–90, an increase over the 1988 Paris agreement by US$384 million, more than 14 percent. This reflected the confidence of the governments of the advanced industrialized countries and the international financial organizations that compose the Consortium that the Government of Pakistan could be financially responsible under democratic rule. In May 1989, Prime Minister Bhutto announced that the IMF was relaxing conditions attached to the IMF structural adjustment loan. Instead of cutting Pakistan's budget deficit to 5.5 percent of GDP, the government was permitted to hold the deficit to 6 percent of GDP. The IMF vigorously denied that there had been a relaxation of economic conditions.[37]

Despite the unpopularity of structural adjustment, Prime Minister Bhutto made solid progress in implementing the IMF agreement. The Pakistan rupee was gradually devalued. At the end of October 1988, the rupee stood at 18.20 to the dollar.[38] Within a year, by October 1989, it shrunk to Rs. 20.95 to the dollar, a devaluation of nearly 12 percent.[39] Within six months, the Pakistan rupee had lost another 4 percent of its October 1988 value.[40] Most importantly, the PPP government reduced the budget deficit to 6.8 percent of GDP in fiscal year 1989–90 by freezing all government spending at the rate of inflation. In fiscal year 1988–89, the deficit had been 8.5 percent of GDP. The PPP government also made overtures to the Pakistani business community. In early April 1989, Bhutto arranged for selected businessmen in Karachi to be included in the framing of the budget. A Board of Investment was also established and chaired by the Prime Minister to facilitate private sector industrialization.

On August 6, 1990, Pakistan's President, Ghulam Ishaq Khan, dismissed the government of Benazir Bhutto and appointed Ghulam Mustafa Jatoi, the IJI opposition leader, interim Prime Minister. Elections were scheduled for October 24, 1990. In late August and early September, an IMF team visited Islamabad to discuss the third tranche of Pakistan's 1988 loan. The third letter of intent had not been signed on schedule because the IMF was not satisfied with Pakistan's refusal to increase immediately the domestic price of oil, gas, and electricity by 40 percent, so as to reach international levels,[41] and Pakistan's failure to keep the fiscal deficit to 5.5 percent as originally projected for fiscal year 1990–91.[42] The IMF and the World Bank had also raised with Mrs. Bhutto, before her dismissal, the political uses of loans and their low recovery by the nationalized banking sector.

Nawaz Sharif's privatization campaign[43]

The IMF closely monitored the government that succeeded the PPP as well. The October 1990 elections led to the victory of the IJI and the National Assembly's selection of Nawaz Sharif as Prime Minister. In his first address to the nation as Prime Minister, Nawaz Sharif announced that the new government intended to move quickly on privatizing the public sector and deregulating private industry. According to Sharif, Pakistan's privatization program would be more rigorous than anything that Margaret Thatcher could implement and would serve as a model for the entire Muslim world.

The IJI government, however, did not satisfy IMF conditionalities as well as the PPP administration had, or as well as the subsequent PPP administration would. In keeping with IMF demands, Sharif did raise oil prices by 41 percent upon his move into office, but resisted price increases in electricity and natural gas. While talks with the IMF over the final disbursement of the 1988 loan continued, the government sought an additional loan of US$1 billion from the IMF under its Extended Structural Adjustment Facility, a facility for countries which have completed an IMF adjustment program.[44] The major concern of the IMF with Pakistan's adjustment program was its difficulties in reducing the fiscal deficit and in effecting tax reform. The IMF, concerned that capital earned from privatization was being used to finance the deficit, made the non-use of privatization proceeds for deficit management a conditionality of the 1990 memorandum.[45]

In November 1990, a Disinvestment and Deregulation Committee was formed to identify enterprises to be privatized and to suggest deregulation measures. The Committee recommended that the government "retire from the production of industrial goods."[46] One hundred and five enterprises were identified for privatization. All nationalized banks were slated for privatization as well as the Telegraph and Telephone Corporation of Pakistan. The Commission decided against privatization in only two of the cases it has considered, the National Bank of Pakistan and Pakistan International Airlines (PIA). The government then established, in January 1991, a Privatization Commission to handle the privatization process. Senator Saeed Qadir, a retired general, was appointed Chairman of the Commission.

Opportunities for personal profits, and to a lesser extent need to finance the deficit reduction stipulated by the IMF, drove the privatization campaign in Pakistan. Senator Saeed Qadir presented the government's privatization program not as an economic necessity, as the reforms in India were presented, but as a victory for the free market. Qadir's enthusiasm for the virtues of the private sector was challenged. At one meeting:

> Senator Saeed Qadir faced a hostile audience which mostly comprised the trade union activists, journalists, academicians and intellectuals and he lost his control on many occasions. He was interrupted when he said industrialization in Pakistan was done entirely by the private entrepreneurs after Partition in 1947 and many persons from the audience reminded him that the actual pioneering role was played by Pakistan Industrial Development Corporation, a public sector institution.[47]

By the time Nawaz Sharif left the Prime Minister's office in 1993 – at the request of the military – the Privatization Commission sold 67 of the 105 public sector enterprises on its 1991 list as well as two of the four national banks. These included 11 cement factories (at Rs. 4.658 billion), eight automobile factories (at Rs. 1.043 billion), five chemical and ceramics factories (at Rs. 1.030 billion), 15 *ghee*, or vegetable oil, mills (at Rs. 626 million), two fertilizer factories (at Rs. 457 million), seven rice mills (at Rs. 165 million), four engineering firms (at Rs. 141 million), and thirteen *roti*, or bread, plants.[48] Under Prime Minister Nawaz Sharif's tenure alone (October 1990–June 1993), the Pakistani public sector shed 60,000 workers through privatization.[49]

The potential windfall in a single privatization deal is illustrated by the privatization of the Pak China Fertilizer company.[50] The Privatization

Commission evaluated the Pak China Fertilizer facility and the 300 acres upon which it stands at Rs. 470 million. The industrial estate included clubs for rest houses, and dozens of living quarters for officers and staff. The Schon group purchased the factory and estate for Rs. 190 million. This included the Rs. 180 million in cash holdings of the enterprise. The Schon group prospered under Zia ul-Haq and maintained close relations with Nawaz Sharif.[51] Having purchased the enterprise, the new owners had the facility appraised. Based on a Rs. 980 million appraisal, the Schon group was then able to arrange for a Rs. 720 million loan.

The Pak China Fertilizer Mazdoor Union, to which all Pak China Fertilizer workers belong, fearing for their jobs, protested against this subsidized transfer of their factory. The Union took their case before the Privatization Commission, where they were told that the transfer was legal. The new management attempted to form a pocket union, but no workers opted to accept the offer to become officers in the new union. The new management had also promised the Mazdoor Union that it would not hire new workers, but has nevertheless hired security staff who are prohibited by law from joining the Pak China Fertilizer Mazdoor Union.

Prime Minister Nawaz Sharif often protested that Pakistan's economic reform program was not "an *ad hoc* exercise, but rather the immediate steps in a well-thought out strategy of industrialization and economic development."[52] His protestations draw attention to the concerns of international financial institutions and investors. Pakistan's adjustment program, under Nawaz Sharif, was essentially *ad hoc* and involved too little consultation with affected social sectors or government ministries to be easily sustained. Indeed, officials in the Ministry of Production claim that they were only appraised of the privatization of the industries under their charge when the managers of the individual enterprises informed them of the Prime Minister's privatization initiative.[53]

The 1993 IMF loan and the interim Qureshi government

In recognition of the reform efforts of the "caretaker" government of Prime Minister Moeen Qureshi, the IMF approved a standby loan of US$377 million over a twelve-month period for the 1993–94 economic and finance program. GDP growth had declined in 1992–93 to 6 percent from 9 percent in 1991–92.[54] The removal of an elected government and approval of an IMF adjustment by the subsequent military-appointed government repeats a pattern begun in 1988.

Deepening adjustment under Bhutto, 1993–1994

As negotiated by the Pakistani military, elections to the National Assembly were held on October 6, 1993. The Pakistan Peoples Party, with the support of smaller parties and independents, formed the government. The National Assembly elected Benazir Bhutto Prime Minister.

Pakistan was hit by massive flooding in 1992, followed by drought and further flooding in 1993, with consequent massive crop infestation and disruptions of hydroelectric-supplied power to industry. These natural calamities had a serious negative impact on Pakistan's economic growth. Growth in gross domestic product in 1992–93 was only 2.3 percent, and only 3.9 percent in 1993–94. As the Economist Intelligence Unit put it, "in the face of such adversity the government's commitment to the adjustment path is laudable."[55] In fiscal year 1993–94, Mrs. Bhutto brought the fiscal deficit down to 5.8 from 8.0 percent.[56] In fiscal year 1994–95, contraction of credit and money supply fell below World Bank and IMF targets, the expansion of exchange reserves exceeded expectations, and the fiscal deficit was to estimated at 4.0 percent.[57]

Between returning to power, in October 1993, and the end of 1994, Mrs. Bhutto sold 22 public sector enterprises.[58] Two state companies were sold in May 1994, a *ghee* mill and a fertilizer factory. In July and October 1994, 16 more enterprises were sold for a total of Rs. 8.83 billion (US$289.5 million).[59] The government initiated the sale of four large financial institutions: the National Development Finance Corporation, the Industrial Development Bank of Pakistan, Habib Credit and Investment Corporation, and Banker Equity.[60]

Nawaz Sharif 1995–1999

The privatization of the oil and natural gas sector in Pakistan suggests that unfettered economic policy decisions are not necessarily economically sound. In May 1999, the Pakistan Privatization Board, chaired by Nawaz Sharif, approved the disinvestment of Oil and Gas Development Corporation gas and oil fields. The Board estimated that the sale of 20 percent to 30 percent of those concerns could bring US$450 to US$560 million. Prime Minister Sharif wanted the complete privatization of the oil and gas sector. "Why every time the country should raise a begging bowl before everybody and why should not we get the money by selling our assets," he asked reporters.[61] The Board-appointed Privatization Commission Financial Advisor on oil and gas reported that consumer prices for oil and gas would need to be raised in order to make the concerns attractive to foreign investors. The Minister of Petroleum, estimating the value of their holdings at several times that amount, opposed the privatization of the industry before the development of a strategic plan.

Pakistan's Privatization Commission sold or closed all central government public sector units in Northwest Frontier Province, resulting in the loss of thousands of the province's best jobs.[62]

Privatization compared

> We've got these desperately poor people and no matter what you do in adjustment it won't affect them. ... The thing we are all after is this exit policy [a policy granting employers the right to fire employees]. We can't move until we buy off labor. After all, we're talking about only 500,000 workers in a labor force of 350 million. An aggressive manager can pretty much buy these guys off.[63]
>
> Richard Cambridge

According to World Bank officials, organized labor remains the greatest obstacle to the full implementation of India's IMF structural adjustment program. Several years into India's structural adjustment program, organized workers and unions have yet to be bought off. Employer federations have not won their demand for labor law reform that would allow employers in large enterprises to fire employees without government permission. And, despite government efforts, no central government public sector enterprise, and few at the state level, has been privatized. In Pakistan, where a similar IMF structural adjustment program was adopted, organized labor posed little impediment to the government's adjustment program. Indeed, those Pakistani public sector unions which first faced de-nationalization negotiated an agreement with the Ministry of Manpower, cleared the way for the privatization of the entire manufacturing sector and, shortly thereafter, all other sectors of the economy. Despite vigorous opposition from Pakistani labor unions, workers have only occasionally delayed privatization, never prevented it, as workers in India have.

Variation in social institutions – not the manipulation of opposition groups – explains why similar economic reform efforts have had widely differing results. I show that political party-based unionism and enterprise unionism have a significant and predictable influence on economic reform initiatives. Political party-based unionism – wherein unions are allied to political party patrons – can succeed in blocking adjustment measures but it is weak at mobilizing support from other social groups, even from other unions, whether or not they are affiliated with political parties. In contrast, enterprise unionism – factory-based unions without political party affiliation – is not able to block adjustment measures but, somewhat surprisingly, is able to forge community alliances and to advance workers' welfare.

To blame Indian trade union centers for intransigence in the face of industrial restructuring and consequent job losses, as many economists and industrialists do, is silly. The criticism is misplaced not merely because the defense of the economic interests of its members is one of the cardinal purposes of a union. Rather, it is misplaced because Indian trade union centers often oppose industrial restructuring because the political parties to which they are affiliated, when they are out of power, often find it politically expedient to challenge the privatization measures of the ruling party. Thus, it is wise to take the perspective suggested by Perry Anderson. "[T]rade unions," Anderson reminds us, "do not *challenge* the existence of society based on a division of classes, they merely *express* it."[64] Unions are best understood as agents operating within the structure and the constraints of existing social institutions.[65] How does political party-based unionism, characterized by a dependence of unions on political parties, influence patterns of economic adjustment? How does enterprise unionism, characterized by factory-level bargaining by politically unaffiliated unions, influence patterns of adjustment? Under what circumstances do labor organizations contribute to promotion of employment, labor standards, human development, and social opportunity?

Indian trade union responses

Indian and Pakistani union responses to privatization converge and diverge in revealing ways. We begin with a brief overview of protests by Indian unions against privatization. Indian trade unions have responded to privatization with strikes and demonstrations. Demonstrations have expressed workers' feelings of betrayal and fears of losing employment. After the announcement of the structural adjustment measures, a one-day nationwide strike was organized by a coalition of national trade union centers, on November 29, 1991, to demonstrate to the government the damage that labor could do to the adjustment program if trade union federations were not consulted. The general strike, and those which followed on June 16, 1992, September 9, 1993, and September 29, 1994, were of national significance because they disrupted the national economy. In Delhi and in other cities, public transport and financial services were suspended. In industrial areas, workers' demonstrations were vocal and, in some places, drew police fire. The November 1991 strike, like the subsequent general strikes, was complete throughout eastern and southern states and was nearly complete elsewhere, reflecting in part the geographical strength of unions other than Indian National Trade Union Congress (INTUC) and the Bharatiya Mazdoor Sabha (BMS) which boycotted the national strike in favor of their respective political parties' positions on structural adjustment.

Although all trade union federations argue that the government's new economic adjustment policies are an assault on organized labor, the central offices of the INTUC and the BMS, in deference to the economic policies of the political parties to which they are affiliated, did not join these general strikes. Officials of the INTUC and the BMS, whose political parties have supported economic restructuring in Parliament, offered the explanation that their decision not to participate was not in support of economic adjustment, but was rather a strategic maneuver. The threat of a general strike, they argued, is a more effective way of ensuring that organized labor is consulted in economic policy than actual strike action. National strikes, they have argued, only exhaust the trade union movement's leverage over government.[66] The actual reason for the INTUC's and the BMS's non-participation is that the political parties to which they are affiliated dictate their policy.

Some local unions affiliated to INTUC and BMS did participate in the general strikes. The Karnataka and Madhya Pradesh enterprises of INTUC, for example, gave support to the strikes of November 1991 and June 1992, despite the non-participation of the central trade union body in the general strikes. Some INTUC officials called for strike action against the new economic policy. Despite the opposition of the Indian National Trade Union Congress to such general strikes, Gopeshwar, General Secretary of INTUC, called for a general strike among public sector workers in West Bengal if the Communist Party of India (Marxist) government there continued with its "retrograde" privatization policies toward the public sector.

Negotiating with Government

Negotiations between government and organized labor over the implementation of structural adjustment measures have been largely inconclusive. In November 1991, the Government of India, responding to pressure from major national trade union federations, initiated negotiations over the new economic policies. Tripartite negotiations began on December 21, 1991 under the direction of the Minister for Coal, P. A. Sangma. Prime Minister P. V. Narasimha Rao chose not to appoint a Labour Minister after the resignation of M. K. Ramamurthy, but rather called upon the Minister for Coal to handle negotiations with the trade union centers.[67] According to Indian trade union center officials, this had the effect of diminishing organized labor's formal access to government policy.

The tripartite committee decided to concentrate first upon the viability of public sector enterprises. Labor representatives wanted to prevent the assignment of decision-making authority on unviable public sector enterprises to the Board for Industrial and Financial Reconstruction (BIFR). They argued that the BIFR was under-staffed and ill equipped to devise proper reconstruction packages. Labor representatives proposed the re-establishment of tripartite committees on an industry basis for those sectors facing widespread sickness. Eventually, the government would accede to this demand. The chief achievement for labor in the tripartite discussions was the agreement, formally made at the second meeting on January 20, 1992, that labor would be "consulted" before the closure of any public sector enterprise. The business press had reported earlier that the Finance Minister had offered to write off the company liabilities of any public sector enterprise that workers purchased.[68] The Finance Minister promised labor leaders at the tripartite gathering that workers would be given priority in buying loss-making enterprises and managing them as workers' cooperatives. The Minister also promised that the liability of enterprises under workers' management would be written off. When the Finance Minister's promise failed to appear in the official minutes of the meeting, prepared by the Ministry of Coal, labor representatives petitioned the Ministry to issue a revised version that noted the Finance Minister's promise. This suggests the lack of seriousness with which the labor consultations were initially met by the government.[69]

Since these initial tripartite meetings, the central government and the largest trade union centers have begun a series of industry-specific tripartite discussions. Trade union officials report that these tripartite discussions are unlikely to lead to a managed restructuring of failing public sector enterprises. In the textile industry, for example, four textile research associations were commissioned to devise a rehabilitation package based on massive labor force reduction and the sale of Rs. 26 billion of surplus land. All the major trade union federations opposed the renewal package by supporting a *jail bharo* (fill the jails) agitation on December 12, 1995.[70]

Preventing privatization

The chief advantage of political party-based unionism to labor is that organized labor might gain a voice, through political parties, in the political process that it could not have gained by merely making economic demands at the enterprise or industry level.

The reversal of the government's decision to privatize the giant Indian Iron and Steel Company (IISCO) demonstrates the strength of political party-based unionism labor in India. The government, in a cabinet meeting in November 1993, decided that IISCO should be privatized. The Steel Authority of India Ltd. (SAIL), under the financial constraints of a tighter government budget, was unable to finance the necessary modernization. The Communist Party of India (Marxist) (CPM)-ruled government of West Bengal, where IISCO is located, supported the move. The central government invited bids and accepted that of an Indian industrialist.

The 30,000 workers at the Burnpur-based enterprise objected to the privatization plan. INTUC, the CPM's chief rival in West Bengal, together with other centers, organized a "lightning strike to oppose the decision."[71] The unions managed not only to stage a strike throughout the entire public steel sector but also to gain the support of public sector officers' associations. A Parliamentary committee, convened to review the privatization decision, recommended that the decision be withdrawn and that SAIL be given the necessary budgetary support to finance IISCO's modernization. The government, despite the Congress's majority in the chamber, withdrew from the Lok Sabha the bill which would have effected the privatization of IISCO. The reversal of the government's decision to privatize the giant public sector enterprise demonstrates the ability of politically affiliated unions, when they are united across party lines, to oppose government privatization efforts.

Labor opposition to privatization in India has not been restricted to the traditional mechanisms of strikes and negotiations. Labor agitations have also employed some unusual and ingenious strategies. The Bombay workers of Hindustan Lever, an Indian subsidiary of the giant Anglo-Dutch transnational Unilever, locked out of their factory, produced their own washing detergent powder under the brand name Lock-Out. Selling 110 tons of the powder won the union considerable public attention. Continuing the innovative strategy, the Hindustan Lever Employees' Union runs parallel annual general shareholders' meetings so as to inform investors of various management and financial irregularities. In August 1992, cotton textile mill workers from central Bombay marched through the streets in underpants and undershirts denouncing India's commitment to the eradication of poverty as a sham.[72]

The ability of political party-based unionism to resist privatization also may be seen in the trade union opposition to one of the early attempts by a state government to privatize a public sector enterprise. In May 1991, the Janata Dal Chief Minister of Uttar Pradesh, Mulayam Singh Yadav, took out advertisements offering to sell the three cement plants within the Uttar Pradesh State Cement Corporation. Nine workers' unions joined to win a UP High Court order to stay the sale. Ignoring the stay, the Chief Minister drew up an agreement with the Dalmia industrial group for transferring the plant for a seriously undervalued sum. The High Court accordingly began proceedings for a contempt of court case against the Chief Minister, but the assassination of Rajiv Gandhi, in the middle of India's tenth general election, forced the court to reschedule the case for after July 1991. Before handing over state offices in June, Mulayam Singh Yadav approved the sale of the Dalla plant and began arrangements for handing over the plant to the Dalmia group.

In June 1991, UP government officials and management personnel of the Dalmia group arrived at the factory in Dalla, UP under police escort to transfer possession of the premises. Workers feared that they would lose their jobs. They protested at the factory gate, preventing the new management from entering the premises.[73] Police clubbed, tear-gassed, and shot workers, killing twelve and injuring over fifty, six of whom were to die later of their injuries.[74] According to an investigative delegation of members of the Rajya Sabha, police fired without provocation, pursued workers over three days, and assaulted workers and their wives in their homes.[75] Despite the BJP's position in favor of de-nationalization, sustained popular pressure organized by the workers of the Dalla plant joined by other state employee unions forced the BJP government to cancel the sale of the plant.[76]

Effort to privatize the Bailadila Mines in Raipur, Madhya Pradesh also reveals how labor organizes effective resistance. Mining and quarrying have been the exclusive preserve of central and state governments in India. The Government of Madhya Pradesh entertained proposals for opening the mineral rich Chattisgarh area to the private sector in 1995. Pramod Mittal's Nippon Denro purchased the mines. The Chattisgarh Mukti Morcha (Chattisgarh Liberation Front) (CMM) organized protests against the privatization plan.

The CMM is an independent trade union organized by tribal mine workers, formed in reaction to intimidation and periodic killing of laborers and labor leaders by local police and industrialists. Twenty-one workers were killed in 1978 when police fired on non-violent demonstrations against the mechanization of the mines. The leader of the CMM, Shankar Guha Niyogi, was murdered, allegedly by local industrialists, in September 1991.[77] Eleven workers were killed and forty injured in 1992 when police fired on a demonstration for a uniform labor law and the prosecution of Niyogi's killers. The CMM Vice-President Sheikh Ansar in March 1996 contemplated contesting a Lok Sabha seat in the April–May 1996 general elections.[78] A mass demonstration was also threatened by the Janata Dal, Communist Party of India, and Communist Party of India (Marxist) to prevent Nippon Denro from entering the iron ore mine site at Mine 11B.[79]

The Bharatiya Janata Party (BJP) also opposed the privatization plan. Congress dissidents in the All India Indira Congress (Tiwari) and Communist Party of India (CPI) activists claim that the National Mining Development Corporation (NMDC) had its proposals for mineral development ignored. The NMDC, with headquarters in Hyderabad, produces 9 million tones of iron ore annually in the Bailadila Sector, one of its major projects, and raises Rs. 400 crore (US$123 million) in foreign exchange on diamond exports. The NMDC planned to double its iron ore output from the Bailadila mining sector within five years.[80] Internationally, the NMDC has successfully competed with foreign firms in the supply of modernization equipment. At issue in the protests over the privatization proposals are foreign ownership and profit making in an industry where the Indian public sector industry has the capacity to develop the sector profitably. One CMM labor leader complains that "they [government officials] say De Beers will bring technology. But just ten percent of the royalty from the mine can buy the technology. Why give it to them?"[81]

The conflict over the privatization of Chattisgarh mining has raised questions about the need for foreign investment and the potential consequence of foreign management in a strategically sensitive sector of the economy. The Bailadila controversy involves the additional element of a local labor force consisting predominantly of a poor tribal population that has been socially and politically marginalized by local industry, administration, and government. State and upper-caste oppression, now combined with the threat of privatization, forged the local labor force's trade union into a political movement. Labor resistance to the privatization of the Bailadila

Mines is one instance in a series of opposition efforts by organized labor that dates to the initiation of economic reforms in July 1991.

A stand-off also developed between organized labor and the government over the privatization of the telecommunications industry, formerly in the exclusive purview of the public sector. In January 1994, in the most important component of India's privatization program to date, the central government decided to end the state monopoly in telecommunications. Department of Telecommunications unions responded by holding a crippling national strike just before the opening of bids for basic telephone contracts. Labor unions, joined by private firms that were dissatisfied with the tendering procedures, won a Supreme Court ruling in December 1995 requiring the government to address their charges before issuing licenses for telecommunications services to the private sector. The Supreme Court regarded the lack of a regulatory authority to supervise the privatization process as the principal concern.[82] In anticipation of the court's verdict, in January 1996 the central government issued an ordinance establishing a regulatory body, the Telecom Regulatory Authority of India (TRAI), to formulate guidelines for the participation of private companies in the privatization of the central government's telephone monopoly. The court's decision constituted a victory for the telecommunications labor unions as it specified that an administered process, subject to the political influence that trade unions could apply, would be established for the privatization of the industry.

The exit policy and industrial disputes

There has been significant public debate on the adoption of a so-called exit policy, a policy that would give employers of large industries the right to fire employees at the discretion of the employer. At present, employers with more than 100 employees are permitted only to dismiss individual workers and only for proven disciplinary problems. Lay-off of workers in enterprises employing more than 100 workers must receive the approval of the government. A 1977 amendment to the Industrial Disputes Act of 1947, requires government approval for the retrenchment of employees at enterprises employing 100 or more workers. The government is almost always unwilling to grant the approval and risk alienating the labor voter. Employers can circumvent the law by declaring that an enterprise is unprofitable, closing the factory, and refusing to pay workers' salaries. If an enterprise is to restructure its labor force without closing down the factory, however, a deal must be struck with the unions. The legal dismissal of employees, without their consent, is demanding. An employee must first be issued a charge sheet, an initial warning in which the violation of the terms of contract is made explicit to a worker. Employers prepare charges, workers prepare defenses, and the case is given a hearing before the Labour Commissioner's office. Individuals who commit even relatively minor offenses may be dismissed in this manner, but the process requires considerable legal involvement at management's expense and is typically drawn out for months.

An Industrial Relations Bill, designed to eliminate the employment security of the Industrial Disputes Act, was proposed by the Janata Dal government in 1978. It was redrafted and circulated to Parliament by the Congress government in 1988 and again in 1993 without sufficient support for enactment. Although the memoranda of understanding signed by the IMF and governments adopting adjustment programs are not made public, it is officially acknowledged in India that an exit policy is an important condition of India's 1991 IMF structural adjustment loan. It was widely expected to be addressed in the Finance Minister's budget speeches in 1992 and 1993. Since the April 1996 parliamentary elections, the expectation of a change to the Industrial Disputes Act's employment protection has receded.

India's trade unions have been particularly concerned about the "exit policy." Employers have been overwhelmingly for it. "Freedom of entry and exit is a basic prerequisite of any competitive environment," begins a publication of the Federation of Indian Chamber of Commerce and Industry on the Exit Policy.[83] In private consultations and in tripartite discussions, the national trade union federations have persuaded the government that such a policy would be politically disastrous. The trade unions have blocked amendment to the Industrial Disputes Act needed for an exit policy. A bill to amend the Industrial Disputes Act of 1947 was drafted by the government in 1993, but the government opted not to press for its enactment. Indeed, then Finance Minister Manmohan Singh told a group of Japanese investors, whose single strongest demand on Indian economic reform is deregulation of terms of employments, that:

> if by exit policy the employers mean hire and fire policy propounded by Western standards, we are not for it. You can not talk of labour glibly as a commodity. ... The pace of India's economic reforms has to be tailored to the objective situation existing in the country.[84]

As then Secretary of Labour V. P. Sawney put it, the government can not permit Indian industry to "just say *talak, talak, talak* (I divorce you)" to labor.[85] Sustained opposition by the trade unions has prohibited the Indian government from moving toward an exit policy.

Public sector closures and the BIFR

The Board for Industrial and Financial Reconstruction (BIFR), a quasi-judicial body designed to evaluate and facilitate the rehabilitation of "sick" industries, provides incentives for industrial failure. Industrialists intentionally drain resources from some of their enterprises, transferring those resources to other enterprises, so that the "sick" enterprise can get additional financing and tax relief from the BIFR. The incidence of industrial failure, measured by the number of enterprises or the amount of bank loans tied up in failing industries, has grown considerably since the 1970s.[86] In 1985, in order to address the growing incidence of industrial failure, the BIFR was legally constituted through the Sick Industrial Companies Act of 1985. The act was signed into law in January 1986 and the BIFR began its work in May 1987.[87] An industry is officially considered "sick" in India, as defined in the Sick Industrial Companies Act of 1985, if its losses are greater than the net worth of the company, if it has incurred cash losses for two consecutive years, and if it has been a registered company for seven years or more. The BIFR operates on the principle that with managerial guidance and financial assistance from the government, a failing business can be made profitable and employment can be saved.

Organized workers and unions prevented the Indian government from establishing a government agency that could determine which public sector enterprises should be sold to the private sector, or be liquidated, and to oversee such sales. The government attempted to implement its policies piecemeal. The BIFR, which was created to reduce the financial burden on the government of industrial failure, was reorganized so as to serve as the principle government agency for industrial restructuring. The World Bank and the IMF evidenced "an interest in the BIFR" early on in India's adjustment process.[88] For it is through the BIFR that the government can gradually effect an exit policy "in reality but not in fact."[89]

Within a few years, the BIFR was transformed from an agency designed to encourage industrialists to restructure industry, to persuade industrialists to commit additional capital, and to reduce thereby the public financial burden of ailing industries, to an agency used by industrialists to gain subsidized credit while siphoning funds between companies. Through an act of Parliament, the BIFR was made the only central government agency with the authority to determine that a sick industry, public or private, be closed and that workers be terminated. In its first three and one half years, the BIFR considered over a thousand cases. The BIFR had generated rehabilitation schemes for over a third of these companies.[90] While strongly defending his agency's record in rehabilitating ailing industries, the past Chairman of the BIFR, R. Ganapathy, acknowledged that industrialists have skillfully used the BIFR to gain access to tax concessions, additional government subsidies, and public capital. Many industrialists purposely siphon funds or supplies in order to profit privately while gaining these concessions, subsidies, and public capital for their "sick" industries. Although the Industrial Disputes Act of 1947, prohibits any change in the "service conditions" of employees in factories in which an industrial dispute is pending, in roughly a quarter of the cases coming before the BIFR, the enterprise in question is already closed.[91]

Sickness has been an important issue in Indian economic policy for two reasons. An immense and unproductive commitment of public funds is tied up in sick industries. In 1990, it was estimated that outstanding public credit to sick industries amounted to more than US$52.5 billion. Industrial sickness is also important because the exchange of accusations by management and labor over the causes of sickness encapsulate the conflict between the two parties over the causes of India's industrial underdevelopment. Industrialists, and the business press, claim that labor problems are the chief cause of sickness. Organized labor claims that sickness is caused by fraud on the part of industrialists and management. A Reserve Bank of India Committee concluded that labor problems contribute to a small minority of the cases of industrial sickness. Management deficiencies and mismanagement contribute three times the number of cases of industrial sickness as labor troubles and poor labor relations.[92]

Amendments to the Sick Industrial Companies (Special Provisions) Act of 1985 made in December 1991 allowed for the closing of chronically loss-making public sector industries. The BIFR is now legally empowered to determine and to order that public sector enterprises which, in the BIFR's view, are unviable be shut down. According to the Sick Industrial Companies Act, which created the BIFR, only sick private sector companies were to fall under the purview of the BIFR. The opposition in Parliament charged that the amendment passed by Congress Members of Parliament, with the support of the BJP, was enacted at the behest of the IMF and the World Bank.

The central trade unions have protested the empowerment of the BIFR to decide on public sector closures. As the BIFR is staffed by government officers rather than elected politicians, the BIFR's expanded mandate would seem to allow the government a certain degree of insulation from unpopular decisions on the closure or privatization of public sector enterprises. The BIFR, however, has not become an instrument of privatization. Not a single "wind-up" order has been issued to a public sector enterprise. The BIFR, staffed by senior officials from India's Finance Ministry who have typically served in national banks, is not pro-labor. Nor does organized labor seem to have an ongoing relationship with the BIFR. Often, labor representatives are not present for the discussions on rehabilitating a "sick industry." The BIFR, however, is not pro-employer either. Under the former Chairman, Ganapathy, the BIFR was deeply suspicious of the accounting practices of allegedly sick industries for an official declaration of sickness enables industrialists to gain concessionary loans and debt and tax relief. Many siphon funds from one enterprise to other enterprises so as to be able to avail themselves of these financial concessions. According to the former Minister of State for Industry, P. J. Kurien, there had been discussion within government circles of creating a separate body for rehabilitating and closing public sector enterprises. But the Indian trade union federations have opposed such a move.

Pakistani trade union responses

While Pakistani trade unions are more legally constrained than Indian unions in calling strikes, like their Indian counterparts, they protested structural adjustment measures through demonstrations and strikes. They met with considerably less success in blocking reforms but greater success in obtaining workplace concessions from the government. Pakistani trade union federations had little choice but to cooperate with the reform agenda while extracting concessions.

Labor unions in banks and financial institutions were at the forefront of the resistance to privatization in Pakistan. They held protests, in which 150,000 employees participated, against privatization in the last weeks of December 1990. In another demostration, in August 1992, Pakistan Bank officers, led by the Officers' Federation of Banks and Financial Institutions of Pakistan, went on a hunger strike to protest cut backs in the incremental pay scale and in related salary conditions. Pakistani unions, like Indian unions, have also used the courts to attempt to slow the adjustment process. Workers of the Thatta Cement Company in Sindh, for example, challenged the government's privatization policy in court on the grounds that the Privatization Commission, appointed by the Prime Minister, has no legal basis.

Trade union federations have opposed the government's policy of privatizing large areas of the public sector. Central to the workers' campaign against privatization was the formation of the All Pakistan State Enterprise Workers Action Committee. The collective bargaining agents of 115 state enterprises, affiliated to 36 separate trade union federations, formed the All Pakistan State Enterprise Workers Action Committee (APSEWAC) in 1990. In one of their first actions in response to the Islami Jamoori Ittehad (Islamic Democratic Alliance) (IJI) government's privatization plans, APSEWAC organized a strike in Lahore in December 1990. More than three dozen trade unions participated.

In opposition to the government's economic policy, processions were organized in various cities on May 18 and June 1, 1992. At a procession in Rawalpindi on 21 June 1992, the All Pakistan Federation of Trade Unions (APFTU) announced that it would declare a tool down strike on July 5, if the government did not initiate a dialogue over the new economic policies. In particular, the APFTU demanded a raising of the minimum wage, a guarantee not to suspend labor laws in special industrial estates and export processing zones, as had been promulgated in a Presidential ordinance, and an agreement not to privatize public sector utilities. The Prime Minister agreed to meet with the APFTU on July 4, 1992. The Prime Minister announced his intention to raise the minimum wage for unskilled workers to Rs. 1,500. He also promised not to privatize power distribution and to take no decision on the privatization of thermal power plants and telecommunications without further dialogue with the concerned trade unions. As regards the suspension of labor law in new industrial areas, the Prime Minister gave vague assurances that policy would give due concern to the interests of workers.[93]

Minimum wage concessions

The Government of Pakistan met the initial upsurge in trade union action through minimum wage concessions. In Pakistan, minimum wage setting is legally the responsibility of the Provincial Minimum Wage boards. In 1990, the Pakistan Peoples Party, fulfilling one of its election promises, raised the minimum wage in Pakistan from Rs. 530 (US$21) to Rs. 1,100 (US$44) per month.[94] The IJI government of Nawaz Sharif further raised the minimum wage, although not as high as promised in the IJI election manifesto.[95]

The IJI made the election promise that the minimum wage would be lifted to Rs. 3,000 per month (US$120). At the December 1991 meeting of the Pakistan Tripartite Standing Labour Committee, however, the government proposed lifting the minimum wage from Rs. 1,500 to only Rs. 2,000. Meeting for the first time in over three years, the Pakistan Tripartite Standing Labour Committee agreed that a standing Tripartite Wage Council ought to be established to review and revise minimum wage levels. Rather than let that Council meet and begin a process of institutionalizing the revision of minimum wages, the government and the largest pro-government union, the APFTU, announced an agreement. Critics in the labor movement alleged that the exchange of APFTU demands and government concessions was engineered to raise the stature of the APFTU and of the government of Nawaz Sharif, but weakened trade union solidarity.

The All Pakistan State Enterprises Workers Action Committee

Nawaz Sharif's Minister of Labour, Manpower, and Overseas Pakistanis, Eijaz Haq, son of the late General Zia ul-Haq, approached Malik Muhammad Yaqub with a proposal for an agreement. Under the direction of Malik Muhammad Yaqub, a Vice President in the Muttahida (United) Labour Federation, with support from the Pakistan Institute of Labour Education and Research in Karachi and the Sungi Development Foundation in Islamabad, the APSEWAC negotiated an agreement with the Privatization Commission. The APSEWAC agreement gives workers of enterprises undergoing privatization the options of retaining their job for one year after privatization, retiring with a pension amounting to four months' salary for every year worked, and making a bid for the purchase of the enterprise in which they are employed. Purchases made by workers are guaranteed the first right of refusal and can be financed by workers' provident and gratuity funds and by private bank loans. At the time of the agreement, workers' representatives voiced a preference for workers' management of 25 industrial enterprises, in the manufacture of cement, chemicals, and transport equipment.[96] As of November 1995, nine of these industrial enterprises were operating at a profit in the private sector under workers' management.[97]

The APSEWAC President met with the then Minister of Labour, Eijaz Haq, on 25 August 1992, to review the progress of the implementation of the government-public sector industrial workers' agreement. They agreed that the Cabinet Committee on Privatisation should decide on the number of shares to workers. They also discussed the provision of financial assistance to involuntarily unemployed workers for the marriages of their daughters and the education of their children. The agreement looks good on paper. The Privatisation Commission, however, has not always honored its agreement with the public sector workers. The government often failed to compensate dismissed workers. Thus, when it came time to give workers at a petrochemical complex in Gharo their golden handshake and the Federal government announced that it could not pay the workers, workers took matters into their own hands. Before they agreed to leave the complex, the new owner – who lost the plant when it was nationalized in 1972 – was forced to pay directly to the workers half of the amount that the Privatisation Commission had earlier promised them. The non-payment of the workers' retrenchment agreement even caught the ire of the World Bank. The World Bank threatened to finance the restructuring of local bodies in Punjab if the government did not fulfill its promise to give workers their golden handshakes.[98]

While workers' ownership schemes have gone further in Pakistan than in India, despite the greater strength of the Indian unions, it would be wrong to suggest that the Pakistan government's attitude toward workers' management's prospects is altogether benign. An attempt by workers to purchase the United Bank Ltd. is a case in point. On August 24, 1992, Abdul Aziz Memon, Secretary General of the Pakistan Peoples Party's (PPP) Peoples Labour Bureau and President of the United Bank Ltd. Employees Federation, along with 15 other PPP-associated labor leaders, were arrested. Memon was arrested on account of his implication in weapons purchases for the Peoples Student Front. The real reason for arrest was his opposition to the privatization of United Bank. Memon had formed an employees' group to purchase United Bank Ltd., but the government refused their offer. In response to the arrests, the United Bank Ltd. Employees Federation declared a one day strike on August 30, 1992, which closed 1,700 bank branches and involved 4,000 employees. Labor leaders of other federations also condemned the arrests. The National Industrial Relations Commission prohibited United Bank workers from striking, under section 16 of the IRO of 1969. According to US government analysis, "[n]ews reports that the government planned to actively support pro-privatization union leaders lends credence to rumors that Memon's arrest was prompted by his anti-privatization stance."[99]

The government announced in May 1992 that a proposed Daewoo industrial complex to be set up at Port Qasim would be exempted from all labor law. The plant, expected to employ between 15,000 and 20,000 people, is to manufacture automobiles, telecommunications equipment, televisions, video cassette recorders, and other electronic goods. In response to the government's announcement, Shafi Malik of the Pakistan National Federation of Trade Unions (PNFTU) complained of "slavery" and "bonded labour" and threatened to begin a nation-wide strike.[100]

Pakistani trade unions have become increasingly opposed to privatization and violation of fundamental labor rights. The APFTU, led by Khurshid Ahmed, had been on record that it would oppose the privatization of utilities.[101] In commenting on the privatization measures under Nawaz Sharif, Khurshid Ahmed made the distinction between public sector utilities and industries, accepting that loss-making public sector enterprises may be made more efficient by privatization.[102] But as regards utilities, he argued that "it is the duty of the state to provide essential services to the people." Such public necessities as water and electricity which private industry would not provide to all areas or which the poor could not afford, he argued, ought to be provided by the state. Thus, the APFTU and its core union, also headed by Khurshid Ahmed, drew the line between acceptable and unacceptable areas of privatization at the provision of public services. But only the later stages of the privatization process have tested the resolve of the large public sector unions.

The government planned to initiate privatization of the 160,000 megawatt Kot Addu power plant, near Multan, in March 1995. When a group of prospective foreign investors sought to examine the premises, the 885 workers there blocked their way and refused the prospective investors access to the facility. The workers held off the privatization in this manner for almost six months, while negotiations took place between the local union, the APFTU, and the government. The Kot Addu union is affiliated to the 160,000-member Hydroelectric Central Labour Union, the collective bargaining agent of Pakistan's giant Water and Power Development Authority (WAPDA). The Economist Intelligence Unit noted the Pakistan trade union's new militancy with unease:

> Another problem is trade union resistance to the disposal of state entities. This has been most vehement in the case of the Kot Addu power station . . . and could result in the planned sale being shelved, or even scrapped altogether. The demonstrations are also making would-be buyers of other enterprises pause for thought. There is a danger of the unrest spreading.[103]

The resistance of the Kot Addu union surprised the government. There had been "little resistance from the small, loosely organized worker groups at privatised small and medium manufacturers."[104] The confrontation was eventually resolved when the government threatened to call in security forces and agreed to make the retirement and severance benefits extended in the APSEWAC agreement the base for negotiations with the workers.[105] The struggle at Kot Addu suggests that as Pakistan's privatization moves into larger industrial enterprises, which are expected to render 250,000 to 300,000 workers unemployed,[106] trade unions may pose a greater obstacle to the government's privatization program.

Limiting the costs of adjustment

Structural adjustment programs produced significant economic changes across the developing world. In opting for International Monetary Fund (IMF) loans and extensive structural adjustment programs in the 1980s and 1990s, economic policy makers in India and Pakistan responded to a financial crisis. They deciding that greater international economic interdependence was a necessity. Success in implementing adjustment programs, however, has differed widely between India and Pakistan. Labor institutions, created by past political regimes, have been central to this differing unfolding of economic adjustment programs.

Trade unions in both countries have deployed a range of strategies to oppose structural adjustment and the deregulation of conditions of work and terms of service, the informalization of production, and the general crisis of formal sector employment, discussed in chapter five. Trade union strategies range from general strikes to consultations with government. This chapter discussed the response of organized labor to the industrial and labor force restructuring in each country. Despite similar challenges to organized labor, the Pakistan trade union movement has not been able to successfully oppose the government's structural adjustment and privatization programs while the Indian trade union movement has emerged as the major obstacle to the governments' structural adjustment program.

This exploration of the development of labor institutions under India's electoral democratic regimes and Pakistan's authoritarian regimes suggests that political regimes lay down deep institutional roots in their political economies. Especially influential are the institutions laid down during the formative period of postcolonial modernization, which in South Asia extended roughly from the mid-1940s to the mid-1960s.

India's structural adjustment program began earlier than Pakistan's and was far more gradual. Both countries have broadly met IMF conditions, although Pakistan has on a few occasions failed to meet IMF targets, provoking hiatuses in loan pay-outs. The most pronounced difference between the Indian and Pakistani privatization experiences is that the government of Pakistan was able to privatize dozens of public sector enterprises, in the industrial and financial sectors, while the government of India has been unable to privatize a single central government public sector enterprise since 1991.

Some claim that structural adjustment programs in India and Pakistan improved, or will in time improve, general public welfare. Others claim that structural adjustment increased poverty and hunger. We cannot know with certainty the costs or benefits of alternative approaches. But one does not need to know the exact costs or benefits of structural adjustment, in the short term or long term, to assess the relative impact of unions on democratic development.

In each country, workers and employers, including the government, faced economic hardship and financial crises. IMF structural adjustment programs in India and Pakistan may have been good for the economy in the long run, but have devastated working people and the general public in the short run. In both countries, workers lost jobs. Terms of service and conditions of work have worsened. Workers in India were able to limit the costs of adjustment; workers in Pakistan were less successful. The involvement of workers and unions in the adjustment program, even as resistors of aspects of the program, led to higher post-reform growth in India.

4

REORGANIZING INDUSTRY, DISORGANIZING WORKERS

> [The informal sector, based on] low working capital, cheap labour and scuttling of all labour laws ... now threaten[s] the very existence ... of the organized sector.[1]
>
> E. Balakrishnan

The previous chapter demonstrated that similar structural adjustment policies were not implemented in similar ways in India and Pakistan. Differences in labor institutions and organizations account for much of that variance. This chapter investigates the changing nature of employment and work in the Indian and Pakistani economies.

In India and Pakistan increasingly fewer workers are recognized under law as workers. This chapter underscores that strategies – both government and union – devised for a presumed future of formal production are now outdated. Not merely public sector employment but all of formal employment is in decline. The chapter explains why a new kind of union organization, focusing on securing protections and benefits for all workers, not only those in formal unions, has emerged. The final chapter, which follows, discusses organized labor's response to these significant changes in the nature of employment and work.

Labor forces in India and Pakistan

It is impossible to see the Indian or Pakistani labor forces well with existing labor force data alone. Some estimates are quite unreliable; basic definitions are restrictive, leaving many workers missing; and definitions, such as employment, are sometimes changed, destroying trend lines. These difficulties are multiplied when data are used comparatively. The government of Pakistan derives labor force statistics from a national labor force survey. The government of India, in contrast, uses figures reported – largely voluntarily – by establishments and unions. The differing bases for estimates make comparison tricky. In each country, hundreds of millions of workers are not recognized statistically or legally. Nevertheless, with the aid of comparison over time, local and provincial surveys, and interviews with workers we can see trends: unemployment, informal terms of employment, and increasingly reliance on informal, especially female, labor.

The Indian labor force

According to the Indian Ministry of Labour, India's labor force consisted of approximately 368.97 million workers in 2000, 26.58 million of whom were unemployed seeking work.[2] In India, employment is defined to include anyone gainfully employed for at least one hour during the week under survey. Estimates for a more recent year are not available.

Indian labor statistical reporting has long made a distinction between "organized" and "unorganized" sectors, sometimes also called the "formal" and "informal" sectors. The application of that distinction in labor force surveys is limiting. The distinction was originally based on recognizing the contribution of organized labor to planned development, not on aiding the "unorganized." Whole categories of workers are considered "unorganized labour" according to their enterprises' size (measured by number of employees), ownership (public or private), industry (whether using electricity, whether a state government or central government subject) and location (whether in a union territory or in Jammu and Kashmir). But if one's "enterprise" is not specified as "unorganized," then one is not counted.

The government of India used to define formal sector workers as employees of all public sector enterprises, all electrified factories and companies employing more than ten people, and all non-electrified factories and companies employing more than 20 people. The formal sector is now defined as including all public sector employment and all private sector employment establishments employing ten or more people (or 25 or more in Mumbai and Kolkota). The number of employees in a single establishment, or whether or not electric power is used in that establishment might once have been a good way to gauge the relative sizes and growth rates of the formal and informal labor force. But these are no longer adequate indicators.

It is more useful to define formality and informality – as I will argue – with reference to whether workers are legally recognized as employees. Security guards are often working informally – without contracts – at public sector enterprises, such as Mumbai Airport. Thus, there is informal sector employment in the public sector. And there is formal sector employment in establishments employing fewer than ten people in the private sector. Thus, we need better ways to see workers.

The figures in table 4.2 significantly underestimate the size of the labor force, especially in industries with few employees per firm. For example, a much larger portion of work in construction and manufacturing is performed

Table 4.1 India: labor force data, 1999–2003

population (2003)	1,064.40 million
economically active population (2000)	368.966 million
paid employment in "formal" sector (2003)	27.000 million
employment in the "informal" sector (2000)	65.560 million
unemployment (1999–2000)	26.58 million
claimed union members (1999)	6.407 million
claimed union members/economically active population	1.7 percent

Sources: Population is from World Bank, *World Development Report 2004*, 256. Economically active population and paid employment in the ILO, *Yearbook of Labor Statistics 2002–03*. Informal sector employment is from *Survey of non-Agricultural Enterprises in the Informal Sector*, 2000. It includes "all unincorporated proprietary and partnership enterprises producing all or some goods or services for sale." Unemployment is based on the National Sample Survey Organization estimate for current daily status, from the Ministry of Labour, "Over 21 million estimated to be unemployed," May 5, 2006, press release. Claimed union members are from the Government of India, *Manpower Profile*, supplied by ILO on June 4, 2006.
Note: The Government defines the formal sector as "public sector and establishments of non-agricultural private sector with 10 or more persons employed" or in Mumbai or Kolkota with 25 or more persons.

by enterprises with fewer than ten employees than in finance and insurance. Thus, it is underestimated relative to the finance, insurance, and real estate sector.

The formal sector in India – both public and private – is in decline, while the number of people demanding jobs is increasing steadily. As we shall see, Pakistani statistics suggest a similar unemployment crisis in Pakistan. In 1991, total employment in the "formal sector" was around 27 million, 19 million in the public sector and 8 million in the private sector. More than two-thirds of the employment in the formal sector in India is in the public sector. It is the non-public "formal sector" that is declining most rapidly. Employment in the public formal sector is declining less rapidly.

The source for figures on unemployment is the National Sample Survey (NSS). The NSS has used comparable definitions of data in five-year surveys since 1972–73. The NSS, unlike the Labour Ministry's figures and those of the Annual Survey of Industries, covers all types of gainful employment, not only that in the "organized sector" (i.e., private sector employment in non-agricultural establishments employing ten (25 or more in Mumbai and Kolkota) or more people and public sector establishments regardless of size).

The Pakistani labor force

In Pakistan, a worker is defined, for labor data collection purposes, as any person ten years of age and above, not in military service, who at any time during the week prior to the survey worked for pay or profit or was willing

Table 4.2 India: employment growth by sector, 1993–2004

	Annual % growth
Agriculture, Fishing, Forestry, Hunting	-.005
Mining and Quarrying	-.016
Manufacturing	-.006
Electricity, Gas, and Water	-.001
Construction	-.019
Trade, Restaurants, and Hotels	+.021
Transport, Storage, and Communications	-.003
Financial, Insurance, Property, and Business Services	+.018
Community, Social, and Personal Services	+.004
Total	-.001

Source: International Labor Organization, *Yearbook of International Labor Statistics*, Geneva: ILO, various issues.
Note: The government defines the formal sector as "public sector and establishments of non-agricultural private sector with 10 or more persons employed" or in Mumbai or Kolkota with 25 or more persons.

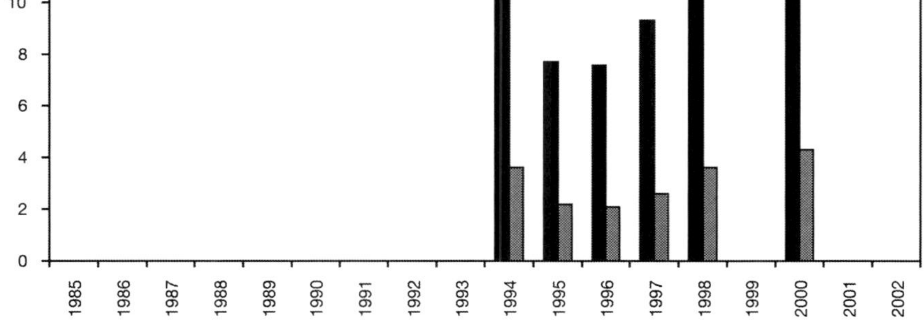

Figure 4.1 India: general unemployment and unemployment rate, 1985–2002

Source: Government of India, Federal Bureau of Statistics, *Labour Force Survey*, 1994–2000.

to work. Labor statistics yield more than 38 million "economically active" workers, including nearly 3.5 million unemployed workers (See table 4.3.)

The labor force in Pakistan in 2002 was estimated at 38.88 million individuals, of whom 3.5 million are unemployed, rendering an unemployment rate of 9 percent.

Until 1991, annual unemployment was officially estimated at a consistent 3.1 percent of the labor force.[3] Such perfect consistency did not give great confidence to users of such data. Unemployment estimates in Pakistan are now more realistic. The true unemployment figure is understood by economic planners, labor economists, and trade unionists to be considerably higher, approximately 15 percent of the labor force.

The Pakistan Labour Force Survey – the dominant labor survey instrument in Pakistan – defines the informal sector, inadequately, to include "persons working in unincorporated enterprises (excluding quasi-corporations) owned by own-account workers irrespective of the size of the enterprise, or by employers with less [sic] than 10 persons engaged." Indian labor data suffers from this same incongruity between concept and measurement. Terms of employment determine informality, not the number of workers at a workplace.

Large numbers of job seekers join the labor force annually in India and in Pakistan. Unemployment is rising. In each country, employment in the organized sector, both private and public, increased rapidly in the initial decades after Independence. Employment in the public sector and in the large formal private sector provided the foundation for trade unionism. Organized sector employment, however, has gradually declined, in both countries, since the 1970s.

Table 4.3 Pakistan: labor force data, 1997–2003

population (2000)	148.4 million
economically active population (2000)	38.005 million
economic activity rate (15+) (2000)	50.4 percent
total employment (2000)	36.847 million
total employment in "informal" sector (1997)	64.6 percent
total employment in "informal" sector (1997)	23.803 million
unemployment (2003)	3.48 million
claimed union members (2001)	276 million
claimed union members/economically active population	0.73 percent

Sources: Population is from World Bank, *World Development Report 2004*, 257. Economically active population excludes armed forces. Paid employment excludes the armed forces and people under the age of 10. Data are from ILO, *Yearbook of Labor Statistics.* Informal sector employment is from the *Labour Force Survey,* 1997, Ministry of Labour, Manpower, and Overseas Pakistanis, *Labour Force Survey, 1999–2000*, and Finance Division, *Pakistan Economic Survey.* Claimed union members is from Government of Pakistan, *Pakistan Statistic Yearbook*, provided by ILO on 4 June 2006.

Table 4.4 Pakistan: employment growth by sector, 1994–2001

	annual % growth
Agriculture, Fishing, Forestry, Hunting	+.076
Mining and Quarrying	+.014
Manufacturing	+.007
Electricity, Gas, and Water	+.104
Construction	+.040
Trade, Restaurants, and Hotels	+.009
Transport, Storage, and Communications	+.022
Financial, Insurance, Property, and Business Services	+.022
Community, Social, and Personal Services	+.022
Total	+.027

Source: International Labor Organization, *Yearbook of International Labor Statistics*, various issues.

For more than two decades, Pakistani and Indian job seekers have faced a declining manufacturing sector. Since the early 1980s, Pakistan has experienced a steady decline in employment in the manufacturing sector. Manufacturing was to lead economic development but reached its height, as

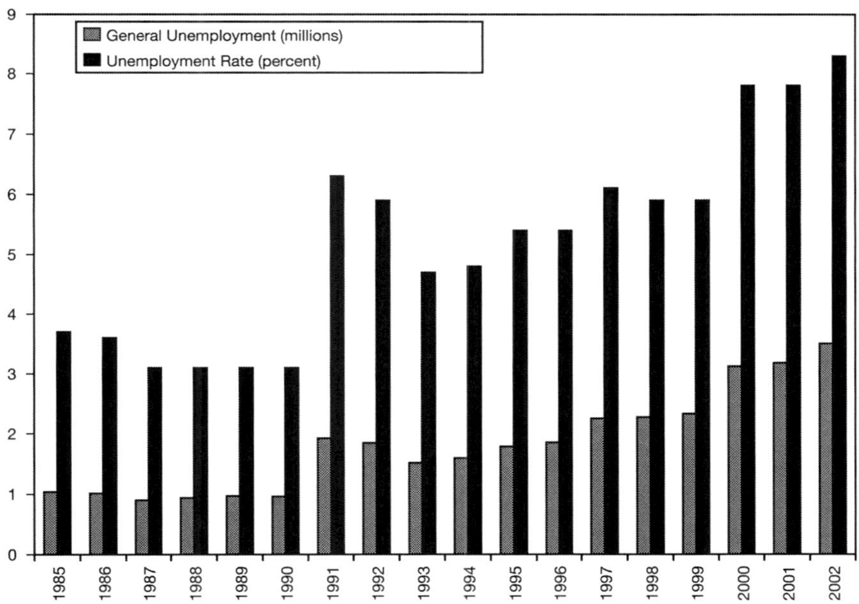

Figure 4.2 Pakistan: general unemployment and unemployment rate, 1985–2002
Source: From Government of Pakistan, Federal Bureau of Statistics, Labour Force Survey 1990–2000.

a percentage of the labor force, in 1979, at just below 15 percent. In India too manufacturing has declined as a percentage of total employment since the late 1970s and in absolute terms since 1993.

There is no evidence that informality has increased because of a push-out effect of standards accrued by workers in the organized sector. But there is evidence that conditions of work and terms of employment have worsened in the organized sector. Management in the private and public sector has succeeded in evading many of the legal protections afforded to workers in large establishments. According to labor economists and trade unionists in both India and Pakistan, since the late 1970s there has been a "management offensive" against trade unionism, aimed particularly at workers in larger industrial enterprises.[4]

Informal and subcontracted employment

Some analyses of India's industrial reforms make journalistic reference to the need to modernize inflexible labor law[5] and to "unproductive organized workers."[6] Largely ignored in the literature advocating more rapid reform of South Asian labor institutions is that these institutions have already been substantially deregulated, even without changed labor legislation. Industry has found ways to evade labor law, even if Indian trade unions prevent the government from legislating labor's deregulation through an amendment to the Industrial Disputes Act of 1947. The Indian economy has been substantially given over to the private sector, even without large or wholesale privatization, because the labor force within it has been progressively deregulated and disorganized. Thus, while privatization has been thwarted, a slow, unofficial process of abandonment of effective labor regulation has been taking place for two decades.

Disorganizing workers

Deregulation of work has been achieved through a combination of techniques and processes. Employers declare bans on new employment but subcontract the new demand for labor to labor suppliers. Employees are reclassified as managers, without change of duties, so that they may not by law join or lead unions. Employees are offered individual wages and benefit incentives upon the achievement of daily individual productivity norms. Management divides production and builds parallel plants in designated "backward areas" with government tax incentives. Management also reduces employees' knowledge of the production processes; threatens to prevent workers from working (a lockout); uses armed thugs to intimidate union leaders and workers at the workplace; and farms out production to areas outside of the scope of labor inspection.

Government statisticians and labor economists note that subcontracted labor is growing. The subcontract labor system (*thekedar nizam*) allows for workers to be provided on demand through a labor contractor (*thekedar*) without any legal or moral relationship between the workers and the person for whom work is done. Employers find labor subcontracting to be an effective way to circumvent labor law. Trade union officials and workers say that subcontracting is increasing in part because management has changed labor processes, often so as to weaken the workplace strength of workers. Trade unionists, labor economists, and workers in both countries suggest that new practices in human resource management and in subcontracting production have undermined organized labor and weakened labor standards. (See interview index.) The production process is being dismembered, as is the common workplace that once provided workers opportunity to organize and, in many factories, to control the workplace. Here, we will look at the growing use of the subcontracted labor system and managerial strategies that transform production processes in ways that undermine the organizational strength of labor.

The deregulation of conditions of work and terms of employment in India and Pakistan is based upon industrial practices rather than government policies. Pakistani and Indian trade unions, therefore, must not only be engaged in influencing government economic policy, but also respond to the restructuring of terms of employment, a threat far more immediate and dangerous to workers and their rights.

Strikes and lockouts

As discussed in chapter two, industrial relations statistics are easier to use in making claims about union or labor power when accompanied by interviews with workers and organizers. When these industrial relations statistics are examined comparatively, then they also become more meaningful.

The challenge that organized labor faces in the restructuring of conditions of work and terms of employment in India is suggested by the steady rise in employment lost to management declared lockouts and the steep decline in the number of workdays lost in strike action (See figure 4.3.)[7] Political or sympathy strikes are not included in either Indian or Pakistani statistics. The Indian Ministry of Labour, however, reported by December 1998 that hundreds of thousands of workdays are lost annually in hundreds of industries in political or sympathy strikes.[8]

Between the early 1960s and the first years of the twenty-first century, the portion of work stoppage – and its burden on workers, waged and salaried – caused by employers (as measured by total workdays lost to lockouts) has risen from approximately 15 percent to approximately 80 percent of total work stoppage. In 1965, employers declared only 16 percent of all work stoppages. In 2005, employers declared 80 percent of all work stoppages. The Indian Ministry of Labour reported that 3,040 workers were retrenched in 2002, a record high, up 39 percent from 2001. But the number of workers locked out of their workplaces was 162,563, in keeping with the trend since the 1970s.[9]

Employers argue that the growth in lockouts is a reflection of two trends. Organized labor, they say, is making increasingly unreasonable demands upon management for wage increases and other benefits. Moreover, employers argue that the rigidities of Indian labor law, particularly the 1977 amendment to the Industrial Disputes Act of 1947, prevent management from dismissing excess workers.

Workers and trade union leaders argue that lockouts are a technique used by management to declare their enterprises unprofitable and thereby to gain access to subsidies and tax concessions. Lockout days surpassed strike-days in India only after 1987, when the Board for Industrial and Financial Reconstruction became operative. This is consistent with to the trade union perspective, that management is using lockouts to close and restructure factories.

Informal labor

The influence of the informal sector in India and Pakistan is ubiquitous. As a proportion of the total labor force, the informal labor force is very large even by lower income developing country standards. And yet it is a sector defined via another sector. It is, literally, what the formal sector is not. The concept of the informal sector has its origins in early economic development theory's distinction between the traditional and the modern. In development economics this distinction was encapsulated in the concept of the dual

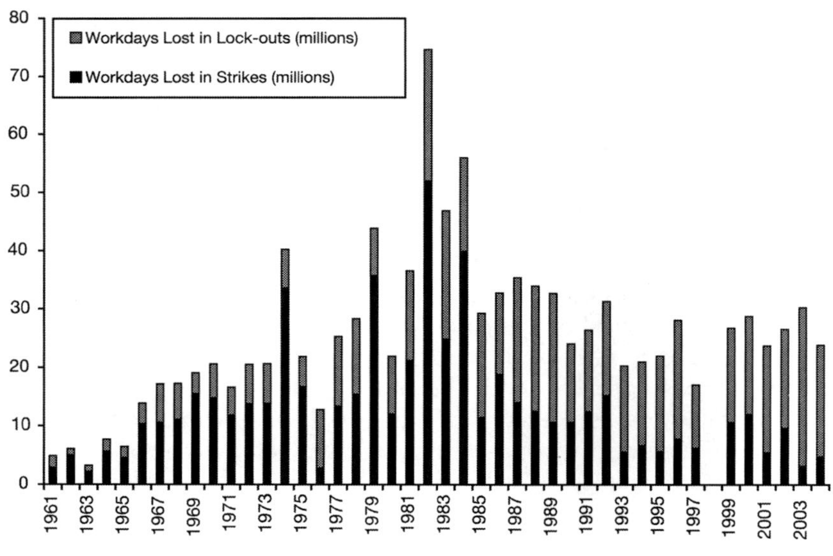

Figure 4.3 India: workdays lost in strikes and lockouts, 1961–2003

Source: Government of India, Ministry of Labour, *Annual Reports*, various issues.

economy. This false dichotomy – a bifurcation of an intertwined whole – allowed for clumsy interpretation of data.

A 1971 International Labour Organization (ILO) mission to Kenya provoked some interest in the potential of the informal sector as a vehicle for employment promotion.[10] The mission report attempted to define the informal sector by characterizing it as comprising those economic activities in which entry is comparatively easy, resources used are chiefly local, ownership is typically family based, the scale of production is small, labor is intensive and unskilled or skills are acquired informally, capital input is low, technologies employed are adapted, and markets are unregulated and competitive.[11] In the ensuing decades, scholars have offered a number of ways to define the informal.

More satisfying than the dichotomy between formal and informal sector employment is an approach that permits one to see the stratified and segmented nature of the labor force. John Harriss, K. P. Kannan, and Gerry Rodgers define distinct categories of nine informal workers: unprotected regular long-term workers, unprotected regular short-term workers, unprotected irregular workers, independent workers, self-employed with capital, marginally self-employed, apprentices, family workers, and the unemployed.[12] Such distinctions are clearly not *a priori*. But they provide a greater sensitivity to the nuances of employment than are on offer by the bifurcation – conceptually – of formality from informality.

Rickshaw drivers

The condition of rickshaw drivers well illustrates the manner in which laws ostensibly designed to protect workers, in practice, make informal sector workers even more vulnerable.[13] Rickshaw driving is typical of the informal sector. Barriers to entry to the enterprise – capital, education, and technical skills – are few. Employment is ready-at-hand. Payment is based on output. An advantage of the industry, over many other informal sector enterprises, is that payment is made upon completion of the task. But, like many informal sector workers, most rickshaw drivers work in a highly noxious environment. Most rickshaw drivers, thereby, suffer from tuberculosis, asthma, and other lung problems. Millions of people ply rickshaws throughout India, with the exception of India's hill and mountain areas. Rickshaw drivers in most northern Indian cities and towns are landless and smallholder peasants, migrants from India's poorer states, chiefly Bihar and Orissa. Most rickshaw drivers in Delhi report that they came to Delhi because there was no work in their villages and not enough produce from their family's farms to feed them.[14]

While some labor organizers have tried, organizing rickshaw driving is extremely difficult. In Kanpur, where an estimated 50,000 people earn their livelihood plying rickshaws, the Rickshaw Mazdoor Union is only influential in the area around the Central Railway station.[15] Most rickshaw drivers are migrants, who return to their villages after a few months of work.[16] Moreover, the vast majority of rickshaw drivers operate illegally, preventing them from organizing legally.

In Delhi, nearly half a million people earn their livelihood peddling rickshaws. Very few rickshaw drivers own their own vehicles. At Rs. 3,500 (US$75), the average cost of a rickshaw is well beyond the means of rickshaw drivers. If an unskilled laborer had Rs. 3,500 in savings, it is unlikely that he would choose rickshaw driving as his means of livelihood. The vast majority of rickshaws plying the roads of Delhi are owned by individuals who have dozens or hundreds of rickshaws, which they rent to drivers for Rs. 20 per day. Ostensibly to prevent the exploitation of rickshaw drivers, article 3, section 1 of the Cycle Rickshaw By-laws of 1960, framed by the Delhi Municipal Corporation, states that:

> no person shall keep or ply [a] cycle-rickshaw in Delhi unless he himself [indeed, all drivers are male] is the owner thereof and holds a license granted in that behalf by the Commissioner on payment of the fee, that may from time to time be fixed under sub-section 2 of Section 430 [of the Delhi Municipal Corporation Act of 1957].[17]

Further, the by-laws require that "no person will be granted more than one such license." According to the man in charge of rickshaw licensing, Additional Commissioner of the DMC, C. P. Gupta, "any individual who is healthy can own a rickshaw if he pays the nominal fee of Rs. 50."[18] But according to drivers, the DMC typically charges Rs. 200 to Rs. 250 for a license. By the DMC's own account, it has issued only 73,000 licenses. Further, the DMC only makes licenses available once a year.[19]

Police often beat rickshaw drivers who cannot produce licenses and confiscate their vehicles. The drivers are made to push the rickshaws to the police warehouses. Even if drivers are willing to pay the police for the return of the vehicle before it is turned over to the DMC, when it begins to accrue storage fees, the process is time-consuming and costly. An application must be made to the Superintendent of Police who must then be persuaded to forward the application to the Traffic Inspector. If the Traffic Inspector approves the application, it must be returned to the Superintendent of Police for his signature and then returned again to the Traffic Inspector, who may release the vehicle. According to one Traffic Inspector, "taking a bribe is out of the question. Who would dare to take money from these poor folks who work desperately to make ends meet?"[20] C. P. Gupta, Additional Commissioner of the DMC, describes things differently. "A rickshaw puller [a term dating to the 1930s when the carriages were pulled rather than peddled] can never complain like that. First of all he refuses to take license. So, he doesn't have any right to complain about the bribe."[21] Not surprisingly, the drivers typically leave the rickshaw owners to recover the impounded vehicles. Successful rickshaw owners stay on good terms with the police and the DMC. Thus, the same regulation that grants the DMC licensing authority permits rickshaw owners, police, and DMC officials to prey on the legal vulnerabilities of rickshaw drivers. Rickshaw drivers in Kanpur, where the Municipal Corporation does not have restrictive regulations related to rickshaw drivers, report that they can earn Rs. 80 to 150 per day[22] – enough to provide for themselves and their families. But rickshaw drivers in Patna, where the Municipal Corporation, under the Bihar Cycle Rickshaw Act of 1979, regulates rickshaws in a manner similar to that in Delhi, consider it "a profession fit for animals."[23] Laws and regulations ostensibly designed to protect the rickshaw drivers, in practice, increase their exploitation and make them vulnerable to harassment.

Subcontracted workers

While the phrase "contract labor" is understood in South Asia to refer to such casual work arrangements, the translation of the Hindi and Urdu word *thekedar* into the English word "contract" is misleading. Neither the labor contractor nor the workers are under contract. The contract labor system enables employers to circumvent contracts and thus circumvent labor legislation and undermine workers' ability to act collectively. Therefore, rather than use the conventional term "contract laborer," I will refer to such workers as subcontracted workers, which, while still imperfect, goes some way toward conveying the distance between workers and their "employers."

The subcontracted labor system is so widespread that even the central, state, and municipal governments in both India and Pakistan make extensive use of subcontracted labor. All the service employees of the central government-owned and operated Mumbai Airport, for example, are subcontracted. By one estimate, the Government of Pakistan contracts out work at a cost of Rs. 150 million.[24] In Karachi, it is estimated that in the textile sector "almost half of the unskilled and semi-skilled workforce is employed through contractor[s] and the trend is increasing."[25]

There is little survey data on the prevalence or the growth of subcontracted labor employment. Government labor force surveys and employment censuses do not include such data. Employers are reluctant to provide such information. Subcontracted workers themselves are difficult to count on a plant basis as contractors normally take their workers from plant to plant in teams, often at irregular hours. On more than one occasion, immediately after talking with subcontracted workers on the premises of a factory, I was informed by factory owners or human resource managers that their factory makes use of absolutely no contractors or subcontracted workers. These factories range from the well organized electronics and engineering factories of transnational corporations, such as Siemens AG in Karachi; to large, modern textile mills, such as Bombay Dyeing; from large, un-modernized mills, such as the Llaylpur Cotton in Multan; to public sector enterprises, such as Mumbai International Airport. When confronted with observation of subcontracted laborers working on company grounds, management typically acknowledges the oversight and explains that these workers are easily forgotten because they are the responsibility of another employer. Trade unions do not want to publicize the extent of subcontracted work in their enterprises as it reflects poorly on the strength of their unions. Available evidence from India and Pakistan suggests that there has been a tremendous increase in the use of subcontracted workers, particularly in the textile and garment, chemical and pharmaceutical, construction, and mining and quarrying sectors.

The Indian government has passed legislation that ostensibly aims to regulate subcontracted labor with the intention of eventually abolishing the practice altogether. In practice, however, the Contract Regulation Act of 1970 prohibits subcontracted laborers from seeking redress in the courts. Instead a separate tribunal, the Contract Labour Board, has been established to hear cases under the Contract Regulation Act. According to one labor lawyer, however, "nobody knows where it sits, who serves on it, or when." Colin Gonsalvez, a Bombay labor lawyer, explains that the Contract Labour (Regulation and Abolition) Act of 1971 sought to legalize and promote rather than to regulate and abolish subcontracted labor. According to Gonsalvez, since the passage of the Contract Labour Act, the use of subcontracted workers has increased greatly. A serious piece of legislation seeking to abolish subcontracted labor would only need to say that if work is of a perennial nature, subcontracted labor is prohibited. "Instead a legally convoluted measure is passed." The Act requires that subcontracted laborers attempt to change their employment status to permanent through courts in which they have no legal standing. "India," says Gonsalvez "is a country where if [the authorities] choose to allow something they pass a law prohibiting it, like the 'Child Labour Prohibition Act of 1986'."[26] Indeed, the regulation effectively provides incentives for manipulation of the legal process.

The Indian government has opted for a proliferation of legislation, partitioning workers into different sectors, such as *beedi* (hand-rolled cigarettes) workers, child laborers, miners, matchmakers, and railway workers. A different instrument of law governs each group. The channeling of court cases to special commissions and boards effectively prevents workers from finding a hearing. The Contract Labour Act, for example, explicitly prevents an appeal to the High Court. According to one Indian government official:

> Certain Labour Laws apply uniformly to all the workers subject to fulfillment of the conditions laid down in the relevant acts or the rules framed thereunder. In some cases, however, the uniformity is not there because these acts have been framed with reference to the specific objectives that they seek to achieve.[27]

According to Colin Gonsalvez, the labor lawyer:

> In the last five or six years, government thinking has crystallized that human rights and labour cases should not be heard in the High Court and Supreme Court. [These] cases have been shunted out. Blocks of workers are excluded from labour law by passage of special bills.[28]

In Pakistan, under section 2(f)(iv) of the West Pakistan Industrial and Commercial Employment (Standing Orders) Ordinance of 1968, workers employed by a contractor are legally to be regarded as employees of the industrial or commercial establishment which employs the contractor, even if that establishment has no direct knowledge of the subcontracted workers and pays only the contractor for services.[29] Subcontracted workers are thereby legally entitled to similar protections to regular employees. The law, however, is not enforced.

Trade union leaders and industrialists in both countries are in sharp disagreement over the subcontract labor system. Trade union leaders point to the appalling working conditions of subcontracted workers, the total lack of job security, and the lack of overtime pay and accident compensation. If a subcontracted worker attempts to join a trade union organization, he or she is likely to be fired. If a subcontracted worker is injured, he or she is similarly likely to be dismissed.

Industrialists claim that subcontracted workers are more "satisfied" than permanent workers because their take home pay is higher and their working hours are more flexible.[30] Further, industrialists argue that subcontracted workers are more productive, because they are effectively paid on a piece rate basis, and that the subcontracted system therefore generates more employment than formal employment could. Mukhtar Sumar, Director of the Farooq Textile Mills, Karachi, explains the employers' point of view on subcontracted labor:

> Under contract labor, the payment to the contract worker is related to productivity; therefore, he produces more than the regular worker. The contract worker can work for every day of the year and in every shift, if he so wishes. This is not the case with the regular worker who gets all the Gazetted holidays and his leave entitlements.[31]

It is not difficult to reconcile the conflicting claims of trade union leaders and industrialists about the subcontract labor system. If the subcontract system is more productive, it is precisely because one subcontracted worker may replace another at any moment. The industrialists' claim that subcontracted workers can earn more than regular workers is highly suspect and is not corroborated by any surveys nor by my conversations with subcontracted workers in textile, pharmaceutical, and engineering plants in and around Mumbai, Kolkota, Lahore, Kanpur, and Karachi.

According to Indian and Pakistani trade unionists, the employers' rationale for the contract labor system is not to achieve higher productivity but to gain greater control over the production process and to weaken the workplace strength of organized labor. As long as the state guided economic development through an organization of production predicated on a formal, recognized, and regularly paid labor force, industrial development in India and Pakistan gave industrial workers in the formal sector considerable control over the production process. A visitor to large organized sector textile mills and factories in India or Pakistan is likely to be impressed by the degree to which the production process is still managed by workers. The workplace management tends to be heads of sections, who are themselves workers. A senior manager or even an owner doing the rounds on the shop-floor of the factory is likely to be met with a great deal of deference from workers but he will not affect the pace of production. The workers themselves, under the protection of the union leadership, determine the rate of work. In visits to dozens of factories on the invitation of the local union, I have never had my investigations questioned or hindered by the plant management, despite the work time I consumed in speaking with workers. Subcontracted workers were the most constrained of the workers with whom I spoke as they often did piece work or were under the close supervision of a contractor.

Labor disorganization in the textile industry

To better understand how the labor force has been affected by industrial restructuring, it is useful to compare the textile industries of India and Pakistan. The sheer size of the industry alone merits its consideration. The textile industry is each country's largest non-agricultural employer. Among the clear similarities of the structurally distinct industries is increasing reliance on subcontracted labor and production in the informal sector. This section examines how terms of employment changed within the textile industry. The disorganization of industry – as is showcased here by the textile industry – has made impossible effective labor organizing by conventional workplace-based, business-tolerated, and government recognized means.

The textile industry has prospered in South Asia for centuries. Since the introduction of the Spinning Jenny and electricity little has changed in the textile industry. Indeed, the major and lasting innovation in the industry has been the powerloom. With the independently operated powerloom, the global textile industry has been transformed from a labor-intensive industry to a capital-intensive industry. The low labor cost advantage of developing countries, which threatened European producers as early as the 1870s, has been nearly offset by the advantage of modern machinery which advanced industrial countries, particularly Japan, the US, Germany, Italy, and the UK, manufacture. The global trade in apparel and textiles was estimated at US$500 billion annually in 2005. Modernization, high speed automated equipment, required computer-aided design and manufacturing, and large outlays of hard currency. There have been difficult for the textile industry in both India and Pakistan.

The management of international trade in textiles has long been contentious. Advanced industrialized countries have restricted textile imports from less-industrialized countries for centuries so as to protect their domestic industry. In the latter third of the twentieth century, the restriction on developing-world textile exports has been achieved through a series of interim international agreements and the repeated extension of the Multi-Fibre Agreement (MFA). A 1962 agreement under the Kennedy Round of the General Agreement on Tariffs and Trade (GATT) was made as a temporary arrangement to allay the growing demand from developing countries that industrialized countries open their markets to textile imports. It was agreed that the importing industrialized countries would relax their import quotas by five percent annually. A clause of the agreement allowed even less liberalization should there be disruption of the home market. The 1962 agreement was designed to last for three years. A more permanent arrangement was to be reached. Unsuccessful negotiations led to the 1962 agreement's extension in 1967 to 1971.[32]

In 1971, the UK replaced its country quota system with a 15 percent import duty on all textiles. The decision was officially conveyed to GATT and textile exporting countries, but was soon reversed. Imports from Pakistan were singled out for a two-month moratorium in March 1972.[33] Pakistani officials alleged that the moratorium was in retaliation for Pakistan's decision to leave the British Commonwealth, while Britain maintained that orders from British importers had exceeded the fixed quota.[34] The United States was the first to use the discretionary clause of the GATT treaty to restrict textile imports. As in 1971, in 1967 Pakistan was the target. The United States cut Pakistan's quota from 30 million to 11.4 million yards. With the United Nations Conference on Trade and Development (UNCTAD) intervention, the United States reviewed its position and gradually increased Pakistan's quota.[35]

Under the MFA, developing countries voluntarily restrained their exports in accordance with assigned quotas. The MFA came into effect on January 1,1974 as a five-year agreement. It was designed to protect the textile industry of advanced capitalist countries while it adjusted to global competition. Instead, it was renewed every five years, giving long-term protection from global production. Despite decades of displeasure on the part of governments and textile producers in developing countries, the MFA was repeatedly extended. It was agreed in the concluding session of the Uruguay Round of negotiations of the GATT that the MFA would be phased out, and it was.

Indian textiles

The textile industry in India is the nation's largest employer outside of agriculture. Since Independence, the industry has been heavily subsidized and regulated for maximum employment, often with less regard for quality or distribution. In Pakistan, it is recognized that "[t]he entire economy of the country owes its ... progress to the healthy performance of the cotton textile and allied industries."[36]

Restructuring the textile industry presents the government with a difficult choice. Labor productivity in the industry is low by global standards, chiefly due to lack of modernization. Both states patronized the textile industry. Indian textile policy, attaching greater importance to protecting existing industrial employment than to modernization and expansion, damaged productivity. Less interventionist Pakistani textile policy permitted a more productive industry, but one structured around the export of cotton yarn, which is relatively low in value added in textile production. Employment in the textile industry in both countries has declined rapidly since the late 1960s and early 1970s, especially among production staff. But the industry still sustains high levels of employment. The restructuring of the industry confronts the government with a choice between employment and international competitiveness. The textile industry is made up of three sectors: the organized mill sector, including spinning and composite mills; the unorganized powerloom sector; and the handloom sector.

The first organized textile mill began operation in 1856. By 1860, there were six mills, each based in Mumbai.[37] Mills soon began to operate in Ahmedabad. Prior to Partition, Sindh and Punjab provided the bulk of the raw cotton for the mills of Mumbai and Ahmedabad. Unlike many other Indian industries in the days of British rule, the textile industry was almost entirely South Asian owned and operated. Though colonial India exported two and half million bales of raw cotton annually, after Partition, India was faced with a raw cotton shortage. Independent India also lost 800 to 900 million yards of cotton cloth sales to the areas that became Pakistan.[38]

The Indian textile industry has long held deep public significance as symbolic of Indian economic independence. The boycott of British textiles in favor of indigenous cotton textile, or homespun, was an important instrument in the struggle for Indian Independence. Indeed an image of a *charka* (spinning wheel), which Mahatma Gandhi made the symbol of the dignity of work and of Indian self-reliance, was a contender for the centerpiece of the Indian national flag.

By 1968, however there were hundreds of sick mills. In 1967, the central government nationalized 111 sick mills and created the National Textile Corporation (NTC) to manage and rehabilitate them. Employment relief was the explicit objective of nationalization. In April 1974, the Indian Parliament under the governance of Prime Minister Indira Gandhi enacted the Sick Textile Undertakings (Nationalisation) Act of 1974.[39] The act nationalized another 103 sick textile enterprises at a cost to the central government of over Rs. 400 million.[40] As in 1967, the rationale for the nationalization was "to secure the principles specified in clause (b) of article 39 of the Constitution," namely "that the ownership and control of the material resources of the community are so distributed as best to subserve [sic] the common good."[41] The NTC produces one-fifth of India's cloth, mostly of coarse and medium variety, as well as cotton yarn. In October 1983, 13 additional mills were nationalized and given over to the management by the NTC (South). At the time of the 1982–83 Mumbai textile strike, the NTC (South) managed 18 mills and the NTC (North) six, while the MSTC managed one.[42] The rationalization of workers and unions in the National Textile Corporation was, as we shall see, the testing ground for the rationalization of workers and unions in the entire industrial sector.[43]

By 1988, employment in the cotton textile industry was at its height, directly employing more than 1.2 million people in India.[44] Eighteen percent of the industrial labor force in India is in cotton textile production. Another several hundred thousand people are estimated to be employed indirectly by the industry.[45] Cotton textile manufacturing contributes 12 percent of the value added of the organized industrial sector. With 16 percent of the world market, India is the second largest exporter of cotton textile in the world, second to Japan.

Textile mill owners in India – mill owners, government officials, and mill workers widely acknowledge – often run their mills at a book loss so as to access government financial rehabilitation assistance. Mill owners fabricate sickness in order to attract public capital. The Indian textile industry contributes more enterprises to the country's list of sick enterprises than any other industry. For decades mill owners and their associations have complained of the burden of an increasing wage bill. However, by their own figures, the wage bill has not increased as quickly as other industrial expenses. Relations between mill owners and government in India have not usually been cordial. By 1956, the central government used excise duties on mill cloth to reduce mill owners' profits, which were thought to be excessive, and to help finance the Second Five-Year Plan.[46] By November 1992, nearly 300 spinning and composite mills were declared sick, of which 140 were closed, leaving 188,000 workers jobless.[47]

The Rashtriya Mills Mazdoor Sangh

Under the Bombay Industrial Relations Act (BIR), trade union recognition in the textile industry is industry-wide rather than by individual enterprises. As a result, the Congress-affiliated Rashtriya Mill Mazdoor Sangh (RMMS) has since the inception of the BIR been the sole recognized union for 60 mills in Mumbai and Gujarat.[48] Few textile workers regard the RMMS as an organization which looks out for their interests, rather than as an instrument of management.[49] Indeed, the BIR was immediately opposed by organized labor on its inception in 1946. One of the principal demands of the 1982–83 textile strike was the repeal of the BIR and the derecognition of the RMMS.

At collective bargaining meetings with the Mill Owners Association, the RMMS is represented by Shankerrao Jadhav, a former RMMS General Secretary. He is alleged to have gained control over the union through physical intimidation, with assistance from alleged crime boss Arun Gavli. In an effort to check the influence of organized crime over the RMMS, Maharashtra government under Chief Minister Sharad Parwar required government approval of collective bargaining arrangements before they are signed by employees and employers.[50]

It is widely alleged that organized crime has been used by the RMMS to persuade workers to agree to the relocation of mills. Khatau Mills workers, for example, were persuaded to move from central Mumbai to the suburbs of Borivli through threats of violence from organized crime. The state government took the unusual step of informing the Board of Industrial and Financial Reconstruction (BIFR) that despite the workers' unanimous consent, the relocation plan was not acceptable because it was secured under duress. A second poll among workers, under government supervision, yielded a similar outcome. In the fatal shooting of textile industrialist Sunit Khatau, organized crime was originally employed by management to persuade workers to agree to Khatau's relocation plans.

The Bombay textile strike

The textile strike of 1982–83 in Mumbai was the world's largest, as measured by number of workdays lost.[51] The strike bore witness to the intense desire of Indian textile workers in Mumbai to escape the confines of political party-based unionism. By a provision under the BIR, a single trade union may be recognized for an entire industry in the states of Maharashtra and Gujarat. As a result, the Indian National Congress-affiliated RMMS has since the adoption of the BIR been the sole recognized union for textile mills in Mumbai, despite challenges to the union's standing in 1950 and 1959.[52] Mumbai textile workers regard the RMMS as an instrument of the mill owners rather than an organization which serves workers' interests. Thus, the principal demand of the mill workers in the historic 1982–83 textile strike in Mumbai was the repeal of the BIR and the de-recognition of the RMMS.[53]

Few leaders commanded sufficient loyalty from workers to lead the Bombay Textile Strike. The senior communist trade union leader, S. A. Dange, who had been active prior to Independence, was still working among textile unions, but after his 1974 42-day textile strike, had no notable achievements. R. J. Mehta had made a name as a responsible trade union leader, a man whom workers could trust to bargain hard for their interests and who would vigorously pursue unfair labor practices in court, and yet whom management could trust to guarantee workers' productivity. R. J. Mehta's style of union leadership represents one aspect of independent trade unionism, which rose in the late 1960s.

Datta Samant began his trade union organizing with quarry workers in Ghatkopar, an outer suburb of Mumbai. "It had been with the support of these grateful workers that he was elected to the State Assembly as an independent candidate."[54] With his success as an independent candidate, the Indian National Congress (I) succeeded in enlisting him as a Congress candidate for the 1972 legislative election, which he won. By the mid-1970s he became a full-time trade union organizer for the Indian National Trade Union Congress (INTUC). Samant gained credibility among workers for his impatience with the legal machinery which often indefinitely postponed solutions to workers' grievances. In the chemical and engineering industries, Samant organized strikes which led quickly to wage and benefit concessions. Samant was critical of the way in which political concern dominated trade unions. Although a member of the Indian National Congress (I), he maintained an uneasy relationship with the INTUC. In 1984, after the failure of the 1982 textile strike, Samant was elected to the Lok Sabha. He was the only non-Congress Member of Parliament from Mumbai to win in the 1984 elections.

Just prior to the strike, Indira Gandhi's government had taken its 1982 IMF loan. The government was therefore determined to demonstrate, both to external creditors and to other Indian workers, that it was capable of defeating labor intransigence. Before the Bombay Textile Strike, mills in Bombay employed some 250,000 regular workers. Today, their numbers have been reduced to 150,000.[55] "N. S. Ansari, president of the Powerloom Weaver's Association, claims that with the exception of NTC mills all mills took sub-contracting" during the 1982–83 textile strike.[56] Datta Samant's Maharashtra Girni Kamgar Union, formed on the eve of the 1982–83 Bombay Textile Strike, has yet to officially call off the strike.

Contracting and powerlooms

The powerloom sector refers to looms in the informal, small-scale sector that use electricity. Of the three textile sectors, the powerloom sector has emerged latest, but registered the fastest growth in production. The first decentralized loom industry to employ power, according to the Powerloom Inquiry Committee (1960), was in the formerly princely state of Ichalkaranji in 1904. In the early 1930s, many of the powerlooms were set up by entrepreneurs who purchased and converted the discarded looms of Mumbai and Ahmedabad mills.[57]

Powerlooms tend to be densely concentrated and located in areas near major industrial cities where access to raw materials and distribution networks are easier than in rural areas. In Maharashtra, where nearly half of the country's powerlooms are located, the major powerloom centers are near Mumbai and Ahmedabad at Bhiwandi, Ichalkaranji, and Malegaon. In Gujarat, powerlooms are concentrated in Surat, possibly the largest concentration of powerlooms in the country.[58] In Tamil Nadu, the state with the second largest concentration of powerlooms, they are concentrated in Madurai.

Bhiwandi, 50 kilometers from Mumbai, is one of largest centers of informal textile production in India. Bhiwandi is, by Indian standards, a productive but impoverished town. The estimated 400,000 looms, powered by electric generators, and operated by 400,000 workers, mostly migrants from other states, create a constant din. Bhiwandi became one of the chief centers of informal sector textile production in India during the prolonged Bombay Textile Strike of 1982–83. Mumbai textile manufacturers, rather than meet Mumbai labor unions' demand for larger productivity-based bonuses, opted to subcontract production to the informal sector. Some Mumbai mills owners even dismantled their mills and sold their looms to "master weavers," individuals to whom textile mill owners transferred nominal ownership of looms and supplies. In Bhiwandi, and other towns, "master weavers" hire workers to operate these mills, often with yarn supplied by the Mumbai mills. Cloth is sent back to Mumbai where textile mill owners have their factory labels attached and have it distributed through company marketing channels.

It is estimated that the powerlooms at Bhiwandi produce "several thousand crore" (roughly two billion US dollars) worth of textiles annually.[59] The workers, however, do not enjoy the fruits of their productivity. Working conditions in Bhiwandi are desperate. Looms are typically installed in small sheds that double as workers' living quarters. As there are no public health or sanitation services available, workers often fall ill. The similarly unsanitary conditions in the town of Surat, the center of informal sector powerloom production for the textile industry of Ahmedabad, were the breeding ground for an outbreak in Western India of plague in 1994.

Workers operate their looms under two 10-hour shifts, typically taking turns between working the looms and sleeping in the adjacent cot. Many of the workers are small children. Daily wages run from Rs. 12 (US40¢) for women and children to Rs. 50 (US$1.65) for adult men. Labor activists have attempted to organize Bhiwandi workers to demand better wages and working conditions, but joining a union is an invitation for dismissal.

Post-Independence policies encouraged the rapid growth of the powerloom sector as a small-scale and cottage-based industry. In 1950, for example, the Government of India prohibited the organized mill sector from producing certain materials that were to be reserved for the handloom sector and for powerloom factories employing four or fewer looms. From 1955, the government adopted a policy of differential excise duties. Fabrics produced by handlooms and powerloom factories employing four or fewer looms were exempted from excise tax while fabrics produced by powerloom factories employing more than four looms enjoyed taxes at rates lower than the mill sector.

Informalization through liberalization

The 1985 textile policy dramatically altered the state's protections and incentives in the textile industry, removing capacity restriction, relaxing the import of synthetic fibers, permitting mills to produce blends of their choice, and extending equal financial assistance. Tens of thousands of handloom workers lost their jobs and numerous mills too became unprofitable and were closed.[60] The 1985 textile policy was one of the major reforms of Rajiv Gandhi's early liberalization efforts. The policy was met with claims that the state was preparing to liquidate the handloom industry as well as remove employment generation as a criterion for economic policy.[61] The unorganized handloom workers, typically also seasonal migrant laborers, were not well positioned to mount a unified opposition or even to monitor economic policy. Workers in the mill sector, organized by party trade unions, went on strike in Madras, Coimbatore, Delhi,[62] and Bombay over the linking of wages to productivity. According to a journalist-author and observer of the textile industry, "what is happening is the complete disaggregation of the textile industry. It's a clear case of disaggregation and disintegration."[63] Spinning is going to the cooperative sector. Weaving has been transferred to the powerloom sector. And processing has been taken up by special processing enterprises. The most profitable textile companies are those whose strengths are not in manufacturing so much as in non-productive factors such as advertising.

The textile industry has provided a greater challenge to the government's liberalization program than any other industry. The Textile Policy of June 1985 and the recommendations of the Abid Hussein Committee expressed the intention of the government to rationalize and remove protections to the industry. These were ultimately politically impossible to impose. As it became clear that neither policy could be implemented, the Ministry of Textiles has repeatedly promised a new textile policy. A Steering Committee of Government Secretaries was constituted to form agreement on a new policy but was unable to reach agreement. But the Prime Minister's Office has been unable to break the stalemate.[64]

One reason for the failure of consensus is that pursuing the strategy of shaping the Indian textile industry into an internationally competitive industry will directly threaten the work and lives of the 3.5 million handloom weavers and their 13 million dependents. The desperation of handloom weavers was brought dramatically to public attention in December 1991 when weavers in Andhra Pradesh died of starvation as a result of government textile policies.[65] Due to increases in the export of cotton yarn, a significant source of income for the Indian spinning mills, the domestic price of cotton yarn was increased, squeezing the already subsistence-level wages of the handloom weavers. As a result, 73 weavers died of starvation in Andhra Pradesh between August 30 and November 8, 1991. Despite the growing concern over the plight of the weavers, the Ministries of Commerce and Finance are committed to the restructuring of the textile industry to meet the export demands of India's structural adjustment program. But politically constrained by the social disruption that would result, the central government has not been able to suddenly abandon the handloom sector.

As contentious as the plight of millions of weavers, is the fate of the National Textile Corporation (NTC). The Ministry of Textiles had decided that workers in NTC mills would be retrenched with compensation drawn from the National Renewal Fund and from the sale of NTC land and machinery. The Ministry, however, was forced to withdraw that plan in the face of opposition from organized labor.

Pakistani textiles

Pakistan's textile industry in cotton alone provides 40 percent of the country's industrial employment, 30 percent of its value added in manufacturing, and 40 percent of its exports receipts.[66] Punjab and Sindh were integral to the cotton textile industry of colonial India, but chiefly as the supplier of raw cotton for Ahmedabad and Mumbai mills. At Partition, the bulk of Pakistan's cotton textile needs were met by imports, chiefly from India. The trade war with India in 1949, however, required Pakistan to develop its own production capabilities.[67] But even prior to 1949, the Government of Pakistan encouraged the rapid development of the textile industry not only through industrial subsidies, protections from foreign competition, and tax incentives, but even by establishing public sector enterprises and transferring these to private ownership once they became viable. Pakistan possessed a strong comparative advantage in cotton textile production, with its cotton production and abundant cheap labor. Even in 1947, Pakistan produced 1.5 million bales of high quality cotton, more than the country's textile industry could use.[68]

From the late 1940s into the 1960s mills sprang up, many of them composite mills with spinning, weaving, dyeing, and finishing sections in a single plant. By the mid-1960s, composite mills began to sell their looms and concentrate in spinning cotton yarn. The concentration of the Pakistan textile industry in the spinning sector reflects business's propensity to seek rapid returns on investment. The induction of high yield varieties of seed, brought about through green revolution agricultural policies, also made the concentration in spinning possible. With a doubling of the cotton yield, it was natural for the spinning industry to expand. In the 1960s, textile manufacturers faced widespread public criticism alleging that mill owners mismanaged mills and were swindling consumers for rapid profits.

The spinning sector has been tremendously successful in Pakistan, but at the expense of other textile sectors with high value added production. The textile industry has concentrated in low value added spinning rather than higher end weaving. The weaving sector has been crowded out of the textile industry as a result of the profitability of yarn production. From 1972 to 1987, the number of looms in the country shrunk from 30,000 to 17,000 and cloth production dropped.

Pakistan's mills (not powerlooms) consume only 10 percent of the cotton yarn produced in Pakistan. The export market consumes 40 percent. Two-thirds of exports go to Japan, Hong Kong, and South Korea for weaving and finishing. Pakistan meets 70 percent of Japan's cotton yarn imports and nearly all of Bangladesh's cotton yarn import requirement. The local ancillary market, predominately the powerloom sector, consumes the remaining 50 percent of the cotton yarn produced.

All Pakistan Textile Mills Association

The All Pakistan Textile Mills Association (APTMA) is the most powerful business association in Pakistan. The APTMA exercises considerable influence over the government's textile policy. Explains one senior government official, "what APTMA wants it usually gets."[69] Any discussion of textiles in Pakistan requires a discussion of APTMA. APTMA has successfully lobbied for government concessions. An example is found in regulation of raw cotton export. The production of cotton yarn is dependent upon the variable cotton crop, which is itself susceptible to infestation and flood. In 1991, the Pakistani cotton textile industry was facing a worldwide glut of cotton yarn. The APTMA announced in August 1992 that all spinning enterprises would remain closed one day each week so as to reduce surpluses across the board rather than risk the closure of whole mills. According to then Chairman of APTMA, Tariq Saeed Saigol, the industry produced 100 million kilograms of cotton yarn per month. But with domestic consumption at 40 to 50 million kilograms and exports stagnant at 35 million kilograms, there was a monthly surplus of 15 to 20 million kilograms. APTMA claimed that this move was not intended to lay off works or to protest government policy, but made clear that, in their view, the total abolition of the export duty and a partial devaluation of the rupee would be necessary to enable Pakistan to maintain its market share in textile exports.[70] Flooding in 1992 and insect damage in 1992 and 1993, however, reduced the cotton crop in 1994 by 15 percent of the previous harvest. APTMA then switched its position on production. APTMA convinced the government likewise to amend its previous position. Having imposed an export ban on cotton yarn to protect Pakistani spinners, the government-lowered export duties effected a partial devaluation of the rupee.

The APTMA has articulated a five-point plan for developing the Pakistani textile industry. It has demanded that the Pakistani rupee be made freely convertible or be seriously devalued, that interest rates on industrial development loans be reduced and debts on outstanding loans be rescheduled for one year, that a refinancing facility be established for yarn exports, that excise taxes be abolished and that duty-free import of long cotton fiber be permitted. Rather than negotiate with the government an industrial development strategy, the APTMA has instead lobbied for special government concessions and facilities for the benefit of spinners.

Pakistani spinners are notorious for failing to pay even the small taxes they are assessed. In 1992, the entire textile industry was assessed Rs. 200 million (US$8 million) on a turnover of over Rs. 30 billion (US$2.2 billion). Pakistani farmers accuse the government of bowing to APTMA at the expense of other enterprises. Powerful agriculturists, including the former Punjab Finance Minister, Shah Mahmood Qureshi, have applied pressure against the government's artificially low cotton prices.[71] Government policy assures that raw cotton supplies to Pakistani spinners are 30 percent below the international price.[72] APTMA has long maintained a hostile position toward organized labor. In 1972, the Sindh-Baluchistan Zone Chairman of the APTMA, A. H. M. Dadabhoy, went so far as to appeal to the government to invoke the Industrial Relations Ordinance of 1969 to prohibit strikes in textile mills by declaring strikes in the industry "prejudicial to the national interest" (using clause 2 and 3 of section 32).[73]

The Pakistani powerloom sector is enormous, consuming on average three times as much as the annual domestic production of yarn of the composite mills and producing 80 percent of the total output of cloth in the country. Estimates on the number of powerlooms operating in the country range from 90,000 to 150,000.[74] A trade unionist, the Vice-President All Pakistan Confederation of Labour, describes the unorganized powerloom sector as follows:

> [I]n the unorganized sector, the owners of ... looms usually sublet them to contractors and many of them work in slum areas and not a single labour law is applied to their workers. Their conditions of work are largely inhuman. To dodge labour laws, the owners of such looms ... divide their factory in a number of small units, each separated by a partition wall, so that each unit has less than 20 workers. In many cases, such small units are sublet to middle men like jobbers or supervisors and there is a paper agreement to do so. In such a situation the owners are not directly responsible for executing any labour law.[75]

The owners of powerlooms are adept at circumventing labor laws. Indeed, the powerloom sector owes its existence to the circumvention of labor law. Loom owners may employ dozens of people, but by hiring subcontractors or jobbers, they are able to avoid registering their enterprises as factories under the Factories Act of 1934.[76]

At present, Pakistan's textile industry employs over one million individuals in the organized and unorganized sectors. The number of individuals at work in the organized factory sector has declined since the mid-1970s, as is evidenced from the census of manufacturing industries.

Government statistics on employment by sector are estimated differently in different years and in many years not calculated at all. (For this reason, I have not provided a line chart.) The employment figures for a number of years are unavailable and the comparability of figures across years is variable. However, the observable trend toward less employment since the mid-1970s is unambiguous. The source for these figures, the Census of Manufacturing Industries, compiled by the Statistics Division of the Ministry of Planning and Development, does not collect data on subcontracted labor. Workers, labor economists, and trade unionists agree that suggest that the proportion of subcontracted workers has risen dramatically since the late 1970s as the number of regular employees has fallen.

This survey of the Indian and Pakistani textile industries shows that in the single largest manufacturing sector, labor relations have transformed rapidly. Once the foundation for formal employment in the organized sector, textiles production is now predominantly in the informal, unregulated sectors, where many of the workers are subcontracted.

Deregulation and workers response

Available data on Indian and Pakistani labor give evidence of a long-term deregulation of conditions of work and terms of service. Trends reflect a transformation of manufacturing worldwide from Fordist production processes toward more "flexible" production processes.[77] The new production methods require networks of local subcontractors. These networks can be activated by many domestic firms but fewer transnational corporations. If some kind of global integration or interdependence of economies is the driving force for informalization, it is nevertheless manifest locally in the national economies of the developing world.

This chapter has shown that the greatest challenge to organized labor in India and Pakistan is that the old social contract with the state is not only neglected, it is irrelevant to most of today's employment situations. In the immediate post-Independence period, the Indian and Pakistani states, although with differing economic objectives, developed a strong formal labor force.

Does policy follows practice?

Some attribute increases in informal terms of employment, subcontracted work, and job insecurity to the IMF structural adjustment policies. Less secure terms of employment are the trend in the Indian and Pakistani economies. However, the beginning of theses shifts predates the adoption of structural adjustment policies. Industrial relations (not industrial relations law) underwent discernible major shifts in India and Pakistan in many

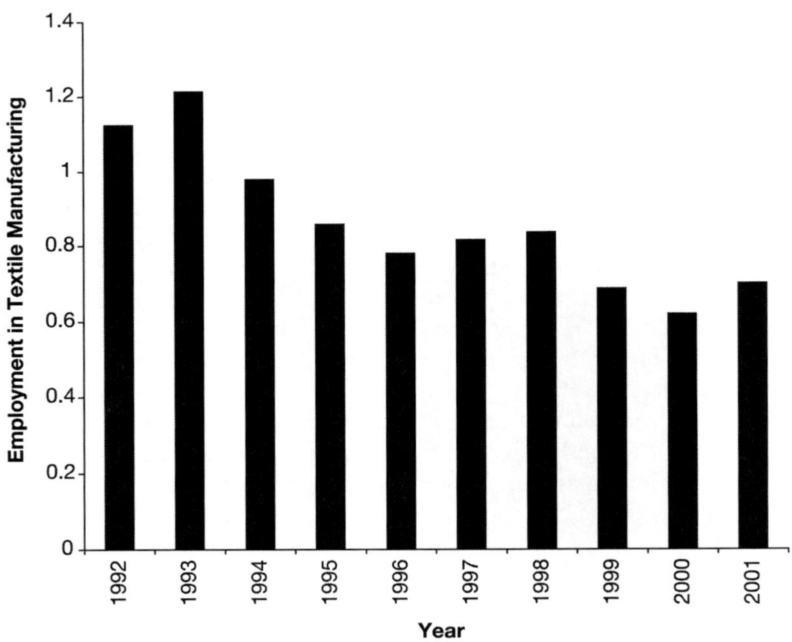

Figure 4.4 Pakistan: employment in textile manufacturing 1992–2001

Source: From Government of Pakistan, Federal Bureau of Statistics, *Labour Force Survey 1990–2000*.

industries from as early as the early 1970s. In India and Pakistan, labor force restructuring preceded the International Monetary Fund (IMF) structural adjustment programs by a decade. Even the earliest IMF adjustment loans in the pre-adjustment days (then called balance of payment stabilization) – in Pakistan in 1980 and in India in 1981 – do not predate significant change in employment patterns. Changes in industrial practices in both countries preceded and prefigured all IMF agreements. It would be difficult to prove that the *de facto* deregulation of industry and of conditions of work and terms of employment promoted its *de jure* deregulation. Nevertheless, the negotiation and implementation of the IMF agreements followed an actual restructuring of conditions of work and terms of employment by Indian and Pakistani employers, including each country's largest employer, the government. The timing of domestic industrial restructuring (earlier) and of external financing for structural adjustment (later) raises the possibility that the Indian and Pakistani states are more affected by local industrial practices than conventional dependency theory – upon which much of the criticism of structural adjustment is modeled – would allow.

Whatever the deeper origins of adjustment, trade unionists claim that since the 1970s many employers and managers have succeeded in undermining the organizational strength of workers and unions on the factory floor by changing work practices. This chapter has examined labor force trends in India and Pakistan. It finds discernible deregulation of conditions of work and terms of employment in India and in Pakistan since the late 1970s – not merely through law but more significantly in practice.

5

ORGANIZED LABOR, DEMOCRACY, AND DEVELOPMENT

> A more nuanced distinction needs to be made between the basic political interests of workers to be articulated by trade unions on the one hand and trade union organizations being tied to political parties on the other. The former kind of trade unionism is consistent with, even demands, trade union unity. The latter ... has only led to progressive fragmentation of the movement.[1]
>
> Bagaram Tulpule

Labor markets, unions, states, and political parties

Some argue that protection of workers impedes efficiency and growth. This study shows that the ability of unions to interfere in government economic reforms is not the price of a competitive political party system. It is an economic benefit. Intractable and resistant social organizations help to prevent governments from enacting policies in reckless or corrupt ways. Thus, the privatization program in India has not only been more gradual than that in Pakistan, it has also been more economically sound and accompanied by far less corruption, as we saw in chapter three.

The previous chapter established that in South Asia, workers are less protected and employers are less responsible for their employees than they were merely two decades ago. The long downward trends are clear even with the limitations of available data. Today, employers and managers are often disassociated from and ignorant of those who provide labor in their enterprises, including public sector employers.

This chapter reports on how unions and other workers' organizations in India and Pakistan have adapted to this era of scarce and increasingly insecure employment. We begin with a brief consideration of relations between labor unions, on the one hand, and states, political parties, and labor markets, on the other. The subsequent section identifies important, new forms of labor advocacy and organizing. These have responded to the changing nature of employment. The concluding section summarizes the major findings of the book and discusses the importance of public institutions that promote solidarity.

Unions and labor markets

Unionized workers are relatively few in India and Pakistan in large part because markets for labor are few. A market for labor, as for any other good or service, entails some relationship between supply and demand. People who have no choice but to accept whatever terms or wages, if any, are offered for their labor, are not in a labor market. Workers who cannot ask for better terms of service (e.g., the recognition of the right to assembly at work) because they fear losing their only source of livelihood are similarly not in a labor market. More than one-third of a billion workers in India and Pakistan do not have the capacity to secure sufficient caloric intake for themselves or their dependents. Lack of income sufficient for minimal food requirements forces hundreds of millions to sell their labor at subsistence wages. The market does not create the price of labor; dire need does. Most workers do not secure employment or wages through demand and supply forces. Even in the most advanced countries labor does not operate according to supply and demand movements.[2]

Economies wherein a significant portion of the population lives at mere subsistence do not give workers, by themselves, such economic power as to secure a living wage. While this proposition is straightforward enough, it has not been very deeply applied to understanding the political economy of development. The notion that labor regulation is an exogenous force and counter to efficiency obviously presumes the existence of a labor market. However, at subsistence levels, individuals cannot be market actors. Dire necessity cannot be the basis of one's estimation of exchange value. In the Indian economy, more than 300 million people live without minimum caloric requirements.[3] Forces more powerful than the estimation of the value of one's labor are obviously at work in employer–employee relations.

The field of labor economics is founded on an assumption that is untenable in much of South Asia. There can be no labor market – no relationship, much less equilibrium between supply and demand for labor – for the 314 million Indians and 28 million Pakistanis who live below the poverty line.[4] One cause of exploitative terms of service and conditions of work is poverty. Under such conditions, workers need unions. But are unions better allying with political parties or with the state?

Unions and the state

In poor, labor-surplus economies – that is, throughout most of the "developing world" – under democratic, non-democratic, and transitional regimes alike, the state once assumed a major role in regulating conditions of work and terms of employment. The state engaged trade unions as partners in this endeavor. Many governments encouraged trade union formation and enacted labor legislation to give workers a measure of protection unavailable to them through the market. The demand for labor can often promote only subsistence wages, not freely and fairly bargained wages. Therefore, governments, gaining state control after long periods of colonialism, conferred upon the state the responsibility for the protection of the common man. Rajni Kothari, in an early analysis of the impact of economic liberalization on India, aptly expressed the sentiment. "In such a poor country, how can you simply dismantle the state? The poor chap what little he has has been provided by the state."[5]

In the present international economic environment, many governments abdicate responsibility for social welfare. In keeping with this trend, governments in many lower-income countries have severed a once sturdy relationship with organized labor. The international economy has made greater demands for lower wages and labor flexibility. Conditions of labor and terms of employment have declined in many countries in many sectors.

India and Pakistan have industrial relations that are similar to many former colonial economies. A development compromise was made possible by the initial affinity between the economic goals of the state and of the formal labor force. Public sector work, from banking to transport to industry, together with organized industrial workers from the private formal sector, grew rapidly under statist economic development. Public sector workers and some workers in private sector industries were able to secure from the state a commitment to decent conditions of work and terms of service, including a high degree of employment protection.

In both the industrialized and industrializing world, the fundamental issues of the formal sector workplace – determination of wages, provision of pensions, payment of bonuses, workers' participation in management, trade union recognition – have been influenced heavily if not decided unilaterally by the state. The Indian and Pakistani states have maintained such a central role in industrial relations since Independence, but not always with benign effects. The Nehruvian package of high tariffs to protect domestic industry, exclusive industrial and financial domains for the public sector, and rigorous obstacles to licensed production might have been socialist in motivation. But it was not very socialist in its effects. Winners in this regulated system – chiefly urban industrialists, urban consumers, and urban formal sector workers – were those with the best connections to state authority.

Beginning in the late 1970s, employment in the formal sectors stagnated, as we saw in chapter four. In many industries, employment has declined in absolute terms. Terms of employment have been made less formal and the subcontract labor system (*thekedar nizam*) has been promoted to avoid labor legislation. Since the 1970s, Indian industry with the support of government agents and policy has instituted managerial and production practices that have circumvented labor legislation, worsened conditions of work, and helped to weaken the unions. These employment and production practices amount to what some organizers refer to as "controlled informalization." India's and Pakistan's emerging political economies, as we saw above in the case of the textile industry, are no longer willing to continue to support that development compromise.

The state's resources, however, remain alluring objects for unions. Many trade unionists and social activists in Pakistan and India regard capture and transformation of the state as key to their strategies. But the influence of the state is often corrupting. States can be repressive and exclusionary. At a minimum, the state's elaborate legislation prevents trade unionists from being more concerned with the affairs of the workers they represent than with organizational maintenance of their unions. In Pakistan, the registration of trade unions, the yearly referenda for collective bargaining agents, and the politics of federation and international affiliations drain the time and energies of trade unions.[6] In India, trade union centers are occupied with the politics of the party to which they are affiliated. Unions in both India and Pakistan are often involved in lengthy court proceedings. Engagement with the state requires tremendous commitment of financial and human resources.

Unions and political parties

Alignment with political parties, themselves aspirants to state power, often prevent unions from achieving their objectives. Political parties, like states, can be untrustworthy allies. Political parties aim to secure or gain some control of the state. Their success in that endeavor poses problems for Marxist or left unions that become associated with the ruling party. Ruling parties in most countries must make debt payments in hard currencies, meet foreign investors' requirements, and satisfy international financial organizations. These international financial obligations promoted a decline in regular employment and in union membership. The interests of ruling parties and left unions associated with them are likely to clash. Jyoti Basu, Chief Minister of West Bengal and energetic salesman of foreign investment in West Bengal, and Basu's colleagues in the Centre for Indian Trade Unions in West Bengal, know this conflict well.

Seeking seats in legislative bodies, or gaining control of some part of the administration of the state, does not always strengthen the capacity of trade unions and their members. The greater benefit of political party-dependent unionism often accrues to the leadership not the members. Further, if these leaders succeed, they often control, manipulate, and corrupt unions allied to them. Unions have little influence over parties once parties become ruling parties.

While political parties may not always be the most effective vehicles for conveying worker interests to government, political parties almost invariably find unions to be effective vehicles for election into government. Indian unions have been able to successfully oppose privatization efforts. In many cases, they have done this through the leverage exercised by the political parties to which they are affiliated. Still, their dependence upon political parties is a source of weakness. The Hind Mazdoor Sabha trade unionist Bagaram Tulpule – in the passage that begins this chapter – points to a vital distinction in trade union politics. An independent labor movement is not one that maintains a cautious indifference to national political developments. Its independence is not a mark of its separation from politics. Rather its independence is marked by its ability to chart political strategies independent of the constraints of political parties.

A distinction can be drawn between the basic political interests of workers (e.g., freedom of association and the right to collective bargaining) and the political interests needed to forge alliances between trade unions and political parties. The evidence from India and Pakistan suggests that the degree to which organized labor can promote the fundamental political interests of its members depends in part upon the degree of democracy within trade unions and upon the independence of trade unions from political parties. The political interests that promote alliances between organized labor and political parties often lead to the fragmentation of the trade union movement. Even the most powerful trade union movements in the world find themselves in the midst of a historic challenge. To make further economic and political gains for workers, trade unions that are allied to the state or political parties must know how to maintain independence from state and political party control.

Unions and workers

Almost all of Pakistan's several hundred public sector enterprises have been privatized over workers' objections because workers were either not organized or not confederated nationally. At the same time, most leaders of Pakistan's trade union federations are well aware that gains made through deals struck with politicians are not necessarily lasting. They know that the gains achieved for the working classes through industrial actions in the late 1960s were quickly lost to political repression. They have seen deals struck between government and some federations on minimum wage increases and promises not to privatize easily give way to austerity and adjustment.

In India, most labor leaders know that unions are less responsive to the interests of their members when political party leadership selects union leaders. Often individuals who run unions do so because they aspire to be leaders in the political party affiliated to the union. If they are not so fortunate as to be recruited by the political party leadership, they often soon regard themselves as labor officials of the party rather than as labor organizers.

Indian and Pakistani trade unionists have been active in developing a new union strategy. For example, in March 1995, three Pakistani federations formed the Pakistan Workers' Confederation, in an effort to form a unified platform for combating economic adjustment and unemployment. The elements of the new union strategy include such inter-federation cooperation, trade union–social movement cooperation, support for workers' management schemes, and a renewed emphasis on workers' education.

New union strategies

Trade unionism in South Asia is responding to the restructuring of industry and the deregulation of conditions of work and terms of service. Indian and Pakistani trade unions have developed strategies to increase their effectiveness in protecting and promoting the rights of workers. In India, this has entailed a focus on the informal sector, where the vast majority of the work force is employed. It has also entailed a softening of the ideological barriers to coordinated action across political parties. Some unions have strayed far from the reach of the party to which they are affiliated. Many workers in many workplaces prefer, and have struggled to win, representation by independent unions. When polled, more than 75 percent of INTUC Working Committee Members wanted to break with the Congress, the party to which it owes its political strength.[7] The two largest trade union federations, the AITUC and the INTUC, took initiatives to "delink themselves from their parent political organizations."[8]

The institutions that enable or constrain labor organization's ability to effectively challenge structural adjustment also affect labor's ability to chart its own future structure. This observation helps to make sense of what many Indian trade unionists, even within the official Indian trade union centers, claim. Political party-based unionism assists the movement in opposing economic policies but can be a hindrance to the social relevance of trade unionism. Most of the official national trade unions that dominate Indian trade unionism usually follow the agenda of their political party yet claim that they are only ideologically allied to that party. A dependent relationship to political parties, not trade unionism itself, nor political party-based unionism, nor the multiplicity of unions, restricts trade unions from serving workers' interests.[9] Communist labor activists in the Communist Party of India (Marxist)-ruled state of West Bengal document that a communist government is no guarantee of better wages, working conditions, job security, or employment promotion.[10] Corporatist control of trade unions, combined with industrial decline in the state, has made unions weak and industrial labor vulnerable, and not only in West Bengal.

In Pakistan, labor federations have formed an alliance – the Pakistan Workers' Confederation (PWC) – in which, among other principles adopted for greater labor solidarity, unions will not compete against fellow PWC unions in collective bargaining agent elections. At the same time, Pakistani unions are embracing the strategy of creating a labor party. The Pakistan Labour Party was established in 1997. The experince of labor federations in Brazil and South Korea is revealing. There too, military governments used the "Japanese" enterprise union system to focus labor's representation on the factory floor. By forming strong confederations and labor parties, unions were able to overcome the divisive logic of factory-based unions.

Indian and Pakistani unions have reconsidered the nature of the state, their relationship to the state, and their roles in economies increasingly unregulated by the state. As well as directly resisting economic adjustment measures, unions in each country are formulating new political strategies and establishing new forms of organizing working people. How are labor organizations responding to deregulation and informalization? What new strategies are they adopting? How can trade unions rise to engage global capital in countries that neglect human development as India and Pakistan do?

The major trade union centers and independent labor organizers have attempted, some successfully, to organize informal sector workers and to educate them about their legal rights. Rajendra Ravi convened the Jan Parivahan Panchayat in Delhi to educate rickshaw drivers on their legal rights.[11] Sanjay Singhvi has organized powerloom operators in Bhiwandi, Maharashtra.[12] Attempts to educate informal sector workers about their rights can be more effective than attempts to organize them as a formal association. These local efforts have not received the scholarly attention they deserve.

A number of significant labor advocacy and organizing initiatives in India and Pakistan – the National Centre for Labour (NCL), the Self Employed Women's Association (SEWA), which was an important member of NCL, the Kamani Employees Union, (each from India), Pakistan's Millat Tractors, the Pakistan Institute for Labour Research and Education, and the Pakistan Workers Confederation – provide illustration in answer to these questions.

National Centre for Labour

One of the most significant developments in the Indian trade union movement since the 1991 economic reforms is the formation, in May 1995, of a confederation of informal sector unions. The National Centre for Labour, made up of 22 labor unions and federations, is the only national trade union confederation that is organized to represent informal sector workers. The emphasis is on "education and information sharing" among informal sector workers and on joint "lobbying and interaction [with] . . . government and its regulatory agencies."[13] The founding convention of the NCL adopted resolutions related to the regulation of the subcontracted labor system;

the rights of women workers and forest workers; a national living wage; a comprehensive social security; and the establishment of local tripartite boards for wage setting.

The NCL represents more than 600,000 workers in activities ranging from garment stitching, embroidery, *beedi* (hand-rolled cigarette rolling), *agarbatti* (incense), and *papad* (chips) making, and food processing to fishing, collecting forest products, and performing domestic work and construction work. The unions with the largest membership in the NCL are the National Federation of Construction Labour and the SEWA. The National Fish-workers' Forum, which spear-headed agitations against commercial trawling and the depletion of fish in coastal waters, and the Forest Producers, Gathers, and Forest Workers Union, which has protested commercial logging, are also vocal members.[14]

Since the earliest discussions to form the NCL in 1991, NCL activists have taken a position against affiliation with political parties. Centre organizers think of themselves as "transcend[ing political] party affiliations."[15] The NCL constitution aims to keep the organization independent from political parties. NCL organizers themselves are associated with different political parties, principally the Communist Party of India, the Communist Party of India (Marxist), and the Janata Party. While the NCL maintains its independence from political parties, it does not believe that it can achieve its goals without an interventionist state.

The NCL focuses on fundamental economic rights, such as a national minimum wage, universal education, and basic health care. A priority of the NCL has been the campaign for a national minimum wage. The campaign was launched in July 1995, shortly after the founding of the NCL, and argues that the government should establish a universal, need-based minimum wage. Minimum wage regulations in India are piece-meal and fragmentary. Workers are accorded different minimum wages according to the industries and states in which they work. Most statutory minimum wages do not afford workers the means for their subsistence. Furthermore, as most informal economic activities are not classified as industries, most workers are denied legal standing. The campaign helped to give considerable support to a national discussion on the need for a national minimum wage, especially under the United Front Government.[16] The NCL devotes its energies not to the negotiation of favorable contracts for their members; it campaigns nationally – through the media and direct legislative action (e.g., demonstrations) – for a uniform minimum wage and universal social security for all workers.

The NCL is also committed to addressing the needs of female workers, who make up more than half of the informal sector. A majority (62 percent) of the office holders of the NCL are women.[17] One of the core and most active members of NCL is the Self-Employed Women's Association.

The Self-Employed Women's Association

The Self-Employed Women's Association (SEWA) not only provides insights about new unionism in South Asia, it has spearheaded much of it. This new unionism, of which SEWA is an example, has two dominant characteristics. The focus of a union is not to aid an allied political party to capture state power, but rather to serve its members. Although legislation is important to new unionism, the focus is not on obtaining state power. The second characteristic is a focus on women informal sector workers. SEWA's participation in the NCL ensured an NCL emphasis on female workers and gender equality. SEWA had a membership in late 2005 of more than 700,000 women, in garment stitching, embroidery, block printing, and silk screening.[18] More than 20,000 of these women work at home.[19]

The Self-Employed Women's Association participation in the NCL has also raised NCL's advocacy for tripartism. SEWA led a successful campaign for the adoption of a Convention on Home-based Workers in the International Labour Organisation.[20] Discussions in the ILO raised understanding among trade unions, business associations, and government officials about the limited protections to this large and growing segment of the labor force. The implementation of the ILO Home Work Convention will help to promote the equal treatment and legal protection of home-based informal sector workers. SEWA is not driven by ideology or even by strong convictions about the workings of the economy.[21] SEWA is focused on developing practical methods for increasing the ability of working women to negotiate and protect themselves.

Independent unionism

Independent unionism has been almost inevitable in Pakistan, where the state and political parties have repeatedly turned against organized labor. Independent unionism has a strong tradition in much of India and Pakistan, especially in Bombay, as discussed in chapter two.[22]

Unionists who have exercised the most independent unionism in India are not apolitical. It is their decisions about the priorities and strategies of their unions that make them independent. Baba Mathew is a member of the Communist Party of India; the union that Comrade Mathew led – the Hindustan Aeronautics Union – is an affiliate to the Communist Party of India (CPI). The Union and Comrade Mathew exercised a strength quite independent of the CPI when they decided, against the party, to permit a large measure of foreign investment in Hindustan Aeronautics.

Indian and Pakistani workers have taken initiatives in cost savings and vigilance against corruption and mismanagement. The recognition that management often has less to lose from unproductive business than do the workers, has convinced workers in many plants that they must actively police the management. Trade unions operate training programs for their workers in developing such skills as reading company balance sheets so as to know when management might be siphoning funds or preparing to declare an industry sick.

Pakistan Institute for Labour Research and Education

The work of the Pakistan Institute for Labour Research and Education (PILER) reveals a great deal about the future of trade unionism in Pakistan and, specifically, Pakistani union responses to structural adjustment and to worsening terms of employment. In a national effort to develop workers' education programs in Pakistan, individuals from trade unions, academia, and other professions established PILER in May 1982. PILER's initial emphasis, given the devastating impact of martial law on labor unions, was on training of workplace level labor leaders. PILER began with a three month Leadership Development Program "aimed at enhancing the social and political awareness" of shop-floor-level trade union leaders.[23] Today, PILER runs 3-day, 2-week, 6-week, and 12-week trade union training programs.

PILER explicitly attempted to involve as many of Pakistan's federations as possible – and managed to achieve this. All Pakistani federations were invited to, and a large number participated in, a National Workshop on Labour Education in June 1988 to draft and approve of the curriculum of the trade unionists education program. Courses were organized in modules on social issues, law, environment, economics, financial analysis, trade unions, and labor law. Courses in the social issues module covered general sociology and political science as well as patriarchy and attitudes toward women. Courses in the law module covered such topics as public interest litigation and human rights. Courses in the module on economics covered the relationship between monetary and fiscal policies, inflation and unemployment, and wages and immigration. Courses in the trade union model examined the role of the ILO in promoting labor standards.[24] Since 1998, PILER has moved from such general education to more specialized trade union educator's programs. It has conducted more than 230 workshops involving more than 7,000 workers, including more than 1,500 working women. Trade union participants are selected from a variety of unions, with different federation affiliations.

All major Pakistani federations participate in PILER training programs. PILER's strongest associate among labor federations is the Karachi-based Muttahida (United) Labour Federation (MLF). The MLF was formed in 1988 by a merger of five "progressive nationalist and anti imperialist"[25] labor federations.[26] The MLF "leadership consists of some of the most experienced and militant trade unionist(s) from all part(s) of the country."[27]

PILER has grown from a facilitator of national labor organization in Pakistan through its trade union education programs to Pakistan's premier labor research center and is as strong as Pakistan's other economic research centers, including the Social Policy and Development Center, also in Karachi, and the Pakistan Institute for Development Education and the Sustainable Development Policy Institute in Islamabad. PILER conducts and publishes research on agricultural and industrial labor, debt bondage, working children, working women, and labor and trade. The Centre for Working Women and the more recently established Centre for Working Children demonstrate a commitment beyond a famously patriarchical trade union movement. PILER has also taken a leading role in Pakistani peace and antinuclear advocacy.

PILER has worked across federation lines and political preferences. Pakistani labor federations are not typically as involved with political party politics as their Indian counterparts. But it is notable that PILER has not sought to concentrate its energies behind a political party. Another notable dimension to PILER's work is its focus on education and training. Only after building a generation of plant-level trade union leaders did PILER begin to undertake substantial research. Early research was program-oriented or action-oriented (e.g., to collect information for better training programs).[28] For example, when brick kiln workers protested their servitude and debt bondage, PILER had already done extensive research and was able to present the government with a detailed plan for abolishing debt bondage and rehabilitating its victims.[29]

Pakistan Workers Confederation

Five Pakistani labor federations with differing ideologies and representing workers in diverse industries, concentrated in separate parts of the country, joined in 1995 to form the Pakistan Workers Confedertaion (PWC). The PWC leadership meets regularly, makes representations to government, and coordinates demonstrations and protests. Federations in the PWC, and the unions that are affiliated to them, overcome the divisive logic of plant-level CBA elections, by refraining from competition in elections against PWC affiliated unions. The PWC is not an alliance of unions representing informal sector unions. But the alliance does, like the NCL, seek to make an impact nationally.

The PWC has worked with non-union organizations to protect rights beyond the workplace. When the private company Dansk Sojakagefabrik (DS) sold a chlor-alkali plant to the Pakistani company Ravi Alkalis for installation in Karachi, Pakistani NGOs, including the Sustainable Development Policy Institute, and Pakistani trade unions, including the PWC, successfully blocked the deal. Together with Greenpeace International, the Pakistani NGOs and trade unions in the Confederation threatened to prevent the unloading at the Karachi Port. The plant, which uses mercury cell technology, the most polluting of the three available chlor-alkali production technologies, had been banned from operating in Denmark on account of workers' health problems.[30]

Not by unions alone

Legal reform

The proliferation of fragmentary laws for classes of workers has made labor legislation inaccessible for most workers. There are 45 ways to recognize (or not recognize) a worker under Indian labor law. As labor is a concurrent subject under the Indian Constitution – a subject of central and state-level law – there are a great number of "scheduled employments" – 1,232 in all – under state law.[31] Labor law effectively prohibits all but a small percentage (fewer than 2 percent) of the labor force in India and Pakistan from bargaining collectively. In Pakistan, union members represent about 0.7 percent of the labor force. (See tables 4.1 and 4.3 for figures and sources.) As the Pakistan Institute of Legislative Development and Transparency puts it, "union activity on the whole is remote from the realities facing the overwhelming majority of the labour force."[32] As a result, unions in each country are advocating universal application of law with greater intensity.

Indeed, unions and labor associations in India and in Pakistan have prioritized universal application of labor law and have obtained significant benefits. Labor associations are focusing increasingly on the fundamental rights of workers, not as workers, who must thereby establish their *locus standi* as workers, but as citizens. The rights of workers should accrue to them as rights, as positive freedoms rather than as consequences of positive, and thereby possibly exclusivist, regulation. Social action, in conjunction with legal protections, wins workers their economic and political rights. Unions persuaded the Indian government, at the 2002 National Commission of Labour, to propose the Unorganized Sector Workers' Social Security Bill, 2005 to establish an authority to oversee collection of contributions from workers and employers. As unorganized sector work often entails having no recognizable employer, the government claims the right to tax or collect from "an industry as a whole."[33]

The law in India and Pakistan is colonial in origin. Moreover, the institutions for its enforcement are not only weak but distort positive plans into actual hardship. South Asian law in general is divisive. One's standing in some cases and before some courts is uncertain. National trade union centers have been criticized for being too legalistic. It would be more accurate to say that they work within a legal apparatus that is designed to apply to only small fragments of the workforce, by no means all workers. Mill workers may file a case here, and miners there, but most workers are excluded from the purview of labor law, and increasingly so.

Indian and Pakistani workers and union leaders have used similar strategies to cope with the loss of regular jobs, the strengthening of management power, and the increased speed of changed employer requirements. The emphases and activities of the National Centre for Labour, the Self-Employed Women's Association, and the Pakistan Workers Confederation use these new strategies.

Foremost, the NCL and SEWA focus on the vast informal sector. Indeed, the NCL recognizes that far from being marginal, or insufficiently integrated into industry, the ordinary Indian worker is an informal sector worker. It is not merely a shift in the image of the Indian worker; it is a recognition that she or he probably works in a section of an industry that makes its workers completely vulnerable.

In both countries, workers are demanding and unions are promoting more internal union democracy. Indian labor federations are increasingly independent from political parties and increasingly allied with social movements representing the large and growing informal sector. Pakistani unions are solidifying their national political power through inter-federation solidarity. Since economic adjustment, national federations in Pakistan have united. Some have formed a labor party, the Labor Party of Pakistan. Left political parties are still very much the party of choice for many left labor unionists, but their view of politics extends greatly beyond party politics. Indian unionists increasingly believe that labor power must be mass-based and movement-oriented.

Legal aid organizations in India and Pakistan fight for legal protection of workers as well as of other citizens. For example, the Indian Centre for Human Rights Law, a public interest law firm, litigates on behalf of subcontracted workers who are doing work in perennial employment positions. The Human Rights Commission of Pakistan has litigated on behalf of exploited brick-kiln workers.

Conclusion

That economies are increasingly exposed to global economic forces is clear enough. How economies and social institutions integrate is not obvious. Similar economic policies have widely differing effects in differing institutional environments.[34] What accounts for the variance?

Social institutions affect the implementation of public policies. The Introduction discussed the limitations of a focus on economic policy choices or political regime types. Social institutions have a profound effect on the direction of economic change, the strength of democratic governments, and the conversion of wealth into wellbeing. Chapter one introduced the book's argument. Social institutions influence economic outcomes, more so than economic policies or even political regime types. Chapter one also discussed the merits of the comparative method and ways to avoid its pitfalls.

Few labor studies show how labor organizations and labor institutions help to produce and reinforce political regimes. Chapter one showed how trade unionism in India and Pakistan had a powerful impact on political developments and on political regime formation in the Subcontinent. In India and Pakistan, workers and unions asserted and fought for fundamental political rights, including universal franchise and the freedom to associate. The involvement of the working classes in the Independence movement helped to consolidate democratic institutions. A habit of selecting candidates for public office from trade union leaders stabilized democracy. Pakistan's weaker unions could not promote a stable democratic political regime, but Pakistani labor movements made significant democratic gains possible in the late 1960s, late 1980s, and 1990s. Chapter one compared Indian and Pakistani political regimes since Independence and presented a comparative political history of the evolution of Indian and Pakistani trade unionism since 1905. That comparative history of Indian and Pakistani trade unionism demonstrated that the contribution of workers to development goes well beyond the workplace.

Workers and unions can shape economic ideologies and economic development strategies. Chapter two focused on the impact of organized labor on Indian and Pakistan economic thought and policies from the 1930s to the late 1980s. Indian workers and unions helped to secure a commitment, albeit not fulfilled, to social and economic justice. In Pakistan, as in other authoritarian regimes without hegemonic political parties, workers and unions could rarely influence national economic goals.

Chapter three provided profiles of the Indian and Pakistani economies, described government efforts to promote IMF structural adjustment, especially privatization, and discussed the relative effects of union responses to privatization. Identical IMF programs, adopted by Pakistan in December 1988 and by India in July 1991, were implemented in both countries. In India, workers and their political party allied unions successfully opposed the privatization program. In Pakistan, workers and their enterprise-based unions permitted a rapid, reckless, and corrupt privatization process. India's political party-based unionism not only made privatization less corrupt but also slowed adjustment in general and softened austerity. The interference of unions in industrial restructuring is not the price of democracy. It is one of its rewards.

Chapter four included a presentation of labor and employment data that indicated a decline in secure terms of employment and a rise in subcontracted work in both India and in Pakistan. Using a comparative overview of employment changes in the textile industry, each country's largest industry and employer, analysis demonstrated that labor strategies – government and union – devised for a presumed future of formal production have become outdated. Changed labor processes and employment practices have made terms of employment, for most workers, increasingly insecure and informal.

This chapter has discussed the changed relationship between unions, political parties, and states in "developing" economies. These might, more accurately, be referred to as economies facing chronic fiscal crises. The chapter paid close attention to the NCL in India and the PWC in Pakistan as illustrations of new forms of political unionism. It demonstrated that durable alliances between organized labor and political parties are no longer possible. Labor law is increasingly used to deny, rather than ensure, that workers' rights are respected. Organized labor's strategic opportunities have changed. Workers in India and in Pakistan are promoting new forms of political unionism to promote social justice and economic democracy. Indian labor federations have gained greater independence from political parties, forged alliances with social movements that represent the large and growing informal sector, and included subcontracted workers in collective bargaining agreements. In addition, Pakistani unions have gained greater political power through inter-federation solidarity. Since economic adjustment, national federations in Pakistan have united. Some have formed a labor party. In both countries, unions are becoming internally more democratic and are using public advocacy campaigns to secure workers' rights.

This comparative political economy study showed that democratic labor institutions and strong labor organizations play a role not only important to broadening the benefits of economic development but also vital to consolidating democracy. Specific kinds of labor institutions affected economic and political, outcomes in predictable and desirable ways.

NOTES

Introduction

1 W. Arthur Lewis, "Economic Development with Unlimited Supplies of Labour," *The Manchester School of Economic and Social Studies*, 22: 2, (May 1954), 155. Lewis was awarded the Nobel Prize in Economics in 1979.

2 Joseph Stiglitz makes this point and a case for government policies aimed at "providing full employment and better working conditions" (p. 10) in "Employment, Social Justice, and Societal Well-Being," *International Labour Review*, 141: 1–2, (2002), 9–29.

3 Here, I use the term "unions" in a broad sense, to refer to membership-based, employer-recognized organizations of workers as well as other kinds of workers' associations.

4 Rob Jenkins, *Democratic Politics and Economic Reform in India*, (Cambridge: Cambridge University Press, 2000).

5 See further Christopher Candland, "Workers' Organizations in Pakistan: Why No Role in Formal Politics?" *Critical Asian Studies*, 39: 1, (March 2007), 35–57.

6 For more on the roots of Pakistan's unequal economic development patterns, see chapter two.

7 Whether the countries that are conventionally referred to as "developing" are developing, even in narrowly economic terms, is debatable. Thus, I avoid the phrase "developing countries." For further discussion on this see Oswaldo de Rivero, *The Myth of Development: the Non-viable Economies of the 21st Century*, (London: Zed, 2001).

8 In Pakistan, unions that have collective bargaining rights represent fewer than 2 percent of the non-agricultural labor force. Calculated from Government of Pakistan, Federal Bureau of Statistics, *Labour Force Survey* and Government of Pakistan, Ministry of Labour, Manpower, and Overseas Pakistanis, *Pakistan Labour Gazette: A Journal of Labour Affairs*. These are the most recent data in 2007. It is usual for South Asian labor publications to be published a few years after the year covered.

9 Chapter three discusses structural adjustment in detail.

10 Chapter two discusses economic policies before the IMF adjustment. Chapter four discusses labor trends, specifically the increasing vulnerability of workers that began before IMF adjustment.

11 See Alice Amsden, *The Rise of "The Rest": Challenges to the West from Late-Industrializing Economies*, (New York: Oxford University Press, 2003).

12 The military cut short both of Benazir Bhutto's terms and the first of Nawaz Sharif's terms in office – through the authority vested in the President, under the Eighth Constitutional Amendment. Among the reasons given for the dismissals was corruption at the highest levels of government. During Sharif's second term, his government removed the Amendment from the Constitution. Sharif's second term ended with General Pervez Musharraf's martial law declaration on October 12, 1999.

13 In India, there was lengthy experimentation with more managerial autonomy in public sector enterprises before the IMF programs. In Pakistan, there was no experimentation with managerial autonomy in public sector enterprises.
14 See Shaheed-ur-Rehman, *Who Owns Pakistan? Fluctuating Fortunes of Business Moghuls*, (Islamabad: Aekia Communications, n.d.).
15 Aristotle, "Metaphysics," Book II, Chapter 3, *The Basic Works of Aristotle*, ed., Richard McKeon, (New York: Random House, 1941), 715.
16 John Stuart Mill, *A System of Logic, Ratiocinative and Inductive Logic*, (London: Longmans, Green and Company, 1961, (1843)), 597.
17 Gunnar Myrdal, *Objectivity in Social Research*, (New York: Pantheon Books, 1969).
18 Reinhard Bendix, "The Mandate to Rule," *Social Forces*, 55: 2, (December 1976), 247.
19 Ayesha Jalal, *The Sole Spokesman: Jinnah and the Making of Pakistan*, (New York: Oxford, 1990).
20 See Maria Victoria Murillo, *Labor Unions, Partisan Coalitions, and Market Reforms in Latin America*, (New York: Cambridge University Press, 2001). A summary appears as Maria Victoria Murillo, "Partisan Loyalty and Union Competition: Macroeconomic Adjustment and Industrial Restructuring in Mexico," in Christopher Candland and Rudra Sil, eds, *The Politics of Labor in a Global Age: Continuity and Change in Late-industrializing and Post-socialist Economies*, (Oxford: Oxford University Press, 2001), 31–68.

Organized labor and democratic consolidation

1 G. V. Joshi, *Writings and Speeches of G.V. Joshi*, (Poona: Aryabhushan Press, 1912), 743. Cited in Bipan Chandra, *The Rise and Growth of Economic Nationalism in India*, (New Delhi: People's Publishing House, 1966), 113. G. V. Joshi was an Indian Civil Service officer and a mentor to prominent Indian industrialists.
2 See David Morris, *The Emergence of an Industrial Labor Force in India: A Study of the Bombay Cotton Mills, 1854–1947*, (Berkeley, CA: University of California Press, 1965) and J. H. Boeke, *Economics and Economic Policy of Dual Societies*, (New York: Institute of Pacific Relations, 1953).
3 A serious discussion on the views of even the major Marxist political parties of the state is a book-length exercise. Baldev Raj Nayar's discussion of the differing perspective of the role of the state in Indian society held by India's two leading communist parties – the Communist Party of India and the Communist Party of India (Marxist) – is almost book length. See "Contending Approaches to the State and Public Sector," *India's Mixed Economy: The Role of Ideology and Interest in Its Development*, (Bombay: Popular Prakashan, 1989), 62–127.
4 Harry Blair, "Mrs. Gandhi's Emergency, The Indian Elections of 1977, Pluralism and Marxism: Problems with Paradigms," *Modern Asian Studies*, 14: 2, (1980), 269.
5 Pranab Bardhan, *The Political Economy of Development in India*, (New Delhi: Oxford University Press, 1984).
6 Tariq Ali provides an insightful discussion of the pivotal role of the military in Pakistan in "The Colour Khaki," *New Left Review*, 19, (January–February 2003).
7 Hamza Alavi, "The State in Postcolonial Societies: Pakistan and Bangladesh," in Kathleen Gough and Hari Sharma, eds, *Imperialism and Revolution in South Asia*, (New York: Monthly Review Press, 1973), 145–73. When Alavi wrote of a bureaucratic-military oligarchy, he referred not to the state, the governmental apparatus, but to a regime, the institutionalized practices of government.
8 Quotations from Alavi, "Class and State," *Pakistan: The Roots of Dictatorship*, (London: Zed Books, 1983), 60 and 65, respectively.

9 According to Alavi, the Indian National Congress took control of the colonial state in the interest of the domestic bourgeoisie, explaining the Indian state's relatively constrained autonomy.
10 One of the strengths of Alavi's analysis is its explicit comparative framework.
11 V. B. Karnik, *Indian Trade Unions: A Survey*, (Bombay: Popular Prakashan, 1978), 1–14.
12 Bakhtiar and his place in the Pakistani labor movement are discussed in greater detail below.
13 See Ranajit Das Gupta, "Social Security and Mutual Assistance in India: A Preliminary Account," *International Social Security Review*, 46: 3, (1993), 53–68.
14 Karnik, *Indian Trade Unions*, 4–9.
15 P. P. Arya, *Trade Unions in India: Growth and Recognition*, (New Delhi: Deep and Deep Publications, 1985), 12.
16 Tanika Sarkar, *Bengal 1928–1934, the Politics of Protest*, (Delhi: Oxford University Press, 1987).
17 B. N. Datar, "Ideology and Trade Unions – Indian Experience," *V. B. Karnik Memorial Lectures*, (Bombay: Maharashtra Institute of Labour Studies, April, 1987), 24.
18 Ibid., 25.
19 Cited in ibid.
20 See G. Kotovsky, "The Origins and Development of the Communist and Workers' Movement in India, with Focus on the CPI," in Berch Berberoglu, ed., *Class, State and Development in India*, (New Delhi: Sage, 1992), 248.
21 Zafar Shaheed, 'The Organisation and Leadership of Industrial Labour in Pakistan (Karachi),' unpublished PhD dissertation, Department of Politics, University of Leeds, 1977, 121.
22 Dick Kooiman, *Bombay Textile Labour: Managers, Trade Unionists and Officials 1918–1939*, (New Delhi: Manohar, 1989), 33.
23 Shaheed, "The Organisation and Leadership of Industrial Labour in Pakistan," 122.
24 Khizar Humayan Ansari, "Roots of Muslim Socialist Activity and Labour Organization in Pre-Partition India," paper presented at the Conference on Labour in Pakistan, Karachi, December 26–28, 1999, 4.
25 Ibid., 7.
26 Shaheed, "The Organisation and Leadership of Industrial Labour in Pakistan," 108.
27 The relevant section of the Indian Penal Code is found in Government of India, Ministry of Labour, *Indian Labour Year Book 1947–48*, (New Delhi: Labour Bureau, 1948).
28 *Indian Labour Yearbook 1946–1947*, 122. Cited in Prafulla Chandra Das, *Trade Unions and Politics in India: A Study of Orissa*, (New Delhi: Discovery Publishing House, 1990), 142.
29 Martin Wainwright, "The Development of India's Defense Industries during the Second World War: Implications for the Partition of the Subcontinent," paper presented at the Association for Asian Studies, 6 April 1990.
30 K.P. Chakravarti, *Law of Industrial Disputes*, (Calcutta: Eastern Law House, 1987), 7.
31 The Indian National Trade Union Congress leader Jagjivan Ram claimed that 90 percent of the seats reserved for labor in the 1937 elections went to Congress. Shachi Rani Gurtu, ed., *Jagjivan Ram on Labour Problems*, (Delhi: Atma Ram and Sons, 1951), 14. In fact, 90 percent of the 20 seats that Congress contested went to the Congress.
32 *Indian Labour Gazette*, (Simla: Labour Bureau, September 1946), 89.
33 G. Ramanujam, *Indian Labour Movement*, (New Delhi: Sterling Publishers, 1990), 19.
34 B. N. Datar, "Ideology and Trade Unions – Indian Experience."

35 Jawaharlal Nehru, *An Autobiography*, (New Delhi: Oxford University Press, 1989, (1936)), 186–87.
36 Kotovsky, "The Origins and Development of the Communist and Workers' Movement in India," 250.
37 Mohandas Gandhi, *Collected Works*, vol. 14, 232–34, as quoted by Judith Brown, *Gandhi: Prisoner of Hope*, (New Haven, CT: Yale University Press, 1989), 121 and 122. Cited in Lloyd Rudolph and Susanne Hoeber Rudolph, "Dependent Labor and the Politics of Economic Reform in India: Left and Right Protectionism in the Nineties," paper presented at the University of California–Harvard University Workshop on Political Parties and Working Class Constituencies, April 25, 1999, 4.
38 For a detailed account of the strike, see Judith Brown, *Gandhi's Rise to Power: Indian Politics 1915–1922*, (Cambridge: Cambridge University Press, 1972), 118–122.
39 The Self-Employed Women's Association (SEWA) emerged from the Textile Labour Association. Ela Bhatt founded SEWA shortly after being expelled from the Textile Labour Association, where she served as Vice President. SEWA, discussed in chapter five, is one of today's most significant trade unions in India.
40 G. Ramanujam, *The Honey Bee: Toward a New Culture in Industrial Relations*, (New Delhi: Sterling Publishers, 1985), 103.
41 Textile Labour Association, "In the Service of Women," (Ahmedabad: Gandhi Majdoor Sevalaya, 1986), 3.
42 Resolution cited by Jagjivan Ram, "Congress and the Workers," in Shachi Rani Gurtu, ed., *Jagjivan Ram on Labour Problems*, (Delhi: Atma Ram and Sons, 1951), 13. Jagjivan Ram was independent India's first Labour Minister.
43 Ibid., 14.
44 Ibid., 12–17.
45 These are Directive Principles 41 through 43. Government of India, *The Constitution of India*, (New Delhi: B. V. P. Press, 1956), 26.
46 For a study of the role of unionists in electoral politics in Orissa, see Prafulla Chandra Das, *Trade Union and Politics in India: A Study of Orissa*.
47 Ajeet Mathur, Professor of Personnel Management and Industrial Relations, Indian Institute of Management, Calcutta, interview with author, December 30, 1991.
48 E. A. Ramaswamy, "A Chastened Trade Unionism," *Business India*, 15th Anniversary Issue, 1993, 161.
49 Rudolph and Rudolph, *In Pursuit of Lakshmi: The Political Economy of the Indian State*, (Chicago, IL: The University of Chicago Press, 1985), 260.
50 Clifford Geertz, *Agricultural Involution: The Process of Ecological Change in Indonesia*, (Berkeley, CA: University of California Press, 1970). Rudolph and Rudolph, *In Pursuit of Lakshmi*, 269.
51 Kamal Muzumdar, a former ILO Director and a senior Indian trade union official with the Indian National Trade Union Congress, argues that the best thing that the Indian trade union centers could do for the labor movement is to disband. Kamal Muzumdar, interview with author, New Delhi, November 28, 1991.
52 Rashid Amjad and Khalid Mahmood, "Industrial Relations and the Political Process in Pakistan, 1947–1977" and Shaheed, 'The Organisation and Leadership of Industrial Labour in Pakistan (Karachi).'
53 Karamat Ali (Multan), "Labour Legislation and Trade Unions," mimeograph, no date.
54 Ibid., 4.

55 See Stanley Kochanek, *Interest Groups and Development Business and Politics in Pakistan*, (Delhi: Oxford University Press, 1983), 69.
56 Khurshid Alam, General Secretary of Bata Mazdoor League Pakistan, interview with author, Lahore, September 4, 1992. Alam has been involved in the trade union movement since 1940.
57 Gulzar Ahmad Chaudhary, General Secretary of All Pakistan Trade Union Federation, interview with author, Lahore, September 5, 1992.
58 Bashir Ahmed Bakhtiar, *Mazdoor Tehriq aur Mai*, ("The Labor Movement and Me"), (Lahore: West Pakistan Hydro Electric Central Labour Union, 1962).
59 Ashraf Ali, "Trade Unions in Pakistan," mimeograph, 1991, 6.
60 Shaheed, "Union Leaders, Work Organization and Strikes: Karachi 1969–72," *Development and Change*, 10, (1979), 181–204, 185.
61 Badiuddin A. Khan, "The Myth of Labour Policy," *Industrial Relations Journal*, 9: 3, (May–June 1992), 29–33, 30.
62 Shaheed, "Union Leaders, Work Organization and Strikes," 185.
63 Iqbal Haidari, ed., *The New Labour Policy: Impact and Implications*, (Karachi: Economic and Industrial Publications, 1972), 165. Haidari describes Malik's policy as paternalistic, based on the lines of Japanese labor policy, presumably referring to enterprise unionism.
64 Riffat Hussain, labor organizer, interview with author, Rawalpindi, September 12, 1992.
65 Khan, "The Myth of Labour Policy," 30.
66 Gulzar Ahmad Chaudhary, interview with author, Multan September 5, 1992.
67 Note that this is not Khurshid Ahmed, General Secretary of All Pakistan Federation of Trade Unions and General Secretary of Water and Power Development Authority (WAPDA)'s State Hydro-Electric Union (SHEU).
68 Kiernan, "A Note on the Author," *Poems by Faiz*, (Lahore: Vanguard Books, 1971), 7.
69 Ali, "Trade Unions in Pakistan."
70 Shaheed, "Union Leaders, Work Organization and Strikes," 186.
71 Ibid.
72 Shaheed has documented the crucial role of workplace leaders and workers' communities in the strike wave of 1963. See Shaheed, 'The Organisation and Leadership of Industrial Labour in Pakistan (Karachi).'
73 "Tributes Paid to Martyrs of March, 1963," paper unknown, clipping in *Dawn* (Karachi) library, March 3, 1969.
74 Shaheed, "Union Leaders, Work Organization and Strikes," 188.
75 Usman Baloch, former President of the Muttahida Mazdoor Federation, interview with author, Karachi, September 27, 1992.
76 Riffat Hussain interview with author, Rawalpindi, September 12, 1992.
77 Usman Baloch, interview with author, Karachi, September 27, 1992.
78 "Labour Body Conference Held," *Morning News*, February 1, 1969.
79 Riffat Hussain, interview with author, Rawalpindi, September 24, 1992.
80 "Workers' Processions, Meetings," *Morning News*, February 24, 1969.
81 "Labour Federations Support Friday's General Strike Call," February 13, 1969.
82 "Workers Walk Out of Joint Council Meeting," *Morning News*, February 22, 1969.
83 Khurshid Ahmed, General Secretary of All Pakistan Federation of Trade Unions, interview with author, Lahore, 3 September 1992.
84 Interviews of author with Maher Mohammad Akram, President, and Syed Akhter Hussain Shah, Deputy General Secretary, Colony Textile Mills Labour Union, Multan, September 24, 1992. Also "6 Workers Hurt in Firing by Multan Mills' Watchmen," *Dawn*, March 18, 1969.

85 "Labour Unrest," *Morning News*, March 7, 1969.
86 "Fair Wages, Right of Strike for Labourers," *Dawn*, April 26, 1969.
87 Noor Khan, interview with author, Karachi, March 28 and 29, 1995.
88 "Government Urged to Announce Revised Labour Policy Soon," *Dawn*, July 1, 1969.
89 The Industrial Relations Ordinance of 1969 repealed four pieces of labor law, two acts passed by the Constitutional Assembly and two martial law ordinances. The annulled labor laws were the East Pakistan Trade Unions Act of 1965, the East Pakistan Labour Disputes Act of 1965, the West Pakistan Industrial Disputes Ordinance of 1968 and the West Pakistan Trade Unions Ordinance of 1968.
90 On record for their support are the APCOL (M. A. Khatib), the APFL (Rehmatulah Khan Durrani), the West Pakistan Textile Mills Employees Federation (Akhtar Husain Kiyani), and the West Pakistan Textile Mills Mazdoor Union (Ghulam Husain). "New Labour Policy Hailed," *Dawn*, July 8, 1969.
91 "Industrial Unrest," *The Pakistan Times*, 15 November 1969.
92 *Daily News*, November 15, 1969.
93 "Protest Rallies by Valika Mill Workers," *Dawn*, November 1, 1969.
94 Faizullah Khan, President, Valika Textile and Woolen Mills Workers Union, interview with author, Karachi, August 31, 1992.
95 "40 Trade Unions Back Striking Workers," *Dawn*, 6 November 1969.
96 "Kaniz Fatma in City," *Dawn*, November 20, 1969.
97 "13 Labourers convicted by ML Court in Karachi," *Political Observer*, November 19, 1969.
98 Maleeha Lodhi, 'Bhutto, the Pakistan Peoples Party and Political Development in Pakistan, 1967–1977', unpublished PhD thesis, London School of Economics and Political Science, University of London, 1980, 130.
99 Manzoor Ahmed, interview with author, September 27, 1992.
100 "Bhutto's Speech at Labour Moot: Text," *Dawn*, November 22, 1973.
101 Riffat Hussain, interview with author, Rawalpindi, September 9, 1992.
102 For fair trade Union perspectives on the policy, see Haidari, *The New Labour Policy: Impact and Implications*, 1972.
103 Ali, "Trade Unions in Pakistan", 103.
104 Mustafa Pasha, conversation with author, February 25, 1995.
105 US Department of Labor, *Foreign Labor Trends: Pakistan*, (Washington, DC: US Government Printing Office, 1990).
106 Haider Zaman, human resource management consultant to the 1979 and 1986 Labour Commissions of Pakistan, Karachi, interview with author, August 26, 1992.
107 Human Rights Commission of Pakistan, *State of Human Rights in Pakistan 1990*, Human Rights Commission of Pakistan, 1990, 49.
108 Haider Zaman, Karachi, interview with author, August 26, 1992.
109 International Labour Office, "Pakistan: Developing a Labour Policy," *Social and Labour Bulletin*, (June 1992), 146–48.
110 British Broadcasting Corporation, Summary of World Broadcasts, "Ban on Railway Workers Lifted," *Radio Pakistan External Service*, 11:00 GMT, May 2, 1995.
111 Left federations have been on record accusing the APFTU of opportunism and of being too willing to enter into agreements with whichever government may be in power. When the APFTU remained in talks with government (which resulted in the 1992 announcement of a new minimum wage for unskilled workers) after all other federations walked out, other federations made the accusation. The APFTU and Kurshid Ahmed, General Secretary since 1972, also receive extensive coverage in the English-language press, while other federations and their leaders are rarely discussed by the press.

112 Ruth Berins Collier and David Collier, *Shaping the Political Arena: Critical Junctures, the Labor Movement and Regime Dynamics in Latin America*, (Princeton, NJ: Princeton University Press, 1991).
113 For details, see Hasan Zaher, "The Communist Connection," *The Times and Trial of the Rawalpindi Consipiracy 1951*, (Karachi: Oxford University Press, 1998, 204–23).
114 Jalal, Ayesha, *The State of Martial Law: The Origins of Pakistan's Political Economy of Defence*, (Cambridge: Cambridge University Press, 1990), 295.
115 Article 21, Section 3 of Industrial Relations Ordinance of 1969.
116 For state-level analysis in India, see Christopher Candland, "Labor Institutions and Industrial Restructuring in India," (College Park, MD: Center on Istitutional Reform and the Informal Sector, India Working Paper, no. 24, 1996).
117 Chapter four discusses the textile industry, the RMMS, the Bombay textile strike, and Datta Samant.

The state and economic development

1 Letter from President of the All India Muslim League to Jawaharlal Nehru, President, Indian National Congress, March 8, 1938, in Syed Sharifuddin Pirzada, ed., *Quaid-e-Azam Jinnah's Correspondence*, third revised and enlarged edition, (Karachi: East and West Publishing Company, 1977), 254.
2 Letter in reply to Mohammad Ali Jinnah, April 6, 1938, in Pirzada, op. cit., 260.
3 Cited by Istaqbal Mehdi (former Pakistan Minister of Production), "State Intervention and Public Enterprises in the Market Place – Some Issues and Problems with Special Reference to Pakistan," manuscript, n.d., 4.
4 Mahbub ul Haq first spoke of the "22 families" in a talk to the Applied Economics Research Centre of the University of Karachi in 1968.
5 Emajuddin Ahmed, *Bureaucratic Elites in Segmented Economic Growth: Pakistan and Bangladesh*, (Dacca: University Press, 1980), 87.
6 Government of India, "The Industrial Policy Resolution," (Simla: Government of India Press, 1956).
7 Bharat Bhushan Gupta, *The Welfare State in India: Theory and Practice*, (Allahabad: Central Book Depot, 1966), 35.
8 Ibid., 47. There was in the 1950s and 1960s considerable academic work on the Indian "welfare state" in Indian universities and much official literature on the development of the Indian welfare state as well. See, for example, P. D. Gupta, *Welfare State in India*, (Agra: Agra University, 1955) and Government of India, Ministry of Information and Broadcasting, *Road to Welfare State*, (Delhi: Government of India, May 1957).
9 All figures in this and the next paragraph, unless otherwise noted, are for 1999 in India and 1998 in Pakistan. See United Nations Development Programme, table 15, "Inequality in Income and Consumption," *Human Development Report 2005*, (New York: Oxford University Press, 2006), 272.
10 On the impact of Gulf migration on Pakistan see Jonathan Addleton, *Undermining the Centre: The Gulf Migration and Pakistan*, (Karachi: Oxford University Press, 1992).
11 Government of Pakistan, Ministry of Finance, *Pakistan Economic Survey 1990*, (Islamabad: Government of Pakistan Printing Press, 1991).
12 Government of India, Ministry of Finance, *Economic Survey 1990–91*, (New Delhi: Government of India Press, 1991), S-9.
13 See United Nations Development Programme, *Human Development Report 2005*, table 20, "Priorities in Public Spending," 286–87.

14 A. R. Kemal, "Privatisation: The Experience of Pakistan," in V. Kanesalingam, ed., *Privatisation: Trends and Experiences in South Asia*, (New Delhi: MacMillan India, 1991), 132. Figures are presumably those current at the time of writing in 1991, prior to much fiscal adjustment and industrial restructuring.
15 Ibid., 139.
16 World Bank, "Pakistan: Country Economic Memorandum FY93: Progress Under the Adjustment Program," (Washington, DC: World Bank, March 23, 1993), 49.
17 The politically significant issue of industrial "sickness" and its relationship to job protection and employment is discussed in chapter three.
18 See Public Interest Research Group, "Structural Adjustment: Who Really Pays?," (Delhi: Public Interest Research Group, 1992), 36.
19 M. S. Narayanan, "Trading Charges," *Economic Times*, May 19, 1991.
20 Naoroji first articulated his "drain theory" in 1871, in a paper titled "Commerce of India." The theory is more fully worked out in *Poverty and Unbritish Rule in India*, (London: S. Sonnenschein, 1901). Rajani Palme Dutt argued that England had de-industrialized India. See Dutt, *The Problem of India*, (New York: International Publishers, 1943) and *India To-day*, (London: V. Gollancz, 1940). Brook Adams, *The Law of Civilization and Decay*, (London: Sonnenschein, 1895), 259–60 argues that England's industrial revolution was financed by India's plunder.
21 Hassan Gardezi, "Neocolonial Alliances and the Crisis of Pakistan," in Kathleen Gough and Hari Sharma, eds, *Imperialism and Revolution in South Asia*, (New York: Monthly Review Press, 1973), 130–44, 134. Also see Bipan Chandra, *The Rise and Growth of Economic Nationalism in India*, (New Delhi: People's Publishing House, 1966).
22 See Clive Dewey, ed., *Arrested Development in India*, (Riverdale, MD: Riverdale Company, 1988), especially Specker, "'De-Industrialization' in Nineteenth Century India: The Textile Industry in the Madras Presidency, 1810–70," 333–46.
23 Specker, "'De-Industrialization' in Nineteenth Century India," 333. David Morris sought to challenge the de-industrialization thesis, arguing that statistical evidence was inadequate, that a rise in domestic demand could have absorbed the growing imports, and that the import of mill yarn strengthened the position of the Indian weaver. See Morris, "Toward a Reinterpretation of Nineteenth Century Indian Economic History," *Indian Economic and Social History Review*, 5, (1968).
24 Jawaharlal Nehru, *The Discovery of India*, (New Delhi: Oxford University Press, 1992, (1946)), 505.
25 Ibid., 505–7.
26 Chatterjee, *Nationalist Thought and the Colonial World*, (London: Zed Books, 1986), 132.
27 Nehru, *Discovery of India*, 524–36.
28 Ibid., 266.
29 See B. N. Datar, "Ideology and Trade Unions – Indian Experience," *V. B. Karnik Memorial Lectures*, (Bombay: Maharashtra Institute of Labour Studies, April, 1987), 39.
30 Nehru, *An Autobiography*, (New Delhi: Oxford University Press), 267.
31 For an elaboration of this point, see Raghabendra Chattopadhyay, "Indian Business and Economic Planning (1930–56)," in Dwijendra Tripathi, ed., *Business and Politics in India: A Historical Perspective*, (Delhi: Manohar, 1991), 308–50.
32 Ibid., 308.
33 The speech was published as G. D. Birla, "Indian Prosperity: A Plea for Planning," and delivered at the annual session of the Federation of Indian Chamber of Commerce and Industry, 1934.

34 Bipan Chandra, "Jawaharlal Nehru and the Capitalist Class, 1936," in *Nationalism and Colonialism in Modern India*, (New Delhi: Orient Longman, 1979), 171–203.

35 Thakurdas sat on government commissions and corporate boards and was later knighted. J. R. D. Tata was then manager of Tata Iron and Steel Company, Chairman of Tata and Sons and chairman or director of over a dozen other companies. G. D. Birla was a successful textile mill owner, a merchant, Managing Director of the vast Birla Brothers industries, and founder, in 1927, with Thakurdas, of the Federation of Indian Chambers of Commerce and Industry. Dalal was a director and partner of the Tata Sons industrial empire and a government officer. Shri Ram was a mill owner and landlord. Shroff was a stockbroker and businessman. John Matthai was a professor of economics and Director General of Commercial Intelligence and Statistics. Each was associated with the Indian National Congress. *Who's Who in India, Burma and Ceylon, 1941–42*, (Bombay: Who's Who Publishers, 1942). Purshotamdas Thakurdas, J. R. D. Tata, G. D. Birla, Ardeshir Dalal, Shri Ram, Kasturbhai Lalbhai, A. D. Shroff, and John Matthai, *Brief Memorandum Outling a Plan of Economic Development for India*, (Bombay: The Commercial Printing Press, part 1, January, 1944, part 2, January, 1945).

36 Ibid., 48.

37 Ibid., 3.

38 K. B. Krishna, *Plan for Economic Development of India: A Critical and Historical Survey*, (Bombay: Padma Publications, 1945).

39 Ayesha Jalal, *The State of Martial Rule: The Origins of Pakistan's Political Economy of Defence*, (Cambridge: Cambridge University Press, 1990), 9.

40 G. Allana, ed., *Pakistan Movement: Historic Documents*, (Karachi: Department of International Relations, University of Karachi, 1967), 7–10. Cited in Stanley Wolpert, *Jinnah of Pakistan*, (New York: Oxford University Press, 1984), 22.

41 Wolpert, *Jinnah of Pakistan*, 29.

42 Syed Sharifuddin Pirzada, ed., *Foundations of Pakistan: The All-India Muslim League Documents: 1906–1947*, volume III, (1906–47), (Karachi: National Publishing House, 1970).

43 Gardezi, "Neocolonial Alliances and the Crisis of Pakistan," 137.

44 Ibid.

45 Pirzada, *Foundations of Pakistan*, 19.

46 Ibid., 99.

47 Ian Talbot, "Planning for Pakistan: The Planning Committee of the All-India Muslim League 1943–46," *Modern Asian Studies*, 28: 4, (1994), 875–89. Also see Khalid Shamsul Hasan, ed., *Quaid-i-Azam's Unrealized Dream: Formation and Working of the All India Muslim League Economics Planning Committee with Background Material and Notes*, (Shamsul Hasa Foundation for Historical Studies and Research, 1991).

48 The commitment to a "socialist pattern of development" was made in the Industrial Policy resolution of 1956.

49 Nehru, *An Autobiography*, (New Delhi: Oxford University Press, 1989, (1936)), 163, 182–83.

50 Niraja Gopal Jayal, "Introduction," in Sidney Webb and Beatrice Webb, *Indian Diary*, (Oxford: Oxford University Press, 1990), x–xi. For important Fabian tracts see Sidney Webb, *The Necessary Basis of Society*, (London: Westminister, 1911) and G. Bernard Shaw, Sidney Webb, William Clarke, Sydney Oliver, Annie Besant, Graham Wallas, and Hubert Bland, *Fabian Essays in Socialism*,

(London: The Fabian Society, 1889). On the role of central planning in Fabian thinking, see John Callaghan, "Fabian Socialism, Democracy and the State," in Graeme Duncan, ed., *Democracy and the Capitalist State*, (Cambridge: Cambridge University Press, 1989), 159–80.

51 Sukhamoy Chakravarty, *Development Planning: The Indian Experience*, (New Delhi: Oxford University Press, 1987), 9–11.

52 Ibid., 10.

53 Ibid.

54 Chakravarty, "Nehru and Indian Planning," *South Asian Research*, 9: 2, (November 1989), 95.

55 Industrial Policy Resolution, 3.

56 George Rosen, *Democracy and Economic Change in India*, (Berkeley, CA: University of California Press, 1966), 91–92.

57 Government of India, Planning Commission, *Papers Relating to the Formation of the Second Five-Year Plan*, (New Delhi: Government Printing Press, 1955). Cited in Rosen, *Democracy and Economic Change in India*, 126.

58 First Five-Year Plan, cited by H. P. Khare, *Current Trends in Indian Trade Union Movement: A Study of White-Collar Trade Unions*, (Allahabad: Chugh Publications, 1987), 203. Khare's work is a study of the Allahabad Textile Labour Association.

59 Ibid.

60 Baldev Raj Nayar, *India's Mixed Economy: The Role of Ideology and Interest in its Development*, (Bombay: Popular Prakashan, 1989), 249.

61 I use the term "Third World" as Jawaharlal Nehru, Abdul Nasser, Mohammad Sukarno, and Chou Enlai did at the Africa–Asia Unity Conference in Bandung, Indonesia in 1955. They referred to the Third World as that alliance of countries that could carve out a way between the inequalities of market dominated societies, specifically that of the United States, and the abuse of political liberties in state dominated societies, specifically that of the Soviet Union.

62 Nayar, 249–52.

63 Ibid., 254, 261.

64 Angus Maddison, *Class Structure and Economic Growth: India and Pakistan since the Moghuls*, (New York: W. W. Norton, 1971).

65 Kuldip Nayar, *India: The Critical Years*, (Delhi: Vikas Publishing, 1971), 29. Cited in Nayar, *India's Mixed Economy*, 262.

66 Ibid., 253–56.

67 Ibid., 262.

68 Life insurance had been nationalized in 1956.

69 Nayar, *India's Mixed Economy*, 273.

70 (O) stands for Organisation.

71 Ibid., 265.

72 Later to become Congress (I).

73 Nayar, *India's Mixed Economy*, 283–84.

74 Government of India, *Economic Survey 1978–79*, (New Delhi: Ministry of Finance, 1979), appendix.

75 Nayar, *India's Mixed Economy*, 332.

76 Mrs. Gandhi was found guilty of using government officials to erect and supply electricity to speaker stands in her constituency. Henry Hart, ed., *Indira Gandhi's India: A Political System Reappraised*, (Boulder, CO: Westview Press, 1976), 3.

77 Andrew Davenport, "Indira's Industrial Balancing Act," *Far Eastern Economic Review*, August 22, 1975, 55–56.

78 Ibid. Also see Ashok Bhargava and Gopalan Balachandran, "Economic Change During the Indian Emergency," *Bulletin of Concerned Asian Scholars*, 9: 4, (October–December 1977), 50–58.
79 Guillermo O'Donnell, *Modernization and Bureaucratic Authoritarianism: Studies in South American Politics*, (Berkeley, CA: Institute for International Studies, 1973), 85.
80 Ibid., 57–58.
81 Lloyd Rudolph and Susanne Hoeber Rudolph, *In Pursuit of Lakshmi: The Political Economy of the Indian State*, (Chicago, IL: University of Chicago Press, 1985), 88.
82 Government of Pakistan, Planning Commission, *The Sixth Five-Year Plan, 1983–88*, (Islamabad: Planning Commission, 1983), 1.
83 Ayesha Jalal, *The State of Martial Rule*, (Cambridge: Cambridge University Press, 1990), 33.
84 Maddison, *Class Structure and Economic Growth*, 158. See Papanek, *Pakistan's Development*, 40–46 for details on trading communities and Pakistan's early entrepreneurs.
85 Maddison, *Class Structure and Economic Growth*, 139.
86 Ibid.
87 Jalal, *The State of Martial Law*, 32–37.
88 Government of Pakistan, Ministry of Finance, *Fiscal Policy in Pakistan – A Historical Perspective*, Volume one, (Islamabad: Government of Pakistan Printing Press, 1972), 71. Cited in Viqar Ahmed and Rashid Amjad, *The Management of Pakistan's Political Economy, 1947–82*, (Karachi: Oxford University Press, 1984), 68–69.
89 Omar Noman, *The Political Economy of Pakistan 1947–85*, (New York: Routledge and Kegan Paul, 1988), 15.
90 Maddison, *Class Structure and Economic Growth*, 139.
91 Emajuddin Ahmed, *Bureaucratic Elites in Segmented Economic Growth: Pakistan and Bangladesh*, (Dacca: University Press, 1980), 87.
92 Government of Pakistan, *Pakistan Statistical Yearbook*, (Islamabad: Pakistan Government Printing Press, 1964), 163 and Papanek, *Pakistan's Development*, 7. Cited in Gardezi, "Neocolonial Alliances and the Crisis of Pakistan," 139.
93 Tariq Ali, *Can Pakistan Survive? The Death of a State,* (London: Verso, 1983), 62.
94 Habibur Rahman, *Growth Models and Pakistan: A Discussion of Planning Problems*, (Karachi: The Allied Book Company, 1962), 5.
95 US economists working as advisors to the Planning Commission included David Bell, Gustav Papanek, Emile Despres, Lionel Hanson, and Richard Mallon. Gardezi claims that there were thousands of US professionals in Pakistan, "Neocolonial Alliances and the Crisis of Pakistan," 139, citing Embassy of Pakistan, *Pakistan's Third Five-Year Plan, 1965–70*, Interim Report Series, December 1969, 2.
96 Albert Waterston, *Planning in Pakistan*, (Baltimore, MD: The Johns Hopkins University Press, 1963). Waterston was an advisor to the Planning Commission who has detailed its administration by American experts.
97 Ahmed and Amjad, *The Management of Pakistan's Political Economy*, 11.
98 Huntington, *Political Order in Changing Societies*, 253.
99 Ayub Khan was later forced to accept the legalization of political parties.
100 Huntington, *Political Order in Changing Societies*, 251.
101 Ahmed and Amjad, *The Management of Pakistan's Political Economy*, 13–14.
102 Maddison, *Class Structure and Economic Growth*, 136–63.
103 Akmal Hussain, *Strategic Issues in Pakistan's Economic Policy*, (Lahore: Progressive Publishers, 1988), 367–73.
104 Rahman, *Growth Models and Pakistan*, 1962.

105 Ibid., 70.
106 W. Arthur Lewis first published his model as "Economic development with unlimited supplies of labour," *Manchester School of Economic and Social Studies*, 22: 2, (May 1954), 139–91, and later published it in *The Theory of Economic Growth*, (London: Allen and Unwin, 1955).
107 Lewis, "Economic development with unlimited supplies of labour," 189.
108 Rahman, *Growth Models and Pakistan*, 72.
109 Ibid., 69.
110 Mahbub ul Haq, *The Strategy of Economic Planning*, (New York: Oxford University Press, 1963), 1–3.
111 Papanek, *Pakistan's Development*.
112 The phrase is the title of the concluding chapter of Papanek's book.
113 Adams and Iqbal, *Exports, Politics, and Economic Development: Pakistan 1970–82*, (Boulder, CO: Westview Press, 1983).
114 Ahmed and Amjad, *The Management of Pakistan's Political Economy*, 11.
115 Mahbub ul Haq, "A Critical Review of the Third Five Year Plan," in M. A. Khan, ed., *Management and National Growth*, (Karachi: West Pakistan Management Association, 1968), 27. Cited and quoted in Maddison, *Class Structure and Economic Growth*, 158. Mahbub ul Haq's widely cited claim was originally made in a lecture in Karachi in 1968.
116 On the negative consequences of economic concentration under Ayub, see Keith Griffin and Azizur Rahman Khan, eds, *Growth and Inequality in Pakistan*, (London: Macmillan, 1972), Stephen Lewis, *Economic Policy and Industrial Growth in Pakistan*, (London: George Allen and Unwin, 1969), and *Pakistan: Industrialization and Trade Policies*, (Karachi: Oxford University Press, 1970).
117 Huntington, *Political Order in Changing Societies*, 261.
118 For analyses of the composition of the movement against the Ayub Khan regime, see Muneer Ahmed, "The November Mass Movement in Pakistan," in *Aspects of Pakistan's Politics and Administration*, (Lahore: University of the Punjab, 1974) and Shahid Javed Burki, "Ayub's Fall: A Socioeconomic Explanation," *Asian Survey*, 12: 3, (March 1972), 201–12.
119 Adams and Iqbal, *Exports, Politics, and Economic Development*.
120 Mohammad Anwar Syed, *The Discourse and Politics of Zulfikar Ali Bhutto*, (London: Macmillan, 1992), 26.
121 See Mohammad Ashgar Khan, *The First Round*, (Lahore: Taabeer Publishing House, 1978), 113. For an appraisal of Bhutto's role and motivations in the 1965 war see Anwar Syed, "Bhutto and the War of 1965: An Assessment," in Syed, *Discourse and Politics of Zulfikar Ali Bhutto*, 47–55.
122 Ibid., 47.
123 Ibid., 51–54.
124 "(A)llegedly under American pressure" reports Syed. Ibid., 54.
125 Maleeha Lodhi, 'Bhutto, the Pakistan Peoples Party and Political Development in Pakistan, 1967–77', unpublished PhD dissertation, London School of Economics and Political Science, University of London, 1980.
126 Pakistan Peoples Party, *Foundation Documents of the Pakistan Peoples Party*, (Lahore, November, 1967).
127 Syed, *Discourse and Politics of Zulfikar Ali Bhutto*, 62.
128 Pakistan Peoples Party, "Election Manifesto of the Pakistan Peoples Party," (Lahore: Classic, 1970).
129 Syed, *Discourse and Politics of Zulfikar Ali Bhutto*, 65. Quotation cited therein.

130 Elections had been held in 1955 to constitute a new Constitutional Assembly. The Assembly was converted into a short-lived National Asssembly by the 1956 Constitution, and dismissed under martial law in 1958.
131 Syed, *Discourse and Politics of Zulfikar Ali Bhutto*, 117.
132 Zulfikar Ali Bhutto, *Speeches and Statements: December 20, 1971–March 31, 1972*, (Karachi: Government of Pakistan, Department of Films and Publications, 1972), 9–12. Cited in Syed, ibid., 118.
133 Stanley Kochanek, *Interest Groups and Development Business and Politics in Pakistan*, (Delhi: Oxford University Press, 1983), 81.
134 Syed, *Discourse and Politics of Zulfikar Ali Bhutto*, 121.
135 Kochanek, *Interest Groups and Development*, 80.
136 Ibid., 80–82.
137 Mustafa Kamal Pasha makes this observation in "Neoliberal Recipe and Pakistan," *South Asia Journal*, 5 (July–September 2004).
138 Noman, *The Political Economy of Pakistan*, 161.
139 For a discussion of the tendency of democratic populists in Latin America to rely on mobilizing mass support, see Robert Dix, "Populism: Authoritarian and Democratic," *Latin American Research Review*, 20: 2, (1985), 29–52.
140 Selig Harrison, *India: The Most Dangerous Decades*, (Princeton: Princeton University Press, 1960).
141 Baldev Raj Nayar, *The Modernization Imperative and Indian Planning*, (New Delhi: Vikas, 1972).
142 Rounaq Jahan, *Pakistan: Failure in National Integration*, (New York: Columbia University Press, 1972).
143 Despite less room for maneuver in the Pakistani budget, under the present adjustment program, fiscal deficits have been reduced more rapidly in Pakistan than in India.
144 Nehru, *Discovery of India*, 505.
145 Angus Maddison suggests a framework for such a comparative historical analysis. See "The Social Origins and Ideology of the Nationalist Movement" in his *Class Structure and Economic Growth*, 71–75.

Organized labor and economic reform

1 Aroon Purie, "Letter from the Editor," *Business Today*, (22 March–6 April 1992), 1. The cover story of the issue of the Indian business magazine is the "frenetic pace" of economic liberalization in Pakistan.
2 Moazzem Hossain, Iyanatul Islam, and Reza Kibria, *South Asian Economic Development: Transformation, Opportunities, and Challenges*, (London: Routledge, 1999), 109.
3 India's 1981 loan from the IMF, the institution's largest to that date, included structural adjustment features, but was made for balance of payment purposes and preceded the establishment of the IMF's Structural Adjustment Facility.
4 See John Harriss, "The State in Retreat? Why has India Experienced Such Half-Hearted 'Liberalisation' in the 1980s," *IDS Bulletin*, 18: 4, (October 1987), 31–38 and Atul Kohli, "Managing the economy: halfhearted liberalization," in Kohli, ed., *Democracy and Discontent: India's Growing Crisis of Governability*, (Cambridge: Cambridge University Press, 1990), 305–38. James Manor made a similar assessment in "Tried, then Abandoned: Economic Liberalization in India," *IDS Bulletin*, 18: 4, (October 1987), 39–44.
5 David Glover, "A Layman's Guide to Structural Adjustment," *Canadian Journal of Development Studies*, 13: 1, (1991), 173–86.

6 In Pakistan, social spending in real terms and as a proportion of total government expenditure initially shrunk between 1988 and 1991. Between 1991 and 1995, even as the economy grew at 4.5 percent, an additional 18 million people were forced into poverty. (Mahbub ul Haq, *Human Development in South Asia 1997*, (Karachi: Oxford University Press) 17. Haq reports an increase in the poverty rate over the period from 20 percent to 30 percent of the total population.) It is difficult to gauge the extent to which adjustment – distinct from other forces, such as the Gulf War and the associated decline in labor remittances – contributed to social and economic distress. For further discussion of the detrimental social impact of adjustment, see Walden Bello, with Shea Cunningham and Bill Rau, *Dark Victory: The United States, Structural Adjustment, and Global Poverty*, (London: Pluto Press, 1994)

7 W. Arthur Lewis, "Economic development with unlimited supplies of labour," *Manchester School of Economic and Social Studies*, 22: 2, (May 1954), 139–91 and Lewis, *The Theory of Economic Growth*, (London: Allen and Unwin, 1955).

8 On Friday, 13 August 1982, Jesus Silva Herzog, Mexico's Finance Minister, explained to officials in the US Federal Reserve Bank, the US Treasury, and the International Monetary Fund that the Government of Mexico would not meet its foreign debt payments. See Albert Fishlow, "Lessons from the Past: Capital Markets during the 19th Century and the Interwar Period," in Miles Kahler, ed., *The Politics of International Debt*, (Ithaca, NY: Cornell University Press, 1986), 35.

9 For details on the economic and political crises surrounding Mrs. Gandhi's Emergency declaration, see chapter two.

10 A list of the points of the program appears in *Keesing's Contemporary Archives*, (6–12 October 1975), 27369–70.

11 The populist thrust and electoral logic of Mrs. Gandhi's economic policies after becoming Prime Minister in 1966 are discussed in greater detail in chapter two.

12 Manu Shroff, "Liberalisation of the Economy: The Indian Experience," *South Asia*, 1, (1990), 5.

13 Baldev Raj Nayar, *India's Mixed Economy: The Role of Ideology and Interest in its Development*, (Bombay: Popular Prakashan, 1989), 341.

14 Government of India, Ministry of Industry, *Report 1977–78*, (New Delhi: Ministry of Industry, 1978), 268–84 cited in Nayar, op. cit., 342.

15 Sushil Khanna, interview with author, Indian Institute of Technology, Calcutta, 26 December 1991.

16 The US chose not to pursue this under the General Agreement on Tariffs and Trade (GATT) because, by GATT rules, countervailing duties on Indian imports would have required the US to show damage to US industries. Indian officials saw in this an attempt to punish India for its refusal to condemn the December 1979 Soviet intervention in Afghanistan.

17 The Bank explained that their decision to cancel the loan was reached because the Indian government had replaced the US firm C. F. Braun and Company with the Danish firm Haldor Topsoe, affiliated to Snam Progetti, as the consultants to the US$812 million project. Under the agreement, the World Bank maintained the right to approve the consultants.

18 The lending rate was raised from 9 percent to 10 percent, while the minimum reserve rate was raised from 34 percent to 35 percent.

19 *Facts on File*, 1982, 38.

20 Ibid.

21 See Manmohan Singh, "1991–92 Budget Speech of Union Finance Minister Dr. Manmohan Singh," in Debendra Kumar Das, ed., *Structural Adjustment in the Indian Economy*, volume 2, (New Delhi: Deep and Deep Publications, 1993), 253–55.

22 A crore is equivalent to ten million rupees, or one hundred lakh (a lakh is one hundred thousand rupees).
23 Vijay Joshi and I. M. D. Little, "Macro-Economic Stabilization in India, 1991–93 and Beyond," *Economic and Political Weekly*, 28: 49, (December 4, 1993), 2659.
24 One hundred and thirty thousand Indian workers were employed in the Gulf at the time of the Iraqi invasion. The repatriation of these workers cost the government of India an estimated US$200 million, while remittances lost totaled US$205 million. Trade with Kuwait and Iraq worth US$250 million was also lost. James Clad, "The IMF cometh," *Far Eastern Economic Review*, 153: 42, (October 18, 1990), 84.
25 A detailed analysis of the causes of the fiscal crisis is provided by Vijay Joshi and I. M. D. Little, *India: Macroeconomics and Political Economy, 1964–1991*, (New York: Oxford University Press, 1993). According to Joshi and Little, external shocks played a small role in the fiscal crisis.
26 These financial institutions included the State Bank of India, the State Bank of India Finance, the Industrial Credit and Investment Corporation of India, and the Oil and Natural Gas Commission. Clad, "The IMF cometh."
27 The Moody's Investor Service's report on India is discussed briefly by Sunanda Sen, "Dimensions of India's External Economic Crisis," *Economic and Political Weekly*, 29: 14, (April 2, 1994), 808.
28 "Privatization – Need for Checks and Balances," *Economic Review*, February 1, 1992, 7.
29 Anwar Syed, *The Discourse and Politics of Zulfikar Ali Bhutto*, (London: Macmillan, 1992), 122.
30 Shahid Zahid, *The Herald*, July 1988, 58.
31 Omar Ashgar Khan, "Impact of Foreign Aid on Economic Development," in Viqar Ahmed and Rashid Amjad, *The Management of Pakistan's Economy*, (Karachi: Oxford University Press, 1984), 303.
32 International Monetary Fund, *1991 IMF Annual Report*, (Washington, DC: IMF, 1991), 51.
33 *Keesing's Record of World Events*, 34: 10, (October 1988), 36219.
34 Economist Intelligence Unit (hereafter EIU), *Pakistan, Afghanistan, 4/1988*, (October 31, 1988), 12.
35 Sayed Wajid, Chief Economist, Pakistan Desk, IMF, interview with author, July 15, 1992.
36 This paragraph and the following is informed by *Keesing's Record of World Events*, 35: 12, (December 1989), 37151.
37 EIU, *Pakistan, Afghanistan, 2/1989*, (May 10, 1989), 12.
38 EIU, *Pakistan, Afghanistan, 4/1988*, (October 31, 1988), 2. The rate of exchange is for 24 October 1988.
39 EIU, *Pakistan, Afghanistan, 4/1989*, (October 23, 1989), 2. The rate of exchange is for 16 October 1989.
40 EIU, *Pakistan, Afghanistan, 2/1990*, (April 6, 1990), 3. The rate of exchange on 4 April 1990 was Rs. 21.49 to US$1.
41 EIU, *Pakistan, Afghanistan, 4/1990*, (October 25, 1990), 17.
42 Sayed Wajid, interview with author, July 15, 1992.
43 Under Nawaz Sharif, foreign exchange regulations were amended so that, unlike India, any individual could hold bank accounts in foreign exchange. Eleven new private sector commercial banks were approved and 49 mutual funds (modarba companies) were allowed to operate in the Karachi Stock Exchange.
44 According to an IMF official, no negotiations were initiated before Sharif's government was dismissed and the interim government of Moeen Qureshi initiated its radical reforms. Sayed Wajid, interview with author, 15 July 1992.
45 Sayed Wajid, interview with author, July 15, 1992.

46 World Bank, "Pakistan: Country Economic Memorandum FY93: Progress Under the Adjustment Program," (Washington, DC: World Bank, March 23, 1993), 49.
47 "Qadir outlines package for employees," *Dawn Business Review*, August 20, 1991. Qadir was later arrested and jailed, charged with bribe-taking during his tenure as Chairman of the Privatization Commission. It is interesting that the Privatization Commission spells its name with a "z" in accordance with American usage rather than with an "s" which is standard in Pakistan.
48 World Bank, "Pakistan: Country Economic Memorandum FY93," 51.
49 Amir Mir, "Pakistan-Labor: Privatization Increases Labor Woes," Interpress Services, May 14, 1995.
50 This and the next paragraph are informed by Mohammad Ishaque, President, Pak China Fertilizer Mazdoor Union, interview with author, Rawalpindi December 5, 1995.
51 This did not dissuade one of the four brothers who run the Schon group from loaning to Benazir Bhutto a helicopter for use in her 1993 election campaign.
52 Cheryl McQueen, "Pakistan: A Bold Agenda for Economic Reform," *Business America*, 113: 1, (January 13, 1992), 8.
53 Naved Ahmed, Experts Advisory Cell, interview with author, Islamabad February 9, 1992.
54 This is according to IMF Resident Representative Harry Snoeq. "IMF supports Govt's economic policies," *Dawn*, (September 29, 1993), i, iv.
55 EIU, *Pakistan/Afghanistan, 2/1994*, (June 8, 1994), 9.
56 EIU, *Pakistan/Afghanistan, 4/1994*, (November 25, 1994), 21.
57 EIU, *Pakistan/Afghanistan, 2/1994*, (June 8, 1994), 9 and EIU, *Pakistan/Afghanistan, 4/1994*, (November 25, 1994), 22.
58 Salman Zahid, interview with author, Islamabad, 7 November 1995.
59 EIU, *Pakistan/Afghanistan, 4/1994*, (November 25, 1994), 30.
60 Ibid., 34.
61 "Six oil wells, new gas finds to be privatized," *Dawn Wire Service*, (May 22, 1999).
62 Workers Education Research and Welfare Society, "Nijkari ke sub Pakhtunkhwa aur mazdooron par asrat," ["The privatization of the entire Pakhtun nation and its effect on workers"] Peshawar: WERWS.
63 Senior World Bank Economist for India, interview with author, Washington, DC, July 17, 1992.
64 Perry Anderson, "The Limits and Possibilities of Trade Union Action," in Robin Blackburn and Alexander Cockburn, eds, *The Incompatibles*, (London: Penguin, 1967), 264.
65 See further Christopher Candland, "The Political Element in Economic Reform: Labor Institutions and Privatization Patterns in South Asia," in Linda Cook and Marsha Pripstein Posusney, eds, *Labor and Privatization: Responses and Consequences in Global Perspective*, (Brookfield: Edward Elgar, 2002).
66 Claims here are based on a number of conversations in October 1991, November 1991, and January 1993 with R. K. Bhakt, General Secretary, Bharatiya Mazdoor Sangh; G. K. Bhardwaj, Centre for Indian Trade Unions; Homi Daji, General Secretary of the All India Trade Union Congress; and S. N. Rao, Secretary, Indian National Trade Union Congress.
67 Ramamurthy resigned in protest not against the government's labor policies but over the federal government's position in a water dispute involving Karnataka and his home state of Tamil Nadu. International Labour Office, "India: Tripartite Cooperation for Structural Adjustment," *Social and Labour Bulletin*, (June, 1992), 143–45.
68 "Let the Workers Take Over," *Business India*, (January 13, 1992).

69 This perspective on the Tripartite Committee meetings is informed by an interview with a labor representative at the meetings, including Damodar Thankappan, Director, Centre for Workers' Management and former Working President, Kamani Employees Union, interview with author, New Delhi, March 22, 1992, and on the memorandum in question, Government of India, Ministry of Coal, "A Record Note of the First Meeting of the Special Tripartite Committee held in Bombay on 21.12.1991 at 10.00 am under the Chairmanship of Shri P. A. Sangma, Minister of State for Coal," mimeograph, n.d. The deliberations of the meeting were conveyed to the conference of state labor ministers on February 6, 1992, reported in ILO, "India: Tripartite Cooperation for Structural Adjustment."
70 S. N. Rao, Secretary, Indian National Trade Union Congress, interview with author, New Delhi, 15 December 1995.
71 C. R. Bakshi, "Bailadila Privatisation," *Trade Union Record*, (October 20 and November 5, 1995), 35–36.
72 Teesta Setalvad, "Workers Mean Business," *Business India*, (July 6–19, 1992), 99–100.
73 "9 killed in U.P. Firing on Workers," *Times of India*, (June 4, 1991).
74 "RS Call for Probe into U.P. Firing," *Times of India*, (June 5, 1991).
75 T. N. Siddhanta, "Brutal Killings at Dalla Cement Factory," (New Delhi: AITUC Publication, August 1991).
76 Subashini Ali, Communist Party of India Member of Parliament from Kanpur district, interview with author, Kanpur, December 22, 1991.
77 See Sharat G. Lin, "Shankar Guha Niyogi: Beyond Conventional Trade Unionism," *Bulletin of Concerned Asia Scholars*, 24: 3, (July–September 1992), 16–25.
78 Narayanan Madhavan, "India: Indian Mining Plan Draws Opposition Ire," Reuters News Service, (March 31, 1996).
79 "Landmarks," *Business India*, (August 14–27, 1995), 32.
80 Bakshi, "Bailadila Privatisation."
81 "Landmarks."
82 Scandal broke when Himachal Futuristics Communications, in a consortium with Israel's Bezeq and Thailand's Shinwarta, was awarded licenses for 9 of the 21 basic service zones. The Minister of Communications, Sukh Ram, was accused of favoritism in selecting Himachal Futuristics, which is based in the Minister's home state of Himachal Pradesh and successfully bid US$24 billion for the nine zones, despite having revenues of only US$57 million.
83 Amita Verma, "Workshop on Exit Policy for Sick Industrial Undertakings," report prepared for the Federation of Indian Chambers of Commerce and Industry, (December 1991), 1.
84 Hari Ramachandran, "India shuns labour reforms to stall unemployment," Reuters, (March 9, 1994).
85 V. P. Sawney, comments before Federation of Indian Chambers of Commerce and Industry's Workshop on Exit Policy for Sick Industrial Undertakings, New Delhi, (December 4, 1991). With these utterances, and with sufficient intervals and attempts at reconciliation, a Muslim may declare divorce.
86 Sickness in Indian industry has consumed Rs. 9,353 crore (US$6.235 billion) of public funds as of 1989. See "More private units falling sick: panel," *Times of India*, July 19, 1993.
87 V. S. Kaveri and Megha Bhalerao, *Sick Industrial Companies Act*, (Delhi: Ajanta, 1991), 17.
88 Steve Talbot, World Bank Economist for India, interview with author, Washington, DC July 15, 1992. BIFR officials interviewed in New Delhi noted that World Bank officials had come from Bank headquarters to examine the operation of the BIFR, review proposals for its reform, and interview BIFR officials.

89 Richard Cambridge, World Bank Economist for India, interview with author, Washington, DC July 17, 1992.
90 R. Ganapathy, Chairperson of the BIFR, FICCI Workshop on Exit Policy for Sick Industrial Undertakings, interview with the author New Delhi, 4 December 1991.
91 Section 3. Government of India, *Industrial Disputes Act of 1947*, (Bombay: Labour Law Agency, 1987).
92 Tiwari *et al.*, *Report of the Committee to Examine the Legal and Other Difficulties Faced by Banks and Financial Institutions in Rehabilitation of Sick Industrial Undertakings and Suggest Remedial Measures Including Changes in the Law*, (Bombay: Reserve Bank of India, 1984), 25–27.
93 Khurshid Ahmed, General Secretary, APFTU, interview with author, Lahore, September 3, 1992.
94 Human Rights Commission of Pakistan, *State of Human Rights in Pakistan 1990*, (Lahore: HRCP, 1990), 50.
95 The minimum wage is not sufficient to meet minimum living standards for a small family.
96 Mohammad Yaqoob, Chairman, APSEWAC, interview with author, March 29, 1992. The agreement was well covered by the press. See "Workers offered three packages," *Dawn*, October 16, 1991, "Govt, workers reach agreement," *Business Recorder*, October 16, 1991 and "Safeguarding workers' interest," *Business Recorder*, October 25, 1991.
97 A. R. Kemal, Member and Chief Economist, Planning Commission, Government of Pakistan, interview with author, November 29, 1995.
98 *Dawn News Service*, "Dishonest Staff in LBs: IBRD Threatens to Stop Aid to Punjab," February 13, 1995.
99 Syed Hameeduddin, "Workers Protest Labor Leader's Arrest," Karachi: Mimeograph, September 1992.
100 Syed Hameduddin, "Government Exempts Daewoo from Labor Laws," (Karachi: mimeograph, September 1992).
101 The APFTU represents both public sector and private sector enterprises, of which the Water and Power Development Authority State Hydroelectric Labour Union (WAPDA SHLU) is central. Khurshid Ahmed is General Secretary of the WAPDA SHLU and the APFTU.
102 Khurshid Ahmed, interview with author, September 3, 1992.
103 EIU, "Outlook: A Tough Budget is in Prospect," May 31, 1995.
104 EIU, Views Wire, "Pakistan Investment: Power Plant Sell-Off Spurs Violence," May 10, 1995.
105 Khurshid Ahmed, interview with author, Lahore, December 8, 1995.
106 Amir Mir, "Pakistan-Labor: Privatization Increases Labor Woes," Interpress Services, May 14, 1995.

Reorganizing industry, disorganizing workers

1 E. Balakrishnan, "Presidential Address to the Working Committee Meeting (annual) of the All India Trade Union Congress," November 2, 1995 (Bhilai), in *The Working Class*, 25: 4, (December 1995), New Delhi: AITUC, 5–6.
2 Government of India, Ministry of Labour, *Indian Labour Yearbook, 2004*.
3 Government of Pakistan, *Pakistan Labour Gazette: A Journal of Labour Affairs* (Karachi: The Manager of Publications, 1995), 130.
4 See, for example, Sujata Gothoskar, "Managerial Strategies in the 1990s and the Case for Evolving New Union Strategies," (Bombay: Workers' Solidarity Centre, 1991).

5 See, for example, Isher Judge Ahluwalia, "Trade Policy and Industrialisation in India," (Bombay: Exim Bank of India, 1992), 6, 17.
6 See "India: How to Keep Out Investors," *Economist*, June 11, 1994, 34 and Kaushik Basu, "Why India Needs Labor Law Reform" *BBC News*, June 27, 2005.
7 The Provincial Directorates of Labour in Pakistan, which submit figures to the central government, do not distinguish between strikes and lockouts.
8 Satyanarayan Jatiya, Minister of Labour, in answer to question number 852 in the Rajya Sabha on 7 December 1998.
9 Sahib Singh Verma, Minister of Labour, answer to unstarred question number 1812, in the Rajya Sabha on 18 December 2003.
10 International Labour Office, *Employment, Incomes and Equality: A Strategy for Increasing Productive Employment in Kenya*, (Geneva: ILO, 1972).
11 Ibid.
12 John Harriss, K. P. Kannan and Gerry Rodgers, *Urban Labour Market Structure and Job Access in India: A Study of Coimbatore*, (Geneva: International Institute for Labour Studies, 1990). The study is based on a survey of 200 households in a south Indian industrial city.
13 This section is largely informed by the collection of articles published in *Labour File: A Monthly Journal of Labour and Economic Affairs*: 6: 8 and 9, (August–September 2000), edited by J. John.
14 Sindhu Menon, "The Relentless Struggle of Rickshaw Pullers," *Labour File*, 6: 8 and 9, (August–September 2000), 3.
15 Vishnu Shukla, "Rickshaw: A Convenient Conveyance," *Labour File*, 6: 8 and 9, (August–September 2000), 14.
16 Menon, "Relentless Struggle," 9.
17 Ibid., 4.
18 Ibid., 5.
19 Ibid., 6.
20 Ibid., 7.
21 C. P. Gupta, interviewed by Menon, "The Relentless Struggle of Rickshaw Pullers."
22 Shukla, "A Convenient Conveyance," 13.
23 Arbind Singh, "Rickshaw to the Puller," *Labour File*, 6: 8 and 9, (August–September 2000), 17.
24 Fasihuk Karim Siddiqi, "Identification of the Problems and Prospects of Contract Labour in Pakistan (Employers' Point of View)," paper presented to the National Institute of Labour Administration and Training/Friedrich Ebert Stiftung National Seminar on Contract Labour, May 25–26,1992, mimeograph, 3.
25 Zulaekha Zar, "Contract Labour," paper presented to the National Institute of Labour Administration and Training/Friedrich Ebert Stiftung National Seminar on Contract Labour, May 25–26, 1992, mimeograph, 14.
26 Colin Gonsalvez, interview with author, Mumbai, 21 February 1993.
27 Lok Sabha unstarred Question No. 7584, addressed by Shri Kashiram Rana, answered by Deputy Minister of Labour, Shri Paban Singh Ghatowar, April 22, 1992.
28 Colin Gonsalvez, interview with author, Mumbai, February 21, 1993.
29 Zar, "Contract Labour," 1992, 7. Dr. Zar's paper includes a lengthy list of labor laws which specify that work on contract is legally considered to be formal employment.
30 Fasihuk Karim Siddiqi, "Identification of the Problems and Prospects of Contract Labour in Pakistan (Employers' Point of View)." A. Khan, interview with author, Karachi, August 25, 1992.
31 Mukhtar Farooq, "The Textile Sector – An Employer's View," in Qutubuddin Aziz, ed., *Working Conditions in the Textile Industry in Pakistan*, (Karachi: Pakistan Media Corporation, 1992), 37.

32 *Business Recorder*, June 20, 1970.
33 "No Textiles from Pakistan: UK for 2-Month Moratorium," *Pakistan Times*, March 20, 1972.
34 "British Textile Embargo a Political Decision," *Business Recorder*, April 4, 1972.
35 "World Cotton Textile Agreement", *Business Recorder*, 20 June 1970, 4.
36 Industrial Research Service, *Cotton Textile Industry in Pakistan*, (Karachi: Economic and Industrial Publications, 1990), 79.
37 David Morris, *The Emergence of an Industrial Labor Force in India: A Study of the Bombay Cotton Mills, 1854–1947*, (Berkeley, CA: University of California Press, 1965), 17.
38 Millowners' Association, "Facts about the Cotton Mill Industry of India," (Bombay: Millowners' Association, 1953), 1.
39 Baldev Raj Nayar, *India's Mixed Economy: The Role of Ideology and Interest in Its Development*, (Bombay: Popular Prakashan, 1989), 309–14.
40 Government of India, Ministry of Law, Justice and Company Affairs, "The Sick Textile Undertakings (Nationalisation) Act, 1974," (No. 57 of 1974), (Gangtok: Government of India Press, 1984).
41 "The Sick Textile Undertakings (Nationalisation) Act, 1974," Art. 29; Ministry of Law, *The Constitution of India*, (New Delhi: Government of India Press, 1967), 26.
42 From Kotwal Committee Report, 1987, 22. Cited by Hubert van Wersch, *Bombay Textile Strike 1982–83*, (Bombay: Oxford University Press, 1992), 236.
43 Ajeet Mathur, "The Experience of Consultation during Structural Adjustment in India (1990–92)," *International Labour Review* 132: 3, (1993), 331–45.
44 Indian Cotton Mills' Federation, *Handbook of Statistics on Cotton Textile Industry*, (Bombay: Indian Cotton Mills' Federation, 1993), 9.
45 *Kothari's Industrial Directory of India, 1990*, (Madras: Kothari Enterprises, 1990), 15.
46 Millowners' Association, "Facts about the Cotton Mill Industry of India," 8. Ramnath Podar, *The Indian Cotton Mill Industry: Nation's Premier Enterprise*, (Bombay: Podar Trading Company, 1959), 15.
47 Ajay Piramal, "Much depends on exit policy," *Business India 15th Anniversary Issue*, 1993, 284.
48 Hariben Naik, President of Rashtriya Mill Mazdoor Sangh, interview with author, Mumbai April 20, 1992.
49 van Wersch, *The Bombay Textile Strike*, 380–88.
50 Mahesh Vijapurkar, "Steps to check criminalisation of textile unions," *The Hindu* (International Edition), 20: 43, (October 22, 1994), 12.
51 This section is informed by van Wersch, *The Bombay Textile Strike 1982–83*, 95–100.
52 Hariben Naik, President of Rashtriya Mill Mazdoor Sangh, interview with author, Mumbay April 20, 1992.
53 Van Wersch's study on the strike is reviewed by Bagaram Tulpule, "Bombay Textile Strike," *Economic and Political Weekly*, January 16–23, 1993, 101–103. Also see Salim Lakha, "Organized Labor and Militant Unionism: The Bombay Textile Workers' Strike of 1982," *Bulletin of Concerned Asian Scholars*, 20: 2, April–June 1988, 42–53 and Bharat Patankar, "The Bombay Textile Workers' Strike of 1982: The Lessons of History," *Bulletin of Concerned Asian Scholars*, 20: 2, April–June 1988, 54–56.
54 van Wersch, *Bombay Textile Strike*, 97.
55 Rajni Bakshi, "The Legacy of a Marathon Struggle," *The Hindu*, September 20, 1992.
56 van Wersch, *Bombay Textile Strike*, 45.

57 Indian National Textile Workers' Federation and Ambekar Institute for Labour Studies, "Problems of Powerloom Industry in India: A Trade Union Point of View," (Brussels: International Textile, Garment and Leather Workers' Federation, 1984), 6.
58 Before the communal disturbances of December 1992 and February 1993 drove Muslim workers out of Surat, one trade union study estimated that over a hundred weavers migrated to Surat for work every day. Indian National Textile Workers Federation and Ambekar Institute for Labour Studies, "Problems of Powerloom Industry in India: A Trade Union Point of View," mimeograph, (October 1984) 13.
59 Nandika Jaitely, "The Triumph and the Tragedy," *Business India*, (March 19–April 1, 1990), 138–40.
60 Omkar Goswami, "Sickness and Growth of India's Textile Industry, Analysis and Policy Options," *Economic and Political Weekly*, November 10, 1990, 2429–2439 and 2496–2505.
61 L. C. Jain, "1985 Textile Policy. End of Handloom Industry." *Economic and Political Weekly,* July 6, 1985, 1121–1123.
62 Sharat G. Lin, "Delhi Textile Strike: Implication of Linking Wages to Productivity," *Economic and Political Weekly*, August 30, 1986, M85–M92.
63 Praful Bidwai, Senior Correspondent, Times of India, conversation with author, New Delhi, January 9, 1992.
64 "PM to Convene Special Meet on Textile Policy Soon," *Economic Times*, April 13, 1992.
65 See further Asha Krishnakumar, "Weavers in Distress," *Frontline*, 18: 8, (April 2001) 14–27.
66 Industrial Research Service, *Cotton Textile Industry in Pakistan*, 1–2.
67 Shahid Javed Burki, "Cotton Industry's New Importance," mimeograph, April 1972.
68 Khalimullah Khan, "Growth of Pakistan's Textile Industry – A Trade Union's View," mimeograph, 1992, 40.
69 Ahmed Rashid, "Easier Said: Pakistan shows how divisive deregulation can be," *Far Eastern Economic Review*, June 2, 1994, 54.
70 Azhar Lari, "Mills One-day Closure to Cut Yarn Output," *The Muslim*, August 3, 1992, 9.
71 Shahid-Ur Rehman, "Textile Crisis Needs a Nationalistic Solution," *Pakistan and Gulf Economist*, 10–11 April, 1993, 8.
72 Ibid., 8–9.
73 "Industrialists demand ban on strikes", *Business Recorder*, 17 January, 1972, 1.
74 The All Pakistan Textile Mills Association report of 1987–88 reports that approximately 100,000 looms are operating in the informal sector. Shabbir Kazmi estimates that the number is more likely 150,000 looms. Shabbir Kazmi, "Charting the Progress of the Textile Industry," *Dawn*, September 5, 1992.
75 Khalimullah Khan, "Growth of Pakistan's Textile Industry: A Trade Union's View," mimeograph, 1992, 41.
76 Guisinger and Irfan estimate that 69.1 percent of the total Pakistan labor force is in the informal sector. Stephen Gusinger and Mohammad Irfan, "Pakistan's Informal Sector," *Journal of Development Studies*, 16, (1980) 413.
77 On Fordism and flexibilization see Alain Lipietz, *Mirages and Miracles: The Crisis of Global Fordism*, trans. D. Marcey, (London: Verso Press, 1987).

Organized labor, democracy, and development

1 Bagaram Tulpule, "Bombay Textile Strike," *Economic and Political Weekly*, 28: 3 and 4, (January 16–23, 1993), 103. Tulpule is a senior leader in the Hind Mazdoor Sabha.

2 See, for example, John Weeks, "The Myth of Labour Market Clearing," in Guy Standing and Victor Tokman, eds, *Toward Social Adjustment: Labor Market Issues in South Asia*, (Geneva: International Labour Office, 1991), 53–77 and Truman Bewely, *Why Wages Don't Fall During a Recession*, (Cambridge, MA: Harvard University Press, 1999).
3 For a brief overview of the debate on poverty estimates in India, see "On New Poverty Estimates," *Economic and Political Weekly*, 42: 13, March 31, 2007, 1067–68.
4 Estimates are for 1999–2000.
5 Kothari, "The Politics of Planning," paper delivered to Jawaharlal Nehru University, 13 November 1991.
6 This is a major argument of Zafar Shaheed's 'The Organisation and Leadership of Industrial Labour in Pakistan (Karachi)', unpublished PhD dissertation, Department of Politics, University of Leeds, 1977. Oxford University Press Karachi will publish the work in 2007.
7 Amir Mir, "Pakistan-Labor: Privatization Increases Labor Woes," Interpress Services, (May 14, 1995): National Centre for Labour, 2486.
8 Mohan Mani, "New Attempt at Workers' Resistance: National Centre for Labour," *Economic and Political Weekly*, (October 7, 1995), 2486.
9 For a largely quantitative assessment of whether union multiplicity leads to union quiescence (the involuted pluralism thesis of Lloyd Rudolph and Susanne Rudolph, *In Pursuit of Lakshmi*, 1985), see Emmanuel Teitelbaum, "Was the Indian Labour Movement Really Coopted: Evaluating Standard Accounts," *Critical Asian Studies*, 38: 4, (December 2006).
10 Nagarik Mancha (Citizen's Forum), *Against the Wall: West Bengal Labour Scenario*, (Calcutta: Spokesman, 1991).
11 See Sindhu Menon, "The Relentless Struggle of Rickshaw Pullers," *Labour File*, 6: 8 and 9, (August–September 2000), 9.
12 Interview with author, Sanjay Singhvi, Mumbai High Court Mumbai labor advocate, December 15, 1995, Mumbai.
13 Mani, "New Attempt at Workers' Resistance," 2486.
14 The other founding member organizations are the Sarva Shramik Sangh, Aaganwadi Karamchari Sangh, Kamani Employees Union, Ibrahim Pattinam Telugu Vyvasaya Coolie Sangam, Gujarat State Women's Cooperative Federation, Agricultural Labour Union of Gujarat, Construction Labour Union of Ahmedabad, Women's Voice, Rice, Oil Mill and General Workers Union, Cotton Mills Workers Union of Bellary, Mines and Mineral Processing Workers Union, APMC Hamali Sangha, Shramik Samithi of Kanpur, Bangalore Gruha Karmikara Sangh, Samajwadi Mazdoor Panchayat, Nirman Mazdoor Panchayat Sangham, and Ghjed Khatna Mazdoor Morcha of Saharanpu.
15 National Centre for Labour pamphlet, no date.
16 Renana Jhabvala, former General Secretary, Self-Employed Women's Association, letter to N. P. Samy, Convenor, National Centre for Labour, January 16, 1997 and M. Arunchalam (Labour Minister), "Design Protection Measures for Unorganized Labour," in *V. V. Giri National Labour Institute Newsletter*, (August–September 1996), 1–5. See also Supriya Roy Chowdhury, "Old Classes and New Spaces: Urban Poverty, Unorganized Labor and New Unions," *Economic and Political Weekly*, December 13, 2003.
17 "National Council (sic) of Labour to Launch Agitation," *The Pioneer*, (Kanpur), (June 26, 1995), 3.
18 Kerri Danskin, "Made In India; Made in Thailand," *Clamor*, May/June 2003, 59.
19 "SEWA Under Attack," November 2, 2005, *Labor Start*, www.labourstart.org/docs/en/000209.html.

20 See Elisabeth Prügl, *The Global Construction of Gender: Home-Based Work in the Political Economy of the 20th Century*, (New York: Columbia University Press, 1999).

21 Renana Jhabvala "Liberalization and Women," *Seminar*, 531, (Footloose Labour: A Symposium on Livelihood Struggles of the Informal Workforce), November 2003.

22 For a discussion of the rise of independent unionism in Bombay, see E. A. Ramaswamy, "Bombay," *Worker Consciousness and Trade Union Response*, (Delhi: Oxford University Press, 1988), 17–78. Also see Paul Kurian and Amrita Chhachhi, "New Phase in Textile Unionism?" *Economic and Political Weekly*, February 20, 1982; Bharat Patankar, "The Bombay Textile Workers' Strike of 1982: The Lessons of History," *Bulletin of Concerned Asian Scholars*, 20: 2, April–June 1988, 54–56; Debashish Bhattacherjee, 'Union-Type, Labor Market Structure, and Bargaining Outcomes in Indian Manufacturing: An Analysis of the New Unionism in Greater Bombay', unpublished PhD dissertation in Labor and Industrial Relations, University of Illinois, Urbana-Champaign, 1987, cf. 197 on the origins and effects of independent unionism in Bombay in the early 1970s and the subsequent formation of the Kamgar Aghadi Party.

23 MLF, "Muttahida Labour Federation: An Introduction," mimeograph, May 1992.

24 PILER, "Trade Union Leadership Development Course," mimeograph, February 1989.

25 MLF, "Muttahida Labour Federation: An Introduction," mimeograph, May 1992.

26 These federations were the United Workers' Federation, the Democratic Labour Federation, the Joint Labour Federation, the Baluchistan Labour Federation, and the Watan Dost Mazdoor Federation.

27 MLF, "Muttahida Labour Federation: An Introduction," mimeograph, May 1992.

28 Farhat Parveen and Karamat Ali, "Research in Action: Organising Women Factory Workers in Pakistan," in Amrita Chhachhi and Renée Ilene Pitkin, eds, *Confronting State, Capital and Patriarchy: Women Organizing in the Process of Industrialization*, (New York: St. Martins Press, 1996).

29 Pakistan Institute of Labour Education and Research, *Unfree Labour in Pakistan: Work, Debt and Bondage in Brick Kilns*, (Geneva: International Labour Office, March 2004).

30 Beena Sarwar, "Pakistan: Greens to Blockade Import of Danish Ship," Interpress Services, November 15, 1994.

31 A "scheduled" employment refers to occupations designated and incorporated in legislation.

32 Pakistan Institute of Legislative Development and Transparency, *Understanding Labour Issues in Pakistan*, Briefing Paper for Pakistani Parliamentarians, 2002.

33 Unorganized Sector Workers' Social Security Bill, 2005.

34 Christopher Candland and Rudra Sil, eds, *The Politics of Labor in a Global Age: Continuity and Change in Late-industrializing and Post-socialist Economies*, (Oxford: Oxford University Press, 2001).

BIBLIOGRAPHY

Adams, Brook, *The Law of Civilization and Decay*, (London: Sonnenschein, 1895).

Adams, John and Mohammad Iqbal, *Exports, Politics, and Economic Development: Pakistan 1970–1982*, (Boulder, CO: Westview Press, 1983).

Addleton, Jonathan, *Undermining the Centre: The Gulf Migration and Pakistan*, (Karachi: Oxford University Press, 1992).

Ahluwalia, Isher Judge, "Trade Policy and Industrialisation in India," (Bombay: Exim Bank of India, 1992).

Ahmed, Emajuddin, *Bureaucratic Elites in Segmented Economic Growth: Pakistan and Bangladesh*, (Dacca: University Press, 1980).

Ahmed, Muneer, "The November Mass Movement in Pakistan," *Aspects of Pakistan's Politics and Administration*, (Lahore: University of the Punjab, 1974).

Ahmed, Viqar, and Rashid Amjad, *The Management of Pakistan's Political Economy, 1947–82,* (Karachi: Oxford University Press, 1984).

Alavi, Hamza "The State in Postcolonial Societies: Pakistan and Bangladesh," in Kathleen Gough and Hari Sharma, eds, *Imperialism and Revolution in South Asia*, (New York: Monthly Review Press, 1973), 145–73.

Alavi, Hamza, "Class and State," in *Pakistan: The Roots of Dictatorship*, (London: Zed Books, 1983).

Ali, Ashraf, "Trade Unions in Pakistan," mimeograph, 1991.

Ali, Karamat, (Multan), "Labour Legislation and Trade Unions," mimeograph, n.d.

Ali, Tariq, *Can Pakistan Survive? The Death of a State*, (London: Verso, 1983).

Ali, Tariq, "The Colour Khaki," *New Left Review*, 19, (January–February 2003).

Allana, G., ed., *Pakistan Movement: Historic Documents*, (Karachi: Department of International Relations, University of Karachi, 1967).

Amjad, Rashid and Khalid Mahmood, *Industrial Relations and the Political Process in Pakistan, 1947–77*, (Geneva: International Institute for Labour Studies, 1982).

Amsden, Alice, *Asia's Next Giant: South Korea and Late Industrialization*, (New York: Oxford University Press, 1989).

Amsden, Alice, *The Rise of "The Rest": Challenges to the West from Late-Industrializing Economies*, (New York: Oxford University Press, 2003).

Anderson, Perry, "The Limits and Possibilities of Trade Union Action," in Robin Blackburn and Alexander Cockburn, eds, *The Incompatibles*, (London: Penguin, 1967), 263–80.

Ansari, Khizar Humayan, "Roots of Muslim Socialist Activity and Labour Organization in Pre-Partition India," paper presented at the Conference on Labour in Pakistan, Karachi, December 26–28, 1999.
Aristotle, *The Basic Works of Aristotle*, Richard McKeon, ed., (New York: Random House, 1941).
Arunchalam, M., "Design Protection Measures for Unorganized Labour," in *V. V. Giri National Labour Institute Newsletter*, (August–September 1996), 1–5.
Arya, P. P., *Trade Unions in India: Growth and Recognition*, (New Delhi: Deep and Deep Publications, 1985).
Bakhtiar, Bashir Ahmed, *Mazdoor Tehriq aur Mai*, (The Labor Movement and Me) (Lahore: West Pakistan Hydro Electric Central Labour Union, 1962).
Bakshi, C. R., "Bailadila Privatisation," *Trade Union Record*, (20 October and 5 November 1995), 35–36.
Bakshi, Rajni, "The Legacy of a Marathon Struggle," *The Hindu*, (20 September, 1992).
Balanandan, E., "Presidential Address to the Working Committee Meeting (annual) of the All India Trade Union Congress," 2 November 1995 (Bhilai), *The Working Class*, 25: 4, (December 1995), New Delhi: AITUC, 5–6.
Bardhan, Pranab, *The Political Economy of Development in India*, (New Delhi: Oxford University Press, 1984).
Basu, Kaushik, "Why India Needs Labor Law Reform," *BBC News*, 27 June 2005.
Bello, Walden, Shea Cunningham and Bill Rau, *Dark Victory: The United States, Structural Adjustment, and Global Poverty*, (London: Pluto Press, 1994).
Bendix, Reinhard, "The Mandate to Rule," *Social Forces*, 55: 2, (1976), 242–256.
Bendix, Reinhard, *Nation-Building and Citizenship*, (Berkeley, CA: University of California Press, 1977).
Berberolu, Berch, ed., *Class, State and Development in India*, (New Delhi: Sage, 1992)
Bewely, Truman, *Why Wages Don't Fall During a Recession*, (Cambridge, MA: Harvard University Press, 1999).
Bhargava, Ashok, and Gopalan Balachandran, "Economic Change During the Indian Emergency," *Bulletin of Concerned Asian Scholars*,, 9: 4 (October–December 1977), 50–58.
Bhatt, Ela, "SEWA is Heading Towards Full Employment at the Household Level: Interview with Sindhu Menon," *Labour File*, 2: 4 (April 1996), 19–22.
Bhattacherjee, Debashish, *Union-Type, Labor Market Structure, and Bargaining Outcomes in Indian Manufacturing: An Analysis of the New Unionism in Greater Bombay*, unpublished Ph.D. dissertation in Labor and Industrial Relations, University of Illinois, Urbana-Champaign, 1987.
Bhutto, Zulfikar Ali, *Speeches and Statements: December 20, 1971–March 31, 1972* (Karachi: Government of Pakistan, Department of Films and Publications, 1972).
Birla, G. D., "Indian Prosperity: A Plea for Planning," speech delivered at the annual session of the Federation of Indian Chamber of Commerce and Industry, 1934.
Blair, Harry, "Mrs. Gandhi's Emergency, The Indian Elections of 1977, Pluralism and Marxism: Problems with Paradigms," *Modern Asian Studies*, 14: 2, (1980).
Boeke, J. H., *Economics and Economic Policy of Dual Societies*, (New York: Institute of Pacific Relations, 1953).
Breman, Jan, "The study of industrial labour in post-colonial India: The informal sector: A concluding review," in Jonathan P. Parry, Jan Breman and Karin Kapadia, eds, *The Worlds of India Industrial Labour*, (New Delhi: Sage Publications, 1999).

British Broadcasting Corporation, Summary of World Broadcasts, "Ban on Railway Workers Lifted," *Radio Pakistan External Service*, 11:00 GMT, 2 May 1995.

Brown, Judith, *Gandhi's Rise to Power: Indian Politics 1915–1922*, (Cambridge: Cambridge University Press, 1972).

Brown, Judith, *Gandhi: Prisoner of Hope*, (New Haven: Yale University Press, 1989).

Burki, Shahid Javed, "Ayub's Fall: A Socioeconomic Explanation," *Asian Survey*, 12: 3, (March 1972), 201–12.

Burki, Shahid Javed, "Cotton Industry's New Importance," mimeograph, April 1972.

Callaghan, John, "Fabian Socialism, Democracy and the State," in Graeme Duncan, ed., *Democracy and the Capitalist State*, (Cambridge: Cambridge University Press, 1989).

Candland, Christopher, "International Labour Rights: Situating the Debate," *New Political Economy*, 1: 2, (June 1996).

Candland, Christopher, "The Cost of Incorporation: Labour Institutions, Industrial restructuring, and New Trade Union Strategies in India and Pakistan," in Christopher Candland and Rudra Sil, eds, *The Politics of Labor in a Global Age: Continuity and Change in Late-industrializing and Post-socialist Economies*, (Oxford: Oxford University Press, 2001).

Candland, Christopher, "The Political Element in Economic Reform: Labor Institutions and Privatization Patterns in South Asia," in Linda Cook and Marsha Pripstein Posusney, eds, *Labor and Privatization: Responses and Consequences in Global Perspective*, (Brookfield: Edward Elgar, 2002).

Candland, Christopher, "Workers' Organizations in Pakistan: Why No Role in Formal Politics?" *Critical Asian Studies* 39: 1, (March 2007), 35–57.

Chakravarti, K. P., *Law of Industrial Disputes*, (Calcutta: Eastern Law House, 1987).

Chakravarty, Sukhamoy, *Development Planning: The Indian Experience*, (New Delhi: Oxford University Press, 1987).

Chakravarty, Sukhamoy, "Nehru and Indian Planning," *South Asian Research*, 9: 2, (November 1989).

Chandra, Bipan, "Jawaharlal Nehru and the Capitalist Class, 1936," *Nationalism and Colonialism in Modern India*, (New Delhi: Orient Longman, 1979), 171–203.

Chandra, Bipan, *The Rise and Growth of Economic Nationalism in India*, (New Delhi: People's Publishing House, 1966).

Chandra Das, Prafulla, *Trade Unions and Politics in India: A Study of Orissa*, (New Delhi: Discovery Publishing House, 1990).

Chhachhi, Amrita and Renêe Ilene Pitkin, eds, *Confronting State, Capital and Patriarchy: Women Organizing in the Process of Industrialization*, (New York: St. Martins Press, 1996).

Chatterjee, Partha, *Nationalist Thought and the Colonial World*, (London: Zed Books, 1986).

Chattopadhyay, Raghabendra, "Indian Business and Economic Planning (1930–56)," in Dwijendra Tripathi, ed., *Business and Politics in India: A Historical Perspective*, (Delhi: Manohar, 1991), 308–50.

Chowdhury, Supriya Roy, "Old Classes and New Spaces: Urban Poverty, Unorganized Labor and New Unions," *Economic and Political Weekly*, 38: 50, (13 December 2003).

Clad, James, "The IMF cometh," *Far Eastern Economic Review*, 153: 42, (18 October 1990).

Collier, Ruth Berins, and David Collier, *Shaping the Political Arena: Critical Junctures, the Labor Movement and Regime Dynamics in Latin America*, (Princeton, NJ: Princeton University Press, 1991).

Cooke, William N., "Product Quality Improvement Through Employee Participation: The Effects of Unionization and Joint Union-Management Administration," *Industrial and Labor Relations Review*, 46: 1, (October 1992), 119–34.

Danskin, Kerri, "Made In India; Made in Thailand" *Clamor*, 20, (May/June 2003), 59.

Das Gupta, Ranajit, "Social Security and Mutual Assistance in India: A Preliminary Account," *International Social Security Review*, 46: 3, (1993), 53–68.

Datar, B. N., *Ideology and Trade Unions – Indian Experience*, (Bombay: Maharashtra Institute of Labour Studies, 1987).

Davenport, Andrew, "Indira's Industrial Balancing Act," *Far Eastern Economic Review*, (22 August 1975), 55–56.

de Rivero, Oswaldo, *The Myth of Development: The Non-Viable Economies of the 21st Century*, (London: Zed, 2001).

Dewey, Clive, ed., *Arrested Development in India*, (Riverdale, MD: Riverdale Company, 1988).

Dix, Robert, "Populism: Authoritarian and Democratic," *Latin American Research Review*, 20: 2, (1985), 29–52.

Dutt, Rajani Palme, *India To-day*, (London: V. Gollancz, 1940).

Dutt, Rajani Palme, *The Problem of India*, (New York: International Publishers, 1943).

Economist Intelligence Unit, *Pakistan, Afghanistan, 4/1988*, (31 October 1988).

Economist Intelligence Unit, *Pakistan, Afghanistan, 2/1989*, (10 May 1989).

Economist Intelligence Unit, *Pakistan, Afghanistan, 4/1989*, (23 October 1989).

Economist Intelligence Unit, *Pakistan, Afghanistan, 2/1990*, (6 April 1990).

Economist Intelligence Unit, *Pakistan, Afghanistan, 4/1990*, (25 October 1990).

Economist Intelligence Unit, *Pakistan/Afghanistan, 2/1994*, (8 June 1994).

Economist Intelligence Unit, *Pakistan/Afghanistan, 4/1994*, (25 November 1994).

Economist Intelligence Unit, Views Wire, "Pakistan Investment: Power Plant Sell-Off Spurs Violence," (10 May 1995).

Economist Intelligence Unit, "Outlook: A Tough Budget is in Prospect," (31 May 1995).

Elster, Jon, "Marxism, Functionalism, and Game Theory," in Sharon Zukin and Paul DiMaggio, eds, *Structures of Capital: The Social Organization of the Economy*, (New York: Cambridge University Press, 1990), 97.

Embassy of Pakistan, *Pakistan's Third Five-Year Plan, 1965–70*, (Interim Report Series, December, 1969).

Erikson, Erik, *Gandhi's Truth on the Origins of Militant Nonviolence*, (New York: Norton, 1969).

Facts on File, "India: Gandhi Gives Up Defence Ministry," *Facts on File World News Digest*, 22 January 1982.

Farooq, Mukhtar, "The Textile Sector – An Employer's View," in Qutubuddin Aziz, ed., *Working Conditions in the Textile Industry in Pakistan*, (Karachi: Pakistan Media Corporation, 1992).

Fishlow, Albert, "Lessons from the Past: Capital Markets during the 19th Century and the Interwar Period," in Miles Kahler, ed., *The Politics of International Debt*, (Ithaca, NY: Cornell University Press, 1986), 35.

Freeman, Richard, "Labor Market Institutions and Policies: Help or Hindrance to Economic Development," Proceedings of the World Bank Annual Conference on Development Economics, (Washington, DC: 1992).

Ganapathy, R., Chairperson of the BIFR, comments to FICCI Workshop on Exit Policy for Sick Industrial Undertakings, New Delhi, 4 December 1991.

Gardezi, Hassan, "Neocolonial Alliances and the Crisis of Pakistan," in Kathleen Gough and Hari Sharma, eds, *Imperialism and Revolution in South Asia*, (New York: Monthly Review Press, 1973), 130–44.

Geertz, Clifford, *Agricultural Involution: The Process of Ecological Change in Indonesia*, (Berkeley, CA: University of California Press, 1970).

Glover, David, "A Layman's Guide to Structural Adjustment," *Canadian Journal of Development Studies*, 13: 1, (1991), 173–86.

Goswami, Omkar, "Sickness and Growth of India's Textile Industry, Analysis and Policy Options," *Economic and Political Weekly*, November 10, (1990), 2429–39 and 2496–2505.

Gothoskar, Sujata, "Managerial Strategies in the 1990s and the Case for Evolving New Union Strategies," (Bombay: Workers' Solidarity Centre, 1991).

Gourevitch, Peter, *Politics in Hard Times: Comparative Responses to International Economic Crises*, (Ithaca, NY: Cornell University Press, 1986), 10.

Government of India, *Indian Labour Gazette*, (Simla: Labour Bureau, September 1946).

Government of India, *First Five Year Plan*, (Simla: Government of India Press, 1950).

Government of India, "The Industrial Policy Resolution," (Simla: Government of India Press, 1956).

Government of India, *Economic Survey 1978–79*, (New Delhi: Ministry of Finance, 1979).

Government of India, Ministry of Coal, "A Record Note of the First Meeting of the Special Tripartite Committee held in Bombay on 21.12.1991 at 10.00 am under the Chairmanship of Shri P. A. Sangma, Minister of State for Coal," mimeograph, n.d.

Government of India, Ministry of Finance, Board for Industrial and Financial Reconstruction, *Industrial Sickness – Case Studies: Metallurgical*, volume 1, part 4, (July 1991), mimeograph.

Government of India, Ministry of Finance, *Economic Survey 1990–91*, (New Delhi: Government of India Press, 1991).

Government of India, Ministry of Industry, *Industrial Policy Resolution of 1956*, (New Delhi: Ministry of Industry, 1956).

Government of India, Ministry of Industry, *Report 1977–78*, (New Delhi: Ministry of Industry, 1978), 268–84.

Government of India, Ministry of Information and Broadcasting, *Road to Welfare State*, (Delhi: Government of India, May 1957).

Government of India, Ministry of Information and Broadcasting, *The Collected Works of Mahatma Gandhi*, K. Swaminathan, ed., (Delhi: Ministry of Information and Broadcasting, 1958–1963).

Government of India, Ministry of Labour, *Indian Labour Yearbook, 1947–2004* (Shimla: Labour Bureau, 1991).

Government of India, Ministry of Law, *The Constitution of India*, (New Delhi: B. V. P. Press, 1956).

Government of India, Ministry of Law, Justice and Company Affairs, "The Sick Textile Undertakings (Nationalisation) Act, 1974," (No. 57 of 1974), (Gangtok: Government of India Press, 1984).

Government of India, National Sample Survey Organization, Employment and Unemployment situation in India, 1999–2000, (Calcutta: National Sample Survey Organization, 2001).
Government of India, Planning Commission, *Papers Relating to the Formation of the Second Five-Year Plan*, (New Delhi: Government Printing Press, 1955).
Government of Pakistan, *Pakistan Statistical Yearbook*, (Islamabad: Government of Pakistan Printing Press, 1964).
Government of Pakistan, *Industrial Relations Ordinance*, (Islamabad: Government of Pakistan Printing Press, 1969).
Government of Pakistan, *Pakistan Labour Gazette: A Journal of Labour Affairs*, (Karachi: The Manager of Publications, 1995).
Government of Pakistan, Ministry of Finance, *Fiscal Policy in Pakistan – A Historical Perspective*, Volume one, (Islamabad: Government of Pakistan Printing Press, 1972).
Government of Pakistan, Ministry of Finance, *Pakistan Economic Survey 1990*, (Islamabad: Government of Pakistan Printing Press, 1991).
Government of Pakistan, Planning Commission, *The Sixth Five-Year Plan, 1983–88*, (Islamabad: Planning Commission, 1983).
Government of the United States, Department of Labor, *Foreign Labor Trends: Pakistan*, (Washington, DC: US Government Printing Office, 1990).
Griffin, Keith, and Azizur Rahman Khan, eds, *Growth and Inequality in Pakistan*, (London: Macmillan, 1972).
Gupta, Bharat Bhushan, *The Welfare State in India: Theory and Practice*, (Allahabad: Central Book Depot, 1966).
Gupta, P. D., *Welfare State in India*, (Agra: Agra University, 1955).
Gurtu, Shachi Rani, ed., *Jagjivan Ram on Labour Problems*, (Delhi: Atma Ram and Sons, 1951).
Gusinger, Stephen and Mohammad Irfan, "Pakistan's Informal Sector," *Journal of Development Studies*, 16, 1980, 412–26.
Haidari, Iqbal, ed., *The New Labour Policy: Impact and Implications*, (Karachi: Economic and Industrial Publications, 1972).
Hameeduddin, Syed, "Government Exempts Daewoo from Labor Laws," (Karachi: mimeograph, 1992).
Hameeduddin, Syed, "Workers Protest Labor Leader's Arrest," (Karachi: mimeograph, 1992).
Haq, Mahbub ul, *The Strategy of Economic Planning*, (New York: Oxford University Press, 1963).
Haq, Mahbub ul, "A Critical Review of the Third Five Year Plan," in M. A. Khan, ed., *Management and National Growth*, (Karachi: West Pakistan Management Association, 1968).
Harrison, Selig, *India: The Most Dangerous Decades*, (Princeton, NJ: Princeton University Press, 1960).
Harriss, John, "The State in Retreat? Why has India Experienced Such Half-Hearted 'Liberalisation' in the 1980s," *IDS Bulletin*, 18: 4, (October 1987), 31–38.
Harriss, John, K. P. Kannan, and Gerry Rodgers, *Urban Labour Market Structure and Job Access in India: A Study of Coimbatore*, (Geneva: International Institute for Labour Studies, 1990).
Hart, Henry, ed., *Indira Gandhi's India: A Political System Reappraised*, (Boulder, CO: Westview Press, 1976).

Hasan, Khalid Shamsul, ed., *Quaid-i-Azam's Unrealized Dream: Formation and Working of the All India Muslim League Economics Planning Committee with Background Material and Notes*, (Dhaka: Shamsul Hasan Foundation for Historical Studies and Research, 1991).

Hossain, Moazzen, Iyanatul Islam, and Reza Kibria, *South Asian Economic Development: Transformation, Opportunities, and Challenges*, (London: Routledge, 1999).

Human Rights Commission of Pakistan, *State of Human Rights in Pakistan 1990*, (Lahore: Human Rights Commission of Pakistan, 1990).

Huntington, Samuel, *Political Order in Changing Societies*, (New Haven, CT: Yale University Press, 1968).

Hussain, Akmal, *Strategic Issues in Pakistan's Economic Policy*, (Lahore: Progressive Publishers, 1988).

IDS Bulletin, "Quality and Productivity in Industry: New Strategies in Developing Countries," 24: 2, (April 1993).

Indian Cotton Mills' Federation, *Handbook of Statistics on the Cotton Textile Industry*, (Bombay: Indian Cotton Mills' Federation, 1993).

Indian National Textile Workers' Federation and Ambekar Institute for Labour Studies, "Problems of Powerloom Industry in India: A Trade Union Point of View," (Brussels: International Textile, Garment and Leather Workers' Federation, 1984).

Industrial Research Service, *Cotton Textile Industry in Pakistan*, (Karachi: Economic and Industrial Publications, 1990).

International Labour Office, "India: Tripartite Cooperation for Structural Adjustment," *Social and Labour Bulletin*, (June, 1992), 143–45.

International Labour Office, "Pakistan: Developing a Labour Policy," *Social and Labour Bulletin*, (June 1992), 146–48.

International Labour Organization, *Employment, Incomes and Equality: A Strategy for Increasing Productive Employment in Kenya*, (Geneva: International Labour Office, 1972).

International Labour Organization, *Bulletin of Labour Statistics, 1992*, (Geneva: International Labour Office, 1992).

International Labour Organization, Asian Regional Team for Employment Promotion, *Employment and Structural Change in Pakistan – Issues for the Eighties*, (Bangkok: ILO, 1983).

International Monetary Fund, *1991 IMF Annual Report*, (Washington, DC: IMF, 1991).

Itzigsohn, José, *Developing Poverty: The State, Labor Market Deregulation, and the Informal Economy in Costa Rica and the Dominican Republic*, (University Park, PA: The Pennsylvania State University Press, 2000).

Jahan, Rounaq, *Pakistan: Failure in National Integration*, (New York: Columbia University Press, 1972).

Jain, L.C., "1985 Textile Policy. End of Handloom Industry," *Economics and Political Weekly*, (6 July 1985), 1121–1123.

Jaitely, Nandika, "The Triumph and the Tragedy," *Business India*, (19 March–1 April 1990), 138–40.

Jalal, Ayesha, *The Sole Spokesman: Jinnah and the Making of Pakistan*, (New York: Oxford, 1990).

Jalal, Ayesha, *The State of Martial Rule: The Origins of Pakistan's Political Economy of Defence*, (Cambridge: Cambridge University Press, 1990).

Jenkins, Rob, *Democratic Politics and Economic Reform in India*, (Cambridge: Cambridge University Press, 2000).

Jhabvala, Renana, "Liberalization and Women," *Seminar*, 531, (Footloose Labour: A Symposium on Livelihood Struggles of the Informal Workforce), November 2003.

John, J. ed., *Labour File: A Monthly Journal of Labour and Economic Affairs*: 6: 8 and 9, (August–September 2000).

Joshi, G. V., *Writings and Speeches of G. V. Joshi*, (Poona: Aryabhushan Press, 1912).

Joshi, Vijay, and I. M. D. Little, *India: Macroeconomics and Political Economy, 1964–1991*, (New York: Oxford University Press, 1993).

Joshi, Vijay, and I. M. D. Little, "Macro-Economic Stabilization in India, 1991–93 and Beyond," *Economic and Political Weekly*, 28: 49, (4 December 1993).

Karnik, V. B., *Indian Trade Unions: A Survey*, (Bombay: Popular Prakashan, 1978), 1–14.

Kaveri, V. S., and Megha Bhalerao, *Sick Industrial Companies Act*, (Delhi: Ajanta, 1991).

Kazmi, Shabbir, "Charting the Progress of the Textile Industry," *Dawn*, (5 September 1992).

Keesing's Contemporary Archives, (6–12 October 1975), 27369–70.

Keesing's Record of World Events, 34: 10, (October 1988), 36219.

Keesing's Record of World Events, 35: 12, (December 1989), 37151.

Kemal, A. R., "Privatisation: The Experience of Pakistan," in V. Kanesalingam, ed., *Privatisation: Trends and Experiences in South Asia*, (New Delhi: MacMillan India, 1991).

Khan, Badiuddin A., "The Myth of Labour Policy," *Industrial Relations Journal*, 9: 3, (May–June 1992), 29–33.

Khan, Khalimullah, "Growth of Pakistan's Textile Industry: A Trade Union's View," mimeograph, 1992.

Khan, Mohammad Ashgar, *The First Round*, (Lahore: Taabeer Publishing House, 1978).

Khan, Omar Asghar, "Impact of Foreign Aid on Economic Development," in Viqar Ahmed and Rashid Amjad, eds, *The Management of Pakistan's Economy*, (Karachi: Oxford University Press, 1984), 288–305.

Khare, H. P., *Current Trends in Indian Trade Union Movement: A Study of White-Collar Trade Unions*, (Allahabad: Chugh Publications, 1987).

Khattak, Saba, "The State and Industrial Policy in Pakistan: The Zia Regime, 1977–88," paper presented to the Association for Asian Studies, 5–8 April 1990.

Kiernan, V. G., "A Note on the Author," *Poems by Faiz*, (Lahore: Vanguard Books, 1971).

Kochanek, Stanley, *Interest Groups and Development: Business and Politics in Pakistan*, (Delhi: Oxford University Press, 1983).

Kohli, Atul, "Managing the economy: halfhearted liberalization," in Atul Kohli, ed., *Democracy and Discontent: India's Growing Crisis of Governability*, (Cambridge: Cambridge University Press, 1990), 305–38.

Kooiman, Dick, *Bombay Textile Labour: Managers, Trade Unionists and Officials 1918–1939*, (New Delhi: Manohar, 1989).

Kothari, Rajni, "The Politics of Planning," paper delivered to Jawaharlal Nehru University, 13 November 1991.

Kothari's Industrial Directory of India, 1990, (Madras: Kothari Enterprises, 1990).

Kotovsky, G., "The Origins and Development of the Communist and Workers' Movement in India, with Focus on the CPI," in Berch Berberoglu, ed., *Class, State and Development in India*, (New Delhi: Sage, 1992), 243–79.

Krishna, K. B., *Plan for Economic Development of India: A Critical and Historical Survey*, (Bombay: Padma Publications, 1945).

Krishnakumar, Asha, "Weavers in Distress," *Frontline*, 18: 8, 14–27 April, 2001.

Kurian, Paul and Amrita Chhachhi, "New Phase in Textile Unionism?," *Economic and Political Weekly*, 20 February 1982.

Lakha, Salim, "Organized Labor and Militant Unionism: The Bombay Textile Workers' Strike of 1982," *Bulletin of Concerned Asian Scholars*, 20: 2, April–June 1988, 42–53.

Lari, Azhar, "Mills One-day Closure to Cut Yarn Output," *The Muslim*, 3 August 1992, 9.

Lewis, Stephen, *Economic Policy and Industrial Growth in Pakistan*, (London: George Allen and Unwin, 1969).

Lewis, Stephen, *Pakistan: Industrialization and Trade Policies*, (Karachi: Oxford University Press, 1970).

Lewis, W. Arthur, "Economic Development with Unlimited Supplies of Labour," *Manchester School of Economic and Social Studies*, 22: 2 (May 1954), 139–91.

Lewis, W. Arthur, *The Theory of Economic Growth*, (London: Allen and Unwin, 1955).

Lin, Sharat G., "Delhi Textile Strike: Implication of Linking Wages to Productivity," *Economics and Political Weekly*, 30 August, 1986, M85–M92.

Lindblom, Charles, *Unions and Capitalism*, (New Haven, CT: Yale University Press, 1949).

Lipietz, Alain, *Mirages and Miracles: The Crisis of Global Fordism*, trans. D. Marcey, (London: Verso Press, 1987).

Lodhi, Maleeha, *Bhutto, the Pakistan Peoples Party and Political Development in Pakistan, 1967–77*, unpublished PhD dissertation, London School of Economics and Political Science, University of London, 1980.

McQueen, Cheryl, "Pakistan: A Bold Agenda for Economic Reform," *Business America*, 113: 1, (13 January 1992), 8.

Macridis, Roy, and Bernard Brown, *Comparative Politics: Notes and Readings*, (Homewood, IL: The Doresey Press, 1961)

Maddison, Angus, *Class Structure and Economic Growth: India and Pakistan since the Moghuls*, (New York: W. W. Norton, 1971).

Mancha, Nagarik, *Against the Wall: West Bengal Labour Scenario*, (Calcutta: Spokesman, 1991).

Mani, Mohan, "New Attempt at Workers' Resistance: National Centre for Labour," *Economic and Political Weekly*, 7 October 1995, 2486.

Manor, James, "Tried, then Abandoned: Economic Liberalization in India," *IDS Bulletin*, 18: 4, (October 1987), 39–44.

Mathur, Ajeet, "The Experience of Consultation during Structural Adjustment in India (1990–92)," *International Labour Review*, 132: 3, (1993), 331–45.

Mehdi, Istaqbal, "State Intervention and Public Enterprises in the Market Place – Some Issues and Problems with Special Reference to Pakistan," mimeograph, n.d.

Menon, Sindhu, "The Relentless Struggle of Rickshaw Pullers," *Labour File*, 6: 8 and 9, (August–September 2000), 3–9.

Mill, John Stuart, *A System of Logic, Ratiocinative and Inductive Logic*, (London: Longmans, Green and Company, 1961, (1843)).

Millowners' Association, "Facts about the Cotton Mill Industry of India," (Bombay: Millowners' Association, 1953).

Mir, Amir, "Pakistan-Labor: Privatization Increases Labor Woes," Interpress Services, (14 May 1995).

Morris, David, *The Emergence of an Industrial Labor Force in India: A Study of the Bombay Cotton Mills, 1854–1947*, (Berkeley, CA: University of California Press, 1965).

Morris, David, "Toward a Reinterpretation of Nineteenth Century Indian Economic History," *Indian Economic and Social History Review*, 5, 1968.

Murillo, Maria Victoria, *Labor Unions, Partisan Coalitions, and Market Reforms in Latin America*, (New York: Cambridge University Press, 2001).

Murillo, Maria Victoria, "Partisan Loyalty and Union Competition: Macro-economic Adjustment and Industrial Restructuring in Mexico" in Christopher Candland and Rudra Sil, eds, *The Politics of Labor in a Global Age: Continuity and Change in Late-industrializing and Post-socialist Economies*, (Oxford: Oxford University Press, 2001), 31–68.

Muttahida Labour Federation, "Muttahida Labour Federation: An Introduction," mimeograph, May 1992.

Myrdal, Gunnar, *Objectivity in the Social Sciences*, (New York: Pantheon, 1969).

Naoroji, Dadabhai, "Commerce of India," (London: W. J. Johnson, 1871).

Naoroji, Dadabhai, *Poverty and Unbritish Rule in India*, (London: S. Sonnenschein, 1901).

Narayanan, M. S., "Trading Charges," *Economic Times*, 19 May 1991.

Narayanan Madhavan, "India: Indian Mining Plans Draws Opposition Ire," Reuters News Service, (31 March 1996).

Nayar, Baldev Raj, *The Modernization Imperative and Indian Planning*, (New Delhi: Vikas, 1972).

Nayar, Baldev Raj, *India's Mixed Economy: The Role of Ideology and Interest in Its Development*, (Bombay: Popular Prakashan, 1989).

Nayar, Kuldip, *India: The Critical Years*, (Delhi: Vikas Publishing, 1971).

Nehru, Jawaharlal, *An Autobiography*, (New Delhi: Oxford University Press, 1989, (1936)).

Nehru, Jawaharlal, *The Discovery of India*, (New Delhi: Oxford University Press, 1992, (1946)).

Niraja Gopal Jayal, "Introduction," in Sidney Webb and Beatrice Webb, *Indian Diary*, (Oxford: Oxford University Press, 1990),

Noman, Omar, *The Political Economy of Pakistan 1947–85*, (New York: Routledge and Kegan Paul, 1988).

O'Donnell, Guillermo, *Modernization and Bureaucratic Authoritarianism: Studies in South American Politics*, (Berkeley: Institute for International Studies, 1973).

PILER, *Unfree Labour in Pakistan: Work, Debt and Bondage in Brick Kilns*, (Geneva: International Labour Office, March 2004).

Pakistan Institute of Legislative Development and Transparency, *Understanding Labour Issues in Pakistan*, Briefing Paper for Pakistani Parliamentarians, 2002.

Pakistan Peoples Party, *Foundation Documents of the Pakistan Peoples Party*, (Lahore, November, 1967).

Pakistan Peoples Party, "Election Manifesto of the Pakistan Peoples Party," (Lahore: Classic, 1970).

Papanek, Gustav, *Pakistan's Development: Social Goals and Private Incentives*, (Cambridge, MA: Harvard University Press, 1967).

Papanek, Gustav, "Market or Government: Lessons from a Comparative Analysis of the Experience of Pakistan and India," *The Pakistan Development Review*, 30: 4.1, (Winter 1991), 601–46.

Parveen, Farhat and Karamat Ali, "Research in Action: Organising Women Factory Workers in Pakistan" in Amrita Chhachhi and Renée Ilene Pitkin, eds, *Confront-*

ing State, Capital and Patriarchy: Women Organizing in the Process of Industrialization, (New York: St. Martins Press, 1996).
Pasha, Mustafa Kamal, "Neoliberal Recipe and Pakistan," *South Asia Journal*, 5 (July–September 2004).
Patankar, Bharat, "The Bombay Textile Workers' Strike of 1982: The Lessons of History," *Bulletin of Concerned Asian Scholars*, 20: 2, (April–June 1988), 54–56.
PILER, "Trade Union Leadership Development Course," mimeograph, February 1989.
Piramal, Ajay, "Much depends on exit policy," *Business India*, 15th Anniversary Issue, 1993.
Pirzada, Syed Sharifuddin, ed., *Foundations of Pakistan: The All-India Muslim League Documents: 1906–1947*, Volume III, (1906–47), (Karachi: National Publishing House, 1970).
Pirzada, Syed Sharifuddin, ed., *Quaid-e-Azam Jinnah's Correspondence*, third revised and enlarged edition, (Karachi: East and West Publishing Company, 1977).
Podar, Ramnath, *The Indian Cotton Mill Industry: Nation's Premier Enterprise*, (Bombay: Podar Trading Company, 1959).
Prügl, Elisabeth, *The Global Construction of Gender: Home-Based Work in the Political Economy of the 20th Century*, (New York: Columbia University Press, 1999).
Public Interest Research Group, "Structural Adjustment: Who Really Pays?," (Delhi: Public Interest Research Group, 1992).
Purie, Aroon, "Letter from the Editor," *Business Today*, (22 March–6 April 1992), 1.
Purshotamdas Thakurdas, J. R. D. Tata, G. D. Birla, Ardeshir Dalal, Shri Ram, Kasturbhai Lalbhai, A. D. Shroff, and John Matthai, *Brief Memorandum Outlining a Plan of Economic Development for India*, (Bombay: The Commercial Printing Press, part 1, January, 1944, part 2, January, 1945), 48.
Rahman, Habibur, *Growth Models and Pakistan: A Discussion of Planning Problems*, (Karachi: The Allied Book Company, 1962).
Ramachandran, Hari, "India shuns labour reforms to stall unemployment," Reuters, (9 March 1994).
Ramanujam, G., *The Honey Bee: Toward a New Culture in Industrial Relations*, (New Delhi: Sterling Publishers, 1985).
Ramanujam, G., *Indian Labour Movement*, (New Delhi: Sterling Publishers, 1990).
Ramaswamy, E. A., "Bombay," *Worker Consciousness and Trade Union Response*, (Delhi: Oxford University Press, 1988), 17–78.
Ramaswamy, E. A., "A Chastened Trade Unionism," *Business India*, 15th Anniversary Issue, 1993, 161.
Rashid, Ahmed, "Easier Said: Pakistan shows how divisive deregulation can be," *Far Eastern Economic Review*, 2 June 1994.
Rehman, Shaheed-ur, *Who Owns Pakistan? Fluctuating Fortunes of Business Moghuls*, (Islamabad: Aekia Communications, n.d.)
Rehman, Shaheed-ur, "Textile Crisis Needs a Nationalistic Solution," *Pakistan and Gulf Economist*, 10–11 (April 1993), 7–9.
Rosen, George, *Democracy and Economic Change in India*, (Berkeley, CA: University of California Press, 1966).
Rosen, George, *Contrasting Styles of Industrial Reform: China and India in the 1980s*, (Chicago, IL: University of Chicago Press, 1992).
Rudolph, Lloyd, and Susanne Hoeber Rudolph, *In Pursuit of Lakshmi: The Political Economy of the Indian State*, (Chicago, IL: The University of Chicago Press, 1985).

Rudolph, Lloyd, and Susanne Hoeber Rudolph, "Dependent Labor and the Politics of Economic Reform in India: Left and Right Protectionism in the Nineties," paper presented at the University of California–Harvard University Workshop on Political Parties and Working Class Constituencies, 25 April 1999.

Rueschemeyer, Dietrich, Evelyn Huber Stephens and John Stephens, *Capitalist Development and Democracy*, (Chicago: University of Chicago Press, 1992).

Sarkar, Tanika, *Bengal 1928–1934, the Politics of Protest*, (Delhi: Oxford University Press, 1987).

Sarwar, Beena, "Pakistan: Greens to Blockade Import of Danish Ship," *Interpress Services*, 15 November 1994.

Sawney, V. P., Comments before Federation of Indian Chambers of Commerce and Industry's Workshop on Exit Policy for Sick Industrial Undertakings, New Delhi, (4 December 1991).

Sen, Amartya, *On Ethics and Economics*, (Basil Blackwell, 1987).

Sen, Sunanda, "Dimensions of India's External Economic Crisis," *Economic and Political Weekly*, 29: 14, (2 April 1994), 808.

Setalvad, Teesta, "Workers Mean Business," *Business India*, (6–19 July 1992), 99–100.

Shaheed, Zafar, *The Organisation and Leadership of Industrial Labour in Pakistan (Karachi)*, unpublished Ph.D. dissertation, Department of Politics, University of Leeds, 1977.

Shaheed, Zafar, "Union Leaders, Work Organization and Strikes: Karachi 1969–72," *Development and Change*, 10, (1979), 181–204.

Shahid, Zahid, *The Herald*, July 1988, 58.

Shaw, G. Bernard, Sidney Webb, William Clarke, Sydney Oliver, Annie Besant, Graham Wallas, and Hubert Bland, *Fabian Essays in Socialism*, (London: The Fabian Society, 1889).

Shroff, Manu, "Liberalisation of the Economy: The Indian Experience," *South Asia*, 1, (1990).

Shukla, Vishnu, "Rickshaw: A Convenient Conveyance," *Labour File*, 6: 8 and 9, (August–September 2000), 13–15.

Siddhanta, T. N., "Brutal Killings at Dalla Cement Factory," (New Delhi: AITUC Publication, August 1991).

Siddiqi, Fasih ul Karim, "Identification of the Problems and Prospects of Contract Labour in Pakistan (Employers' Point of View)," paper presented to the National Institute of Labour Administration and Training/Friedrich Ebert Stiftung National Seminar on Contract Labour, 25–26 May 1992, mimeograph.

Singh, Arbind, "Rickshaw to the Puller," *Labour File*, 6: 8 and 9, (August–September 2000), 16–19.

Singh, Manmohan, "1991–92 Budget Speech of Union Finance Minister Dr. Manmohan Singh," in Debendra Kumar Das, ed., *Structural Adjustment in the Indian Economy*, volume 2, (New Delhi: Deep and Deep Publications, 1993), 253–75.

Skocpol, Theda, "Emerging Agendas and Recurrent Strategies in Historical Sociology," in Theda Skocpol, ed., *Vision and Method in Historical Sociology*, (Cambridge: Cambridge University Press, Institute of Policy Studies Working Group on Economy, 1984), 369–70.

Solow, Robert, *The Labor Market as a Social Institution*, (Cambridge: Basil Blackwell, 1990).

Specker, Konrad, "'De-Industrialization' in Nineteenth Century India: The Textile Industry in the Madras Presidency, 1810–70," in Clive Dewey, ed., *Arrested Development in India*, (Riverdale, MD: Riverdale Company, 1988)

State of Employment in Pakistan: Report of a Working Group, (Islamabad: Institute for Policy Studies, 1987), 15–17.

Stiglitz, Joseph, "Employment, Social Justice, and Societal Well-Being," *International Labour Review*, 141: 1–2 (2002), 9–29.

Syed, Mohammad Anwar, *The Discourse and Politics of Zulfikar Ali Bhutto*, (London: Macmillan, 1992).

Talbot, Ian, "Planning for Pakistan: The Planning Committee of the All-India Muslim League 1943–46," *Modern Asian Studies*, 28: 4, (1994), 875–89.

Teitelbaum, Emmanuel, "Was the Indian Labour Movement Really Coopted: Evaluating Standard Accounts," *Critical Asian Studies*, (forthcoming October 2006).

Textile Labour Association, "In the Service of Women," (Ahmedabad: Gandhi Majdoor Sevalaya, 1986), 3.

The All Pakistan Textile Mills Association report of 1987 (Karachi: IPS Publications, 1987).

Tiwari, *et al.*, *Report of the Committee to Examine the Legal and Other Difficulties Faced by Banks and Financial Institutions in Rehabilitation of Sick Industrial Undertakings and Suggest Remedial Measures Including Changes in the Law*, (Bombay: Reserve Bank of India, 1984).

Tulpule, Bagaram, "Bombay Textile Strike," *Economic and Political Weekly*, 28: 3 and 4, (16–23 January 1993).

United Nations Development Programme, *Human Development Report 2005*, (New York: Oxford University Press, 2006).

Uphoff, Norman, *Learning from Gal Oya: Possibilities for Participatory Development and Post-Newtonian Social Science*, (Ithaca, NY: Cornell University Press, 1992).

van Wersch, Hubert, *Bombay Textile Strike 1982–83*, (Bombay: Oxford University Press, 1992).

Verma, Amita, "Workshop on Exit Policy for Sick Industrial Undertakings," report prepared for the Federation of Indian Chambers of Commerce and Industry, (December 1991).

Vijapurkar, Mahesh, "Steps to check criminalisation of textile unions," *The Hindu* (International Edition), 20: 43, (22 October 1994), 12.

Wainwright, Martin, "The Development of India's Defense Industries during the Second World War: Implications for the Partition of the Subcontinent," paper presented at the Association for Asian Studies, 6 April 1990.

Waterston, Albert, *Planning in Pakistan*, (Baltimore: The Johns Hopkins University Press, 1963).

Webb, Sidney, *The Necessary Basis of Society*, (London: Westminister, 1911)

Weeks, John, "The Myth of Labour Market Clearing," in Guy Standing and Victor Tokman, eds, *Toward Social Adjustment: Labor Market Issues in South Asia*, (Geneva: International Labour Office, 1991), 53–77.

Who's Who in India, Burma and Ceylon, 1941–42, (Bombay: Who's Who Publishers, 1942).

Wolpert, Stanley, *Jinnah of Pakistan*, (New York: Oxford University Press, 1984).

Workers Education Research and Welfare Society, "Nijkari ke sub Pakhtunkhwa aur mazdooron par asrat," ["The privatization of the entire Pakhtun nation and its effect on workers"] Peshawar: WERWS., n.d.

World Bank, "Pakistan: Country Economic Memorandum FY93: Progress Under the Adjustment Program," (Washington, DC: World Bank, 23 March 1993).

World Bank, *India: Poverty Study*, Washington, DC: International Bank for Reconstruction and Development, 1997.

World Bank, *World Development Reports*, (New York: Oxford University Press, 1990–2006).

World Resources Institute, United Nations Environment Programme, United Nations Development Programme, and The World Bank, *World Resources 1996–97*, (Washington, DC: World Resources Institute, 1997).

Zaher, Hasan, "The Communist Connection," *The Times and Trial of the Rawalpindi Conspiracy 1951*, (Karachi: Oxford University Press, 1998), 204–23.

Zar, Zulaekha, "Contract Labour," paper presented to the National Institute of Labour Administration and Training/Friedrich Ebert Stiftung National Seminar on Contract Labour, 25–26 May 1992, mimeograph, 14.

Newspaper articles

"13 Labourers convicted by ML Court in Karachi," *Political Observer*, (19 November 1969).

"40 Trade Unions Back Striking Workers," *Dawn*, (6 November 1969).

"6 Workers Hurt in Firing by Multan Mills' Watchmen," *Dawn*, (18 March 1969).

"9 killed in U.P. Firing on Workers," *Times of India*, (4 June 1991).

"Bhutto's Speech at Labour Moot: Text," *Dawn*, (22 November 1973).

"British Textile Embargo a Political Decision," *Business Recorder*, (4 April 1972).

Daily News, editorial, 15 November 1969.

"Dishonest Staff in LBs: IBRD Threatens to Stop Aid to Punjab," *Dawn News Service*, (13 February 1995).

"Fair Wages, Right of Strike for Labourers," *Dawn*, (26 April 1969).

"Government Urged to Announce Revised Labour Policy Soon," *Dawn*, (1 July 1969).

"Govt, workers reach agreement," *Business Recorder*, (16 October 1991).

"IMF supports Govt's economic policies," *Dawn*, (29 September 1993).

"India: How to Keep Out Investors," *Economist*, (11 June 1994).

"Industrial Unrest," *The Pakistan Times*, (15 November 1969).

"Industrialists demand ban on strikes," *Business Recorder*, 15 January 1972, 1.

"Kaniz Fatma in City," *Dawn*, (20 November 1969).

"Labour Body Conference Held," *Morning News*, (1 February 1969).

"Labour Federations Support Friday's General Strike Call," *Morning News*, (13 February 1969).

"Labour Unrest," *Morning News*, (7 March 1969).

"Landmarks," *Business India*, (14–27 August 1995).

"Let the Workers Take Over," *Business India*, (13 January 1992).

"More private units falling sick: panel," *Times of India*, (19 July 1993).

"National Council (sic) of Labour to Launch Agitation," *The Pioneer*, (26 June 1995.

"New Labour Policy Hailed," *Dawn*, (8 July 1969).

"No Textiles from Pakistan: UK for 2-Month Moratorium," *Pakistan Times*, (20 March 1972).
"PM to Convene Special Meet on Textile Policy Soon," *Economic Times*, (13 April 1992).
"Privatization – Need for Checks and Balances," *Economic Review*, (February 1992), 7.
"Protest Rallies by Valika Mill Workers," *Dawn*, (1 November 1969).
"Qadir Outlines Package for Employees," *Dawn Business Review*, (20 August 1991).
"RS Call for Probe into U.P. Firing," *Times of India*, (5 June 1991).
"Safeguarding Workers' Interest," *Business Recorder*, (25 October 1991).
"Six Oil Wells, New Gas Finds to be Privatized," *Dawn Wire Service*, (22 May 1999).
"Tributes Paid to Martyrs of March, 1963," paper unknown, (3 March 1969).
"Workers Offered Three Packages," *Dawn*, (16 October 1991).
"Workers' Processions, Meetings," *Morning News*, (24 February 1969).
"Workers Walk Out of Joint Council Meeting," *Morning News*, (22 February 1969).
"World Cotton Textile Agreement," *Business Recorder*, 20 June 1970, 4.

Interviews

Ahmed, Khurshid, [General Secretary of Bata Mazdoor League Pakistan], Lahore, 4 September 1992.
Ahmed, Naved, [Privatization Commission, Experts Advisory Cell], Islamabad, 9 February 1992.
Ali, Subashini, [Communist Party of India Member of Parliament from Kanpur district], Kanpur, 22 December 1991.
Baloch, Usman, [former President, Muttahida Mazdoor Federation], Karachi, 27 September 1992.
Bhakt, R. K., [General Secretary, Bharatiya Mazdoor Sangh], New Delhi, 18 February 1992.
Bidwai, Praful, [Senior Correspondent, *Times of India*], New Delhi, 9 January, 1992.
Cambridge, Richard, [Senior Economist for India], World Bank, Washington, DC, 17 July 1992.
Chudhary, Gulzar Ahmad, [General Secretary, All Pakistan Trade Union Federation], Lahore, 5 September 1992.
Gonsalvez, Colin, Mumbai High Court Labor Advocate, Mumbai, 21 February 1993.
Hussain, Riffat, [trade union leader], Rawalpindi, 9, 12 and 24 September 1992.
Ishaque, Mohammad, [President, Pak China Fertilizer Mazdoor Union], Rawalpindi, 5 December 1995.
Kemal, A. R., [Member and Chief Economist, Planning Commission, Government of Pakistan], Islamabad, 29 November 1995.
Khan, Ahsanullah, [Chairman, Human Resources Committee, Sindh Industrial and Trading Estate Association of Industry and Member of the Standing Committee on Labour], Karachi, 25 August 1992.
Khan, Faizullah, [President, Valika Textile and Woolen Mills Workers Union], Karachi, August 1992.
Khan, Noor, Deputy Martial Law Administrator 1969–1971, Karachi, 28 and 29 March, 1995.
Khanna, Sushil, [Professor, Indian Institute of Technology, Calcutta] Calcutta, 26 December 1991.

Mathur, Ajeet, [Professor, Indian Institute of Management, Calcutta], Calcutta, 30 December 1991.
Muzumdar, Kamal, [INTUC official], New Delhi, 28 November 1991.
Naik, Hariben, President of Rashtriya Mill Mazdoor Sangh], Bombay, 20 April 1992.
Pasha, Mustafa, [Professor, American University], Washington, DC, 25 February 1995.
Rao, S. N., [Secretary, Indian National Trade Union Congress], New Delhi, 15 December 1995.
Singhvi, Sanjay, [Mumbai High Court labor advocate], Mumbai, 8 March 1993.
Talbot, Steve, [World Bank Economist for India], Washington, DC, 15 July 1992.
Thankappan, Damodar, [Director, Centre for Workers' Management and Working President, Kamani Employees Union], New Delhi, 22 March 1992.
Wajid, Sayed, [Chief Economist, Pakistan Desk, IMF], Washington, DC: 15 July 1992.
Yaqoob, Malik Muhammad, [Chairman, APSEWAC], New Delhi, 29 March 1992.
Zahid, Salman, [Privatization Commission], Islamabad, 7 November 1995.
Zaman, Haider, [Human resource management consultant to the 1979 and 1986 Labour Commissions of Pakistan], Karachi, 26 August 1992.

INDEX